Good Intentions Aside

D0615163

A Manager's Guide to Resolving Ethical Problems

Laura L. Nash

HARVARD BUSINESS SCHOOL PRESS
Boston, Massachusetts

97 96 95 94 93   5 4 3 2 1

The recycled paper used in this publication meets the requirements of the American National Standard for Permanence of
Paper for Printed Library Materials Z39.49-1984.

Library of Congress Cataloging-in-Publication Data

Nash, Laura L.
    Good intentions aside : a manager's guide to resolving ethical
problems / Laura L. Nash.
        p.   cm.
    Originally published: Boston : Harvard Business School Press,
1990. With new preface.
    Includes bibliographical references and index.
    ISBN 0-87584-429-4 (pbk. : acid-free paper)
    1. Business ethics.   I. Title.
[HF5387.N35 1993]
174'.4—dc20   93-14788
                                                        CIP

Contents

87915

Preface to the Paperback Edition

Good Intentions Aside was originally written with a strongly pragmatic, behavioral bias. My goal was twofold: to describe systematically the components of ethical business conduct in accessible language; and to explore the main factors underlying typical breakdowns and restoration of this ethic among managers. Recently, however, the normative aspects of the Covenantal Ethic have captured more attention as executives and public policymakers consider the moral foundations on which socially legitimate forms of capitalism rest.

The need for a moral model of capitalism becomes urgently clear as we witness the tentative and often ambivalent first steps of Eastern European, South American, and Southeast Asian nations toward a new economic order. Capitalism, like democracy, will not take hold simply because a socialist regime has fallen. Issues of moral legitimacy and effectiveness must be articulated if citizens and governments are to make the hard sacrifices and trade-offs needed to get a democratic economy under way. History tells us that good business ethics has not been a distinguishing feature of industrialized capitalism in its early stages. Cartels, corruption, and a lack of accountability for injury to the public are far more common. The first steps toward a free market economy must include a model that provides guideposts for integrating morally acceptable and economically sound business behavior.

Developed economies may be equally in need of such a model. Today we are bombarded with examples of "Recessionary Ethics": in the name of survival, decision makers adopt a "me-first" approach to the exclusion of ethical norms. Naturally this only takes them further from quality, customers, employees, and public acceptance of free markets. Unfortunately the primary motivation now dictating the rules of business—profit-maximization—comes very close to condoning such behavior in the name of efficiency.

The covenantal model offered here strongly supports

free markets, but sets up a contrasting approach to decision making. It tries to capture the essential other-orientedness of responsible business in a profit-making context. The term "Covenantal Ethic" reflects the idea that capitalism is at heart a *voluntary* social contract between the public and business to fulfill certain mutually beneficial obligations. Briefly stated, it understands the chief goal of business to be the creation and deliverance of value to a voluntary or democratically controlled marketplace. Concomitantly, it is the obligation of the marketplace (via buyers and the law) to see to it that business receives a fair return for such provision of value. Thus profit becomes the *result* of other first conditions rather than *the* first condition of business, and efficiency is a subset rather than driving definition of delivered value. Similarly, the model discards the inconsistent notion that no matter how valued a business decision might be, it cannot be considered ethical as long as a profit is made.

The Covenantal Ethic sounds deceptively obvious. In fact, as a statement of purpose, it implies profound considerations for mutual welfare, and as I argue in the book, the questions and values that managers bring to their decision making are radically changed when approached from this viewpoint. Short-term, illegitimate manipulations of the market are distinguished from long-term, socially legitimate endeavors. If the Covenant is broken, both the public and business are injured. This can be seen repeatedly as companies go for the edges only to be punished after the fact for harming people or cheating the system. Each time this occurs, the very legitimacy of capitalism is dealt a blow.

The covenantal model is not theoretical in origin. It is based on observation and interviews with managers whose businesses have been more than healthy on the balance sheet, innovative in the marketplace, and accepted well by the public in terms of reputation. Discussions of the Covenantal Ethic with other managers interested in ethics, quality, and customer service have confirmed for me the power and the "makes sense" nature of this approach.

For management groups wishing to explore ethics and business, two questions are good discussion starters: Does this model make sense? If it does, what is confirmed and what changes in the way our company approaches problems?

In the spirit of further stimulation, I cite here three examples of how the Covenantal Ethic helps enlighten ethical decision making.

Example 1. Developing Economies

I recently traveled to Brazil under the sponsorship of the United States Information Agency on the occasion of the Portuguese translation of *Good Intentions Aside*. Several Brazilian and American business groups sponsored a series of lectures and workshops. Much to my surprise, the Covenantal Ethic sparked great interest, but on precisely the opposite issues as in the United States.

U.S. managers tend to find the first and third conditions of the model (value creation and a service orientation) most interesting. Brazilian executives focused on the second condition, namely the right to a fair return. They pointed out that this social/legal contract does not exist in their country. The model helped explain their frustrated attempts at responsible capitalism. Among their examples: closed markets, tax laws favoring narrow interests, systemic bribery, lack of legal enforcement, or make-work jobs such as the mandated accreditation of every industry. Such practices systematically undermine the ability of well-intentioned managers to serve the public. They impose value-insensitive, costly, and corrupting conditions on business. To make a profit, one need not consider how to provide a quality product at a good delivered price that includes fair wages for employees, but how best to engage in illegal or socially illegitimate practices. Under such conditions the only way ethical business practice can survive is among executives with extraordinarily high personal morals operating businesses with highly distinctive competencies or tremendous size with which to dominate their market.

It struck me how infrequently the rationale for reform in new democracies is understood in terms of value delivery to the end-user and service to stakeholders. Rather, policy reform is dominated by macro-economics and broadly defined social welfare measures for people outside the economic loop. Some people may also place their hopes in a personal spiritual conversion of business leaders. But no amount of personal goodness or public largess will meet the economic needs of a country unless the system itself is modelled on a moral view that demands businesses stay close to their markets so as to provide value *and* guarantee a reward for doing so honestly.

The rationale for reform must be accompanied by a fundamental understanding of the moral grounds of capitalism to which a democratic public and business can make a commitment. A covenantal model brings these values to the table while still considering efficiency. Inflation, for example, which currently runs over 25 percent monthly in Brazil, is a complete breakdown of the covenant despite its profitability to certain interests. What is being rewarded is not delivered value. Planning and investing are impossible, thus thwarting product innovation, global competitiveness, and job creation. Unless the country chooses total economic isolation, there is no possibility of honest profit under these conditions, and the social costs of stagnation will continue to rise.

Example 2. International Laws on Intellectual Property

There are innumerable factors in the monumental efforts of GATT to achieve internationally recognized laws on intellectual property. Most of these cannot be discussed here. It is helpful, however, to consider how the Covenantal Ethic model can inform this discussion, and link the familiar stakeholder approach to wealth creation rather than to state social welfare mechanisms.

To continue the previous example, take a U.S. pharmaceutical company wishing to establish operations in Brazil. It refuses to do so, however, because intellectual property laws there currently make it impossible to realize a fair return on its investment. Meanwhile, Brazilians fear that any strengthening of the law would exclude local companies from the market, invite exploitation of local labor, transfer profits out of the country, and bring higher prices of drugs for poor people.

The current standoff on this issue has unacceptable social consequences. New cures for illness are not being researched. Potential jobs are not being created. An economically viable new strategy for conservation of the rain forest is being frustrated. Any solution will require difficult trade-offs, but a Covenantal Ethic would frame this question with an integrated consideration of value to affected stakeholders and a fair return to the companies. First of all, the pharmaceutical companies would have to face up to the complexity of providing value under these conditions: simply providing local jobs and drugs to Americans will not do. Stakeholders in the conservation of Brazil's natural resources will need guarantees of productive development and conservation tactics before people become dependent on monopolistic job markets or wholesale destruction of species. In contrast to their treatment under past agricultural policies, workers will deserve a fair return for value provided. To give access to the poor, a favored price-of-origin should be negotiated for the value the country provides with its natural resources (and perhaps a 20-year discount for poor neighbors, internationally negotiated). Similarly, the pharmaceutical companies must be guaranteed a fair return for delivering value to these stakeholders and the marketplace, and that means some kind of intellectual property guarantee. Note the emphasis on delivered value. Subsidized monopoly games and "dry-hole" scams are out.

The question—Can a business be too ethical?—is especially relevant here. Under a Covenantal Ethic the answer is yes: a company should not commit its resources unless there is a foundation for making a profit from good business practice in that area either through legal guarantees or spillover goodwill from the marketplace.

Example 3. Health Care Management

An elderly patient, confined to a nursing home hospital bed, has recovered sufficiently to leave the building for 24 hours, after which treatment must be continued. In the doctor's view, a visit home for a day would lift the patient's flagging spirits. Home, however, is distant, and requires an overnight. Current policy states that an empty bed must be filled immediately. There is a three-week wait list for beds. If the patient leaves, he will have to go to a hospital, which would remove him from the familiar caretakers and friends at the home. He stays put, and after two weeks begins to show a marked depression and there is a decline in treatment progress.

Both the administrator and the doctor would like to send the patient home for a weekend. The difference is in how they view the ethics of the situation. The doctor feels the current policy, nay, the whole system, is unethical: it violates her ability to carry out her medical obligation to do whatever is in her knowledge to promote healing. The administrator, however, sees the overall cost picture and feels the hospital cannot afford an empty bed; the national medical insurance plan agrees. The decision is not unethical.

Many aspects of health care management create just such an "ethics gap" between managers and physicians. One looks at service and the other at efficiency or profit. The result is often a dysfunctional enmity between the two groups, causing both to prematurely abandon the search for a creative solution. The covenantal model incorporates both views in determining the ethical policy for the nursing home. From the standpoint of service, and value provided to the end-user, the physician's concerns are legitimate guidelines that no ethical administrator can ignore. However, *delivered* value has an efficiency component which also cannot be ignored. Both the physician and the administrator need to develop their points of view to include all the components of the covenantal model.

Many accepted medical practices—such as redundant tests or having sophisticated equipment at every facility—feel like service to the patient and profession, but bring little delivered value. Their costs preclude development of resources that might deliver more value to the same patient. In this case, there seems an obvious need to have a furlough policy despite the cost of an empty bed for 24 hours. The patient would be better served, and his or her treatment might actually cost less over time. These costs need to be documented fully. Should it turn out that overall costs are raised, the physician must help in advising how to cut costs elsewhere. Right to a fair return for the business—not just the doctor—demands it.

Obviously the above examples are not exhaustive. As several perceptive reviewers have noted, the covenantal paradigm invites consideration of many issues not addressed in this book. Two important ones are determining "fair return," and balancing conflicting stakeholder claims to value. My hope is that the first steps taken here will provoke continued exploration of such questions through a covenantal lens.

Cambridge, Massachusetts   Laura L. Nash
February 1993

Preface

When I arise in the morning, I am torn by the twin desires
to reform the world and enjoy the world. This makes it
hard to plan the day.

Many management books have ended with a paean
to ethics. Forty years ago, Philip Selznick's classic *Leadership
in Administration* finished with a thoughtful essay on the
moral responsibilities of leadership. Today, Donald Trump's
best-selling self-portrait of a deal-maker ends with a few remarks on philanthropy and working in the service of others.[1]
Tom Peters's latest work, *Thriving on Chaos*, ends with the
prescription to "Demand Total Integrity." Successful organizations, claims Peters, must shift from "an age dominated by
contracts and litigiousness to an age of handshakes and trust."
His advice: "Set absurdly high standards for integrity—and
then live them, with no fuzzy margins."[2]
While such testimonials are important and inspiring,
they seem to imply that business integrity is simply a matter
of "really meaning it." Such advice fails to help the already
well-minded manager who nevertheless finds the ethical aspects of business sometimes painful, frequently confusing,
and occasionally a matter for personal disappointment—in
oneself or one's company.
And so this book begins where many others leave off.
It examines the specific managerial assumptions and behavioral issues that impede or encourage a decent manager to act
on his or her good intentions. It is for those executives who
intuitively suspect or fervently hope that good ethics makes
business sense, but who do not have at hand a choate explanation of why and how this happy combination might occur.

[1]Donald J. Trump with Tony Schwartz, *Trump: The Art of the Deal* (New York: Random House, 1987), p. 243.
[2]Tom Peters, *Thriving on Chaos* (New York: Harper & Row, 1987), p. 46.

xii GOOD INTENTIONS ASIDE

There is already ample documentation of how business behavior can run to immoral extremes; what we urgently need now is help in understanding what to do about these tendencies. A manager's typical patterns of decision making can either subvert or sustain basic moral norms. The achievement of high ethical standards in today's competitive environment requires a radical realignment of the basic ways in which managers typically approach problem solving. The realignment suggested here, which I call a Covenantal Ethic, does not abandon the profit motive and other assumptions of capitalism, but it does put them in a different contextual framework. While the theoretical framework is my own, it is drawn from and describes the management philosophies of some of the best known and most successful leaders in business today.

In addressing the wherefores and how-tos of business integrity, I faced the terrible paradox of the sort E.B. White describes in the above (*Essays*) quotation. I have a personal conviction that reform of business behavior is imperative, but I also respect many business people and products of business. To write an indictment of the worst kinds of corporate criminality would not be to the point.

My subject instead is the executive approach and behavior of the inherently decent, average managers, who are neither saints nor fiends, and who make up the overwhelming majority of the business population today. After teaching and consulting with thousands of such managers at all levels of the corporation, I have concluded that they have the normal range of ethical instincts and a desire to see that these instincts are not compromised at work. At the same time, their good intentions do not necessarily provide automatic immunity from wrongdoing. Decent instincts are not always strong enough to hold up under the adverse and complex conditions that managers inevitably encounter.

Up to now, management concern about ethics has seemed to center on two great fears: the fear that living up to ethical obligations will impose an immediate cost on the bottom line, and the fear that employees who adopt unethical standards will pose a financial liability down the road. The second fear has certainly been justified. The financial fallout from recent scandals in nearly every industry in America—from Wall Street to Main Street—has made it abundantly clear that no manager can afford to leave company standards to chance. A response is necessary if for no other reason than that economics demands one. At the same time, fear of ethics costing too much prevents the formulation of an effective response.

There is now an urgent need to move beyond fear to understanding. It is crucial to understand how ethical assumptions can be made to work effectively in the marketplace and in a manager's life. This requires not only a strong commitment to integrity but also an informed view of why the normal moral values of private life seem to break down or be ineffectual in a business context. The answers lie in the analytical frameworks that managers use, the goals they set, the organizational structures they adopt, the language they use to motivate others, and their personal assumptions about the intrinsic worth of other people.

These are the issues that form the crux of this book. My purpose is to provoke an explicit self-diagnosis of those mindsets and conditions that typically contribute to moral malfunctions at work, and to suggest a problem-solving framework for meeting these moral challenges more successfully.

There are many good books about how to manage other people: what incentives to provide, what laws to pass, what constraints to place upon an industry's competitive behavior. This book is primarily about self-management. It is an explicit exploration of the basic values that inform responsible business conduct *at the individual level.* Although many of the moral problems described here are deliberately of the garden-variety kind, when taken together they are meant to provide managers with a thorough testing ground for moral leadership in the corporation.

Obviously some ethical problems in business will exceed the boundaries of this discussion. In particular, I have avoided macroissues such as environmental hazards or specific institutional programs such as benefits plans. Important as these topics are, their discussion requires political considerations that are beyond the scope of this book. Moreover, it would be unwise to measure business morality only in macro terms. Individual discretion will always play a crucial role in securing high corporate standards.

Many of my examples may seem to be as much a case of bad economic judgment as of intentionally unethical behavior. This choice was deliberate, for two reasons. First, I wanted examples that would be close to the experience and thinking of the noncriminal manager. Hence, most of the ethical problems described here are not horrendously evil. Unlike many examples in medical ethics, they do not represent life or death choices. They are nevertheless significant tests of a manager's personal integrity, and the building blocks of business legitimacy in our society.

Second, the examples describe situations where ethical assumptions and commercial decisions are inextricably connected, as they are in reality. This pragmatic bias is also deliberate. To separate economics from morality and both from commonsense "people skills" is to construct an artificial analysis that would fail to provide the tools needed to deal with reality. Rather, the critical discussion of moral values and managerial choices must be firmly rooted in common business experience. To put the discussion of moral values in a separate compartment reserved for Sunday School teachers, legendary acts of philanthropy, or major criminal trials is to entertain two wishes that are unlikely to be fulfilled: that the topic of business ethics would disappear for the average person, and/or that one's own moral mettle holds an impregnable position in the face of normal business pressures and conflicting organizational needs.

If we've learned nothing else in the 1980s, it is that business ethics will not go away. It is here already, at the heart of every economic transaction, resource allocation, and human resource decision. The issues are difficult and the track record filled with failures even by the well-intentioned. Future threats to traditional ways of doing business—from sudden ownership disruptions to new alliances with foreigners whose values and culture may differ from ours—only sharpen the need for a coherent and practical approach to achieving high standards of business conduct.

The stakes in this arena are high. Democratic capitalism, resting on a system of voluntary exchange and political commitments to individual freedom and discretion, is at heart a system dependent on the creation of trust. Without a framework of basic moral values such as truth-telling, fairness, and personal accountability, trust will elude even the most idealistic management group. While many management concepts, from discounted cash flow to matrix organizational plans, have their day in the sun and then are abandoned in light of new techniques, ethics and the creation of trust remain constant factors in the viability of the corporation. An effective standard of business integrity is crucial to the welfare of the corporation today, for its people, and for those who are affected by its operations.

That includes everyone. Directly or indirectly, we all rely on the private sector for our well-being. Given our increasing difficulty in ensuring external oversight of corporate activities, and the new technological avenues to internal fraud, it is crucial to our economic system that managers in the private sector increase their capacity to rely on themselves for moral integrity in the pursuit of an honest dollar.

It is also crucial to our national sense of self-worth. I am reminded of Anton Chekhov's haunting description in *The Letter*, when he described "the pathetic forced smile of people who do not respect themselves." The reality of business morality cannot be glossed over with public relations expertise or personal indifference. Real people work in the corporation, with real ideals, and a soul to evaluate. This book is written in the hope that it will be a meaningful resource to managers engaged in these efforts.

ACKNOWLEDGMENTS

Robert Frost wrote that there were no beginnings and ends, only middles. It is very difficult to isolate an exact beginning and end for a work of this kind. Ethics in business is a new field looking at age-old questions. This particular manuscript has gone through several evolutionary stages before reaching its final form. In the process, many people deserve special thanks for their help along the way.

Most notably, Kenneth R. Andrews, former editor-in-chief of the *Harvard Business Review* and Donald K. David Professor Business Administration, Emeritus, at the Harvard Business School, provided critical advice and support at every stage of the project. His reflections on the topic have been a valuable resource and standard. I am very grateful for his continued encouragement and advice. These provided a crucial impetus to see this project through to completion.

Eliza Collins and Harriet Rubin provided valuable editorial advice in the first stages, and Carol Franco and Natalie Greenberg added the final improvements. Alan Kantrow, Paul Sheehan, and David Warsh gave of their journalistic expertise to coax me into being more relevant. Several professional women, who are also close friends, contributed invaluable advice. In deference to their privacy, they remain unnamed but not unappreciated.

Many colleagues are due thanks for their extensive advice and help. At Harvard: Richard Rosenbloom, David Ewing, C. Roland Christensen, Raymond Corey, John Matthews, and Winthrop Knowlton. Ronald Berenbeim at The Conference Board deserves thanks for his excellent work in this field. Participating with Charles McCoy, Kirk Hanson, Tom Donaldson, Manuel Velasquez, and Richard DeGeorge on various ethics projects helped shape the ideas presented here, and I am appreciative of their collegiality.

A large number of top executives offered valuable insights and help during the development of this book. Andrew Sigler's Task Force on Corporate Ethics for the Business Roundtable in 1988 was particularly valuable. My work with his group, particularly the executives at Johnson & Johnson and the Norton Company, provided renewed evidence of the importance of this topic and the need for more work. Elmer Johnson, formerly of General Motors and now partner at Kirkland & Ellis, provided both management insight and editorial help.

The quotations in this book are taken from personal interviews with the CEOs and managers cited, unless otherwise noted. Among the CEOs (current or retired) who gave of their time and to whom I owe thanks are: Rand Araskog (ITT), Robert Baldwin (Morgan Stanley), James Bere (Borg-Warner), James Burke and David Clare (Johnson & Johnson), Philip

Caldwell (Ford Motor Company), Trevor Chinn (Lex Service Group P.L.C.), Wes Christopherson and Donald Perkins (the Jewel Companies), Dick Capen (*The Miami Herald*), Alvah Chapman (Knight-Ridder), Max DePree (Herman Miller), Pehr Gyllenhammar (A.B. Volvo), Arnold Hiatt (Stride Rite), Mitchell Kapor (Lotus Development), Donald Melville and David Nelson (Norton Company), Thomas Phillips and Charles Adams (Raytheon), Edmund Pratt (Pfizer), William Smithburg (Quaker Oats), Delbert Staley and William Ferguson (NYNEX), William Thurston (GENRAD), and Thomas Wyman (CBS). David Collins and Fritz Wenzler at J&J, Bo Ekman and Berth Jonnson at Volvo, and Ronald Marcks at the Norton Company also deserve special attention, as do the divisional presidents at Lex Service Group. Tom Samuelson, formerly of Union Pacific, and the entire corporate staff of the Management Development group at NYNEX have also contributed greatly to the development of this book.

Finally, Peter L. Berger, University Professor at Boston University, has and continues to provide the intellectual model and personal encouragement for stretching the study of the humanities to the realm of practical economic behavior. I owe him and his wife, Brigitte, many thanks for their support over the years.

Cambridge, Massachusetts   Laura L. Nash
April 1990

Part I

The Need to Attend to Business Ethics

1

Why Business Ethics Now?

Reader, suppose you are a businessman. Now suppose you are of ruthless and greedy character. But I repeat myself.

The activity of moneymaking has always stood in somewhat uneasy alliance with people's private sense of morality. Jokes about business ethics—the above epigraph is a paraphrase of Mark Twain's description of a congressman—have regularly appeared in the popular press over the past two centuries. Many an executive today voices a similar cynicism about the relevance of moral inquiry to managerial practice. For many reasons, from the eternal fact of greed to the very different ways in which we tend to think about managing and morality, ethics and business have often seemed if not downright contradictory, at least several worlds apart. Even those wedded to the notion that integrity in business might be an obtainable ideal have nevertheless tended to leave the exploration of ethical dilemmas to each manager's private conscience.

In the past ten years American business has blasted through the Chinese wall that traditionally separates the discussion of management problems and personal morality. Whereas the voicing of ethical standards was formerly a concern of a few exceptional leaders, today the topic of business ethics is acknowledged to pervade every area of the corporation just as it is a recurrent issue in the media. Corporate codes of conduct are now the norm rather than the exception.[1] Corporate leaders have become more vocal about their own commitment to ethical standards. Respected national business groups such as the Business Roundtable, the American Management Association, and The Conference Board are sponsoring major ethics programs. In the consulting world, business ethics seminars and conferences comprise a new cottage industry. And many a respected corporation has embarked on an organized attempt to encourage ethical conduct among its employees.

The reasons for the newly elevated place of ethics in business thinking are many. Managers have seen the high costs that corporate scandals have exacted: heavy fines, disruption of the normal routine, low employee morale, increased turnover, difficulty in recruiting, internal fraud, and loss of public confidence in the reputation of the firm. A body of literature has even developed, at this point tentative, outlining the economic costs of a damaged reputation. Business leaders at such outstanding companies as Johnson & Johnson, IBM, Goldman Sachs, Hewlett-Packard, Ford, 3M, Wal-Mart, General Mills, and many others are emphasizing that high personal standards of conduct are a major asset, as economically valuable as that equally elusive intangible called goodwill.

Although many managers are committed to high ethical standards, many others are unconvinced that ethics can be reconciled with economics, or they regard morality as being exclusively a matter of personal character. In a recent MBA business policy class the students were asked to critique an impressive corporate credo that combined practical business functions with ethical ideals. One student asserted that the document was flawed because it tried to combine two very different things. It violated his sense of order. "After all," he said, "ethics doesn't have any direct relation to market share or earnings. It should be in a separate document. You know, ethics are very personal, they're about yourself." Most of the

[1]Ronald E. Berenbeim, *Corporate Ethics* (New York: The Conference Board Research Report No. 900, 1988).

students nodded sagely. A few days later I heard a similar group agreeing with Albert Carr's classic article in which he contended that it was morally acceptable to lie in business as long as you played within the unwritten rules of the game.[2]

The challenges of today's marketplace and the serious ethical lapses that are occurring in nearly every industry demand a more sophisticated approach to ethical dilemmas, one that is more than simply game playing or indulging in personal feelings about oneself. The root of the word *integrity* means "to hold together." Integrity in business today requires incredible integrative powers; the power to hold together a multitude of important and often conflicting values, and the power to bring personal morality and management concerns into the same dimension. No manager can afford, from an economic or moral standpoint, to keep his or her moral notions off in a separate compartment, reserved for the narrowest and most obvious cases.

FACING UP TO FALLIBILITY

The idea that ethical conduct in business is a fairly straightforward notion is at first glance persuasive. One could argue that most if not all of the values that comprise ethical business conduct—honesty, fairness, respect for others, service, promise-keeping, prudence, and trustworthiness—are a familiar part of most managers' upbringing. However, it is an unfortunate fact that these "commonsense values" have frequently suffered meltdown in the marketplace. The headline-gathering corporate scandal and the petty whisperings of office gossip are evidence that business managers—like the rest of humankind—are not always capable of making good ethics an actual fact of business conduct.

When you couple the undeniable pervasiveness of human fallibility with the age-old temptations of money and power, the need for a deliberate exploration of the moral challenges of management becomes clear. Throw in the organiza-

[2]Albert Z. Carr, "Is Business Bluffing Ethical?" *Harvard Business Review* (January–February 1968), pp. 143–153.

tional factors of delegating the execution of one's decisions and having to defer to higher authorities, and the realities of moral fallibility slam home with all the force of a year-end earnings loss.

Unless one is the sole owner of a company that produces no products and hires no employees and creates no waste, merely being raised right will not provide sufficient ammunition against the ever-present opportunities to abandon one's basic moral standards. Every manager regularly faces decisions that are problematic from a moral standpoint and over which he or she does not have total control: decisions where people will inevitably get hurt; where trade-offs must be made between equally desirable values and constituencies; where the commitments of the organization and a manager's performance goals are at odds with the individual needs of certain employees or customers. On these occasions it may or may not be legitimate to compromise professional standards, but clearly the inevitable compromise of moral values which accompanies such decisions should be seen as truly problematic. The gap between a well-thought-out policy at the top level and the messy, hurtful people problems surrounding its execution is great. A good leader cannot assume that by merely plugging in a decent person the moral lights will shine like beacons for every activity in the company.

Achieving and sustaining business integrity is harder and less automatic than that. What is more, every manager has a responsibility not only to *be* above reproach, but for the *perception* that he or she is above reproach, and expects the same standards from others who execute company policy. Otherwise, the well-intentioned and personally upright manager becomes an unintentional contributor to a "look-the-other-way" climate which invites ethical abuses. Thus from the standpoint of managing the large organization, a manager is not an autonomous moral entity. Rather, he or she must be a moral leader, responsible for the behavior of other people and the institution itself, as well as his or her own character.

Addressing this responsibility requires at a minimum an explicit investigation and stand on the ethical aspects of corporate activity, from strategy to compensation.

DEFINING BUSINESS ETHICS

But what, exactly, is to be investigated? Surely most executives already believe that they support honesty, fairness, and apple pie? What else needs saying? As a first step, then, in understanding the nature of ethical decision making in business—as well as the reasons for moral failure—it is important to agree on some general term for the inquiry.

What is business ethics? *Business ethics is the study of how personal moral norms apply to the activities and goals of commercial enterprise. It is not a separate moral standard, but the study of how the business context poses its own unique problems for the moral person who acts as an agent of this system.*

Aristotle defined virtue as a matter of habit or the trained faculty of choice (*Nichomachean Ethics* II.6). Business ethics reflects the habits and choices managers make concerning their own activities and those of the rest of the organization. These activities and choices are informed by one's personal moral value system, but that system often suffers a transformation of priorities or sensitivities when it operates in an institutional context of severe economic constraints and pressures, as well as the potential for acquiring power.

Although there are many different moral aspects of business, business ethics generally falls into three basic areas of managerial decision making:

1. **Choices about the law**—what it should be and whether or not to obey it.
2. **Choices about the economic and social issues that are beyond the law's domain**—usually called the "gray areas" or "people values." These concern the tangible and intangible ways one treats others, and include not only the moral notions of honesty, promise-keeping, and fairness, but also the avoidance of injury and the voluntary reparation for harm done.
3. **Choices about the preeminence of one's own self-interest**—the degree to which one's own well-being comes before the interests of the company

or of other people inside and outside the company. Included are decisions concerning rights of ownership and how much money is to be retained or distributed elsewhere.

The ways in which such choices are framed, analyzed, and either maintained or abandoned form the basis of the business ethics inquiry. The validation of *business ethics*, however unpopular the term, is simply a way of acknowledging that, indeed, there are choices to be made concerning the means and ends of business which have an essentially moral ingredient.

SHIFTING CONCERNS

Often the discussion of these choices grows out of a major collapse of moral standards in a specific business activity. The issues that receive widespread attention are in those areas where the normal rules have broken down. Thus the topical issues of business ethics shift over time. In the 1950s, two major concerns were price-fixing and dehumanization in the work force (e.g., Arthur Miller's *Death of a Salesman* and Sloan Wilson's *The Man in the Gray Flannel Suit*). In the 1960s, the Vietnam War aroused general moral indignation over the political and military aggressiveness of the military-industrial complex and its "multinational conglomerates." Perhaps in reaction to the demonstrated destructiveness of business overseas, managers were also faced with new constraints on environmental and social destructiveness. A series of social conscience reforms—from pollution control to EEO standards—were instituted inside the corporation and in the legislative arena.

In the 1970s, corporate internationalism and newfound markets in Asia and the Mideast shifted the nation's corporate conscience to issues of bribery here and abroad. Watergate raised an outcry against political contributions activity, and led to a major revamping of reporting requirements and internal auditing procedures. Corporate codes of conduct were a tangible response. Meanwhile, a rapidly rising consumer movement was forcing attention on the deceptive and/ or injurious practices in the development, advertising, packaging, and labeling of goods.

Consumer issues and cultural differences abroad continued to dominate business ethics in the first half of the 1980s. But in the last half of the decade, the central issues of collective moral concern took new shape. Whereas during the past two decades most business ethics issues centered on problems of *institutional* responsibility and *institutional* mechanisms for encouraging conformity to high standards, the focus is now on the *moral capacity of individuals*. Insider-trading, hostile takeovers, and the breakup of well-known and dependable corporate entities such as the major retail chains have shifted public attention back to the age-old problems of individual greed and dishonesty. The egregious behavior of extremely wealthy individuals in both the insider-trading and S&L debacles has ruptured the thin membrane of impersonality that formerly surrounded most discussions of business ethics.

A manager's personal values and strength of character have become urgent issues for the corporation. In a recent survey by Korn/Ferry and Columbia University Graduate School of Business, over fifteen hundred executives from twenty countries rated personal ethics as the number one characteristic needed by the ideal CEO in the year 2000.[3] As Delbert "Bud" Staley, former chairman of NYNEX, remarked, personal integrity is a business leadership essential: "We have to depend on every one of our employees for the good reputation of this firm." So, too, Johnson & Johnson's Jim Burke has asserted that most individuals in his company welcome the emphasis on high ethical standards which their Credo represents. "After all," he said, "everybody wants to believe in something."

EVEN THE BEST PEOPLE HAVE ETHICAL PROBLEMS

Despite the widespread agreement today on the need for ethical *people* in business, it is still hard for individuals to

[3]Korn/Ferry International and Columbia University Graduate School of Business, *21st Century Report: Reinventing the CEO* (Los Angeles: 1989), p. 41.

feel that they personally face ethical problems. This point was made succinctly when NYNEX's current chairman, William Ferguson, remarked that he never viewed "Gab-lines" as his own ethical problem, because he was so clear on his own moral stand: he was personally against pornography. And yet first amendment issues and legal obligations of the carrier demanded that the company provide service for these activities. In retrospect, says Ferguson, he had a moral obligation to address the issue more aggressively. The service was reexamined and NYNEX made a breakthrough in selective blocking technology, which allowed consumers to exercise choice in this matter.

FAMILIAR ETHICAL QUANDARIES

Such circumstances arise daily. The rules of the marketplace and pluralism of our society present opportunities and needs for action which do not on the surface seem to give rise to personal moral doubt, but which do, on closer examination, represent important moral problems for the individual. Ethics is everywhere. A quick survey of most managers would be likely to include participation in, if not direct initiation of, at least twenty of the thirty following situations. All are important from a managerial standpoint, and all contain moral issues of honesty, fairness, respect for others, or fulfillment of promises. I have compiled the list simply from the comments of executives with whom I have worked. The reader may wish to check how many he or she has personally encountered in the past two years.

1. Greed
2. Cover-ups and misrepresentations in reporting and control procedures
3. Misleading product or service claims
4. Reneging or cheating on negotiated terms
5. Establishing policy that is likely to cause others to lie to get the job done
6. Overconfidence in one's own judgment to the risk of the corporate entity

7. Disloyalty to the company as soon as times get rough
8. Poor quality
9. Humiliating people at work or by stereotypes in advertising
10. Lockstep obedience to authority, however unethical and unfair it may be
11. Self-aggrandizement over corporate obligations (conflict of interest)
12. Favoritism
13. Price-fixing
14. Sacrificing the innocent and helpless in order to get things done
15. Suppression of basic rights: freedom of speech, choice, and personal relationships
16. Failing to speak up when unethical practices occur
17. Neglect of one's family, or neglect of one's personal needs
18. Making a product decision that perpetrates a questionable safety issue
19. Not putting back what you take out of the environment, employees, and/or corporate assets
20. Knowingly exaggerating the advantages of a plan in order to get needed support
21. Failing to address probable areas of bigotry, sexism, or racism
22. Courting the business hierarchy versus doing the job well
23. Climbing the corporate ladder by stepping on others
24. Promoting the destructive go-getter who outruns his or her mistakes
25. Failing to cooperate with other areas of the company—the enemy mentality
26. Lying by omission to employees for the sake of the business
27. Making an alliance with a questionable partner, albeit for a good cause

28. Not taking responsibility for injurious prac-
    tices—intentional or not
29. Abusing or just going along with corporate perks
    that waste money and time
30. Corrupting the public political process through
    legal means

What is most interesting to me about this list is its
length. Moreover, these are not hothouse problems that occur
once in a career, they are familiar dilemmas. A company has
at least twenty on the table every day. A manager has at least
twenty on his or her desk every year. What I find equally impressive is their elusive nature. These are the kinds of situations that seem obviously wrong from a distance, but are so
embedded in other concerns and environmental circumstances that the demarcations between right and wrong are
blurred. Even price-fixing has been regarded by many otherwise high-minded executives as not really significant from a
moral standpoint.[4]
    With the possible exception of number 13, each exam-
ple poses a choice to step over the moral line or not. An ethical
resolution to these situations requires discretional judgment
about degree, overall goals, immediate logistical problems,
other trade-offs, chances of success, and so on. There is no
canned program or magical mirror to help you determine
what is right and wrong.
    Such dilemmas are at the core of every manager's job,
and their resolution rests partly on the foundation of values he
or she brings to the task, but also on many conditions beyond a
manager's direct control. Being raised right presumably provides the foundation for moral conduct. But how many managers with good backgrounds nevertheless end up as players in
a commercial effort that puts other people's lives at risk?[5] How
many succumb to an "everybody-for-him-or herself" culture

[4]Relatively low penalties for the act indicate that the judicial system concurs. For a discussion of
attitudes toward price-fixing, see Marshall Clinard and Peter C. Yeager, *Illegal Corporate Behavior*
(Washington, DC: National Institute of Law Enforcement and Criminal Justice, 1979).
[5]For example, over 100,000 deaths per year are attributed to occupationally related diseases, the
majority of which are caused by willful violations of health and safety laws by corporations. See
Ronald C. Kramer, "Corporate Crime: An Organizational Perspective," in *White Collar and Economic Crime*, eds., Peter Wickman and Timothy Dailey (Lexington, MA: Lexington Books, 1982),
p. 76.

because those who were greedy and dishonest seem to get all the rewards? How many employees, disgruntled over a superior's conduct, feel no qualms when they choose to lie to a customer rather than solve the customer's problem?

Or say you are confronted with a potentially flawed product that would not physically injure a customer but certainly would cost him or her time and money. You have to determine whether to delay its introduction, and for how long, while you run time-consuming tests and make adjustments. Meanwhile the company has set your division a hard and fast sales target for the quarter, you are in a declining market with unethical competitors and have a smaller staff, and the investment community is breathing down your boss's neck. How does being raised right provide an automatic solution, even at the theoretical level, to the many ethical choices that must be made about one's obligation to customer, shareholder, boss, and organization?

Good business leadership and ultimately the fate of capitalism depend on the deliberate maintenance of a complex web of ethical values in the face of these many conflicting pressures. No moral artifice such as the law or corporate policy can mechanically solve the difficult trade-offs and painful decisions a responsible manager continually faces.

The moral calculus with which a manager would evaluate the current currency of his or her corporate activities must include more than what was learned at parental knees. It is cavalier to imply that maintaining ethical standards is easy as long as you're strong enough. Everyone faces hard issues whose solutions are not always obvious. The reconciliation of profit motives and ethical imperatives is an uncertain and highly tricky matter.

What is more, theoretical frameworks for reconciliation, though important, are obviously not enough. There is an old proverb: "The road to hell is paved with good intentions." Many analysts of business ethics have noted that most instances of business wrongdoing are committed by people who never deliberately set out to commit unethical acts.[6] The po-

---

[6]For example, Gerald E. Ottoson states: "Most of the unethical acts I have seen committed in business were performed by essentially honest people." "Winning the War Against Corporate Crime," *ethikos* 2.4 (January–February 1989), p. 3.

tential for fallibility is not confined to the business person, but it also does not escape him or her. One is reminded of Hannah Arendt and Primo Levi's sobering conclusions that the truly frightening thing about the Holocaust was that it was carried out not by the fiendishly evil or maladapted, but by ordinary people who, under other circumstances, would appear to fit our common definitions of goodness. Wrote Levi in a moving analysis of the average Nazi in the SS:

> They were made of the same cloth as we, they were average human beings, averagely intelligent, averagely wicked: save the exceptions, they were not monsters, they had our faces, but they had been reared badly. They were, for the greater part, diligent followers and functionaries . . . many indifferent, or fearful of punishment, or desirous of a good career, or too obedient.[7]

History and developmental psychology have indicated that members of almost any group, though individually well intended, can sink to immoral depths they would never dare test as individuals.

Today's manager needs to be armed with an awareness of what habits of thought and action are most likely to subvert moral common sense and the intellectual tools for breaking through these ethical snags.

A SYSTEM AT RISK

The need for a second look at one's own approach to business ethics is particularly urgent as we enter the 1990s. In the past, attention to the ethics of business centered largely on money matters. Corporate standards were primarily a matter of procedural rules about the pursuit of self-interest and welfare state instructions about the responsible distribution of the assets accrued. In a simplistic perversion of the Hebrew commandments, these standards consisted of a promise and

[7]Primo Levi, *The Drowned and the Saved* (New York: Summit Books, 1986).

a curse: Do this and you will prosper, fail to do this and you will be cursed. "This," to put it in free-market terms, was the pursuit of self-interest within the bounds of law and custom.

This contract for conduct has informed the basic motivational and allocation mechanisms in the corporation for at least the past forty years. Its assumption that personal goodness will follow fairly easily has rested on four important conditions:

1. Sustained economic growth
2. An expectation of lifetime employment
3. A homogeneous work force
4. A national educational system that stresses literacy, math ability, and basic Judeo-Christian values

Immediate and dependable cash rewards, people whose norms were similar, an effective educational background, and the prospect of working with much the same group throughout one's career were sufficient to stimulate teamwork and productivity. People were relatively competent by the time they finished their higher education goals, and they were willing to cooperate and be self-sacrificing and work hard because it paid to do so. They stayed more or less within the bounds of acceptable behavior because 1) the players were all reasonably like-minded, 2) the pie was big and growing, and 3) the legislative arena was relatively benign. George Gilder's description of the humane nature of the free market would generally have been said to be accurate, if somewhat exaggerated.

Granted there were downsides to this ethos—smothering conformity, humiliating obedience to a hierarchical social system, and more recently the decline of market responsiveness—but in general, business could rely on informal cultural mechanisms and formal controls to motivate success within acceptable bounds of conduct and still use profit as the driving concept. A manager could informally voice a question about the "right way of doing business" and likely be understood by others without seeming to invade someone else's privacy or putting the business at unacceptable risk.

It was also possible for a manager to have direct oversight of other people's behavior. Robert Baldwin, former chairman of Morgan Stanley, recounted how in his early days at the firm all the traders sat in a circle with Mr. Morgan occupying a prominent position on a platform at one end. "You can believe me," said Baldwin, "this was a powerful incentive to conduct yourself ethically."

Even as late as the early 1980s, the established reaction to scandal—whether it was environmental pollution, consumer injury, or overseas bribery—was to increase the control mechanisms within the company, pass laws or set company restrictions, and leave it at that. The essential motivational patterns and approaches to problem solving remained firmly rooted in a "my profit/my company's profit–first" orientation.

As one astute manager expressed it in 1989, "Essentially you motivate for greed and set up a strong system of controls to ensure that if someone steps over the boundaries, they'll get caught and be penalized."

Although this formula for ethics and success may still hold strong currency in some managers' thinking about business morality, the environment that supported it has been steadily eroding since 1970. In 1990, it is all but gone. Economic recession in many industries and a multipolar array of strong competitors have undermined the promise of universal and immediate cash rewards among like-minded people. Downsizing, mergers, and extreme work force mobility have destroyed any remaining illusions about lifetime employment. Homogeneity and coincident value systems are all but gone. The work force is now international, multiracial, dual sexual, and on its way to being even more so. The legislative arena is redefining (with customary difficulty) every standard of corporate behavior from import quotas to drug testing. The schools have abandoned values education for so long that even a free-market president speaks of a values crisis in this country and calls for a kinder, gentler nation. As for hard work and sacrifice, U.S. personal savings rates dropped from over 10 percent of income to under 2 percent between 1973 and 1987.

In short, the familiar free-market ethos of managed greed has become unmanageable. The already fragile bonds between people in the marketplace are fast disappearing as the cash rewards fail to materialize, and traditional methods of leadership such as personal contact and communication with the top become all but obsolete as the corporation becomes larger and geographically more scattered.

The situation is further exacerbated by massive disruptions of company traditions through ownership changes and the increasing impersonalization of work as technology progresses into everyone's backyard. Excessive wage gaps between the top and the bottom distance people still further and breed resentment. A resentful worker is one more likely to rip off a company or at least fail to go the extra mile for its customers. Moreover, without massive investment in reeducation, many workers could not effectively respond to entrepreneurial opportunities even if they wished to do so.

These environmental changes have meant bad news for many companies' performance records as teamwork, cooperation, and self-sacrifice fail to inform managerial attitudes and behavior. The accompanying decline in trust levels makes it increasingly difficult to motivate intracompany cooperation and responsiveness to customers, or to count on employee loyalty in situations where the rewards must be down the road, and not guaranteed at that. Meanwhile, consumers are able to survey a wider and wider arena of alternatives to choose from.

The impact of these changes is not just economic. They also spell danger for the moral capacity of business and the people in it. Technology and financial complexity have created many more opportunities to cheat and many more corners to hide in. New environmental concerns and a more educated consumer pose additional quandaries about products, markets, manufacturing, and financing. When growth is relatively constant and lifetime membership in the corporate family assured, it is easier for a person to invest time, money, and reputation to solve such problems. But today's survival environment stimulates a me-first business ethic which seems to justify exploitation and cheating because the lifeboats are filled. Game playing and indifference to others are inevitable results. The trust factor is eroded at every level of corporate activity. The spontaneity, enthusiasm, and personal risk-taking that characterize many startup, high-growth businesses are being lost in the economic and social turmoil that embroils most large corporations today.

In such an environment the old models of motivating

for self-interest and passively leaving other values to chance or outside regulation simply fail to be effective moral or market motivators. In the 1980s, we have seen the emergence of a materialistic, get-rich-quick, "lean-and-mean" ethos which is creating a self-destructive confidence gap in individual corporations and the marketplace. It has also set up many executives for a certain identity crisis as their material achievements either diminish in the face of economic downturn or fail to nourish their spiritual needs.

Those who voice confidence in the private sector's ability to carry on as usual in face of such changes should not forget that until quite recently the securities industry, resting on a bedrock of self-regulation and after-the-fact regulatory oversight, was frequently cited as the model for encouraging high ethical standards in business. As the moral fabric of this industry unraveled in the late 1980s, all the environmental factors mentioned above battered the companies at which wrongdoing occurred: dramatically abrupt changes in ownership and leadership patterns, a more diverse work force with more individualistically centered values, heightened complexity of transaction procedures providing more places to hide, a globalized and faster-paced playing field, and legislative rules that did not keep up with changing practices and increased volume.

MOVING BEYOND COMPLIANCE CONCERNS

The quiet tragedy is that so many securities companies, by failing to address the devaluation of personal standards, which would be the inevitable fallout of such conditions, ended up victimizing not only the public but themselves as well. As one executive in the industry put it, the system worked in the sense that some people eventually got caught, but what do you do next? For many whose business approach was formed by this system, the only operating questions on the table are, will we be staying within the procedural rules, and will we make money? In such questions one finds no deep foundation of values to help reverse the recent overemphasis on greed.

Theologian Paul Tillich has described the truth of a faith as its ability to express adequately an ultimate concern. He defines adequacy of expression as something that "creates reply, action, and communication."[8] Laissez-faire ethics, i.e., relying on everyone's home rearing or creating a lot of sticks to punish after the fact, is no longer able to create the kind of communal reply, communication, and action that is adequate for expressing the ultimate concerns about profit and morality, namely, 1) whether there is real value-creation, and 2) how the standard way of doing business affects people in the system and those who are objects of its activity.

The chief issue for business ethics and the manager intent on sustaining high corporate standards of behavior is not the detection of all the business people who are unethical. Compliance oversight is needed, but it is not the whole answer to ensuring ethical business conduct. The task at hand for every corporate leader is to concentrate not just on what should *not* be done, but also on what the ethical manager *should* be thinking from moral and economic standpoints. Here is where the real moral leadership will occur in corporations.

ENLIGHTENED SELF-INTEREST?

To begin the journey, it must be recognized that standard managerial approaches to problem solving and motivation are failing to keep basic moral standards and the overarching goals of a capitalistic society alive in today's changed competitive and social environments. Traditional self-interest models of problem solving and motivating do not adequately stimulate either the moral or performance outcomes for which they were developed. They no longer provoke truly enlightened self-interest, with its implication of suspended self-interest for long-term self-enhancement. Rather, they are being perverted into a justification for what I call the survival ethic, i.e., everyone for him- or herself for the sake of the company's survival. As increasingly dire depictions of Ameri-

---

[8]Paul Tillich, *Dynamics of Faith* (New York: Harper Torchbooks, 1965), p. 96.

can industry's demise are accompanied by calls for "breaking the rules," the survival ethic becomes more and more persuasive and equally unmanageable. The obvious outcome is a no-holds-barred approach to business which renders impotent our hoped-for constraints on predatory behavior. It also introduces into the system a hidden and lethal "exploitation virus" that causes well-intended team building and joint venture efforts to self-destruct.

New kinds of competitive alliances, new arrangements of the work force, and old problems of unresponsiveness call for a more socially oriented approach to management which can stimulate the ethical values that build rather than impede cooperation, hard work, personal empowerment, and value-creation as a first goal. If business and society are to thrive, we need a stronger moral ballast for business than thoughts of self-advancement.

It is time to strike a new bargain for capitalism, one that recognizes that voluntary exchange, individual and social health, and the cooperation of large groups of people are based on more than the management of personal self-interest. To the degree that they fail to go beyond the appeal to self-interest, current goal setting and other motivational frameworks for problem solving are setting companies up for moral and financial failure.

A new foundation of assumptions is needed that elicits the normal array of ethical values *despite* the current economic and social upheavals. Without these values, which would include honesty, trust, value-creation, fairness, and self-sacrifice, potentially destructive ethical dilemmas such as the thirty mentioned above can become the unremarkable norm. Should that occur, current corporate efforts toward innovation, responsiveness, and teamwork will be futile. A company's reputation, for that matter the integrity of our economic system, ultimately rests not on self-aggrandizement but on the cultivation of genuinely self-respecting employees who have the welfare of others firmly seated in their value system. The legitimacy of capitalism depends on managers who have the necessary understanding and skill to maintain these other-oriented standards as the pressure to abandon them increases.

The ethics issue of the 1990s will surely be the search for a set of management assumptions that can stimulate personal integrity and responsiveness to others in the market-place within the changing competitive context of most industries. To be successful, this inquiry cannot remain isolated from other business issues today. One must understand the moral underpinning of a success theory, if excellence is ever to be obtained and sustained.

Some business leaders and long-standing corporate traditions have already found the kind of business philosophy needed to respond to the ethical complexities of commercial endeavor. Increasingly, they are shedding the traditional anonymity of the CEO's role in favor of a more explicit assertion of ethical standards. This new style of leadership, exemplified by such people as Wal-Mart's David Glass, Johnson & Johnson's James Burke, and Xerox's David Kearns, *has underscored the importance of individual integrity and the relevance of private moral values to the achievement of excellent performance.*[9] Likewise, Tom Peters echoes the thinking of a number of his admired executives when, in *Thriving on Chaos*, he cites "integrity" as the capstone of his forty-five-point list of competitive attributes. These people not only have a theoretical commitment to ethical conduct, they have already successfully applied familiar ethical values like honesty, trustworthiness, loyalty, fairness, self-knowledge, and beneficent results to the realm of moneymaking and managing. John Casey's *Ethics in the Financial Marketplace* and Max DePree's *Leadership Is an Art* are two outstanding examples of this leadership philosophy.[10] My purpose here will be to build on the tenor of such works and to systematically explore the major themes of the "excellence" literature in terms of the *moral* premises on which outstanding performance is based and motivated.

THE COVENANTAL ETHIC

The most noteworthy feature of a Johnson & Johnson Credo, or Max DePree's management approach, is the way in which self-interest is reoriented. It is not that these business

[9]For a recent study of "values-driven" leadership, which describes some of this new explicitness, see Joseph L. Badaracco, Jr., and Richard R. Ellsworth, *Leadership and the Quest for Integrity* (Boston: Harvard Business School Press, 1989).
[10]John L. Casey, *Ethics in the Financial Marketplace* (New York: Scudder, Stevens & Clark, 1988); and Max DePree, *Leadership Is an Art* (Garden City, NY: Doubleday, 1989).

leaders ignore profit motives—far from it. But they subordinate self-interest to other motivations, the most prominent of
which are value-creation and service to others. Their experience, the way they define goals, and how they describe the
way they resolve problems provide the basis for what I will
call a Covenantal Business Ethic. This label is a deliberate
echo of the social contracts that early New England communities established for the mutual well-being of their members.
The Covenantal Ethic provides a coherent blending of profit
motive and the other-oriented values that help create trust and
cooperation between people. It has three essential aspects: 1)
It sees value-creation in its many forms as the primary objective; 2) it sees profit and other social returns as a result of
other goals rather than the overriding objective; and 3) it approaches business problems more in terms of relationships
than tangible products.

Building upon this framework, a Covenantal Ethic
stresses service to others and deliberately draws on some of
the nonrational impulses, such as "caring," which secure people's commitment to organizations and tasks even when doing
so is not obviously to their immediate advantage. As such, this
ethic differs from traditional approaches not just in focus but
in the vehicles by which moral conduct is made an active part
of management. Emotional phenomena have for the most part
been absent from the vocabulary and theoretical frameworks
that business people have applied to moral problems. Morality
has been a question of legal obligation, a weighing of rights,
a cost-benefit calculation of consequences. A Covenantal Ethic
does not preclude these kinds of thinking, but it also draws on
the workings of the heart. It is a radical departure from the
eat-or-be-eaten, sweat-or-be-beaten theories of motivating
hard work and innovation one hears so often in executive
seminars and analyses of, for example, why we've fallen behind, say, Japan.

Not only does a Covenantal Ethic promise a more
communal morality in business thinking, it also holds the
prospect of increasing a manager's sense of self-worth. Covenantal thinking's foundation is the belief that *all* individuals
are worthy of respect and service, rather than being of worth
only in terms of what they might cost or gain you. Simply

stated, it is an assertion of humanism, in that it holds every life to be of value, even in the economic context of serving a corporate entity. Thus a Covenantal Ethic, or for that matter any other business ethic, is a statement about the relative significance of individuals and the society to which they are committed. I see these significances not just in terms of productivity, though that is important, but also in terms of vitality. A Covenantal Ethic places the energy and intrinsic worth of individuals above the mechanics of an organizational system and its preordained financial strategy. As such, it is an ethic that directly complements recent arguments such as Tom Peters's or Rosabeth Kanter's about the need for increased individualism and autonomy in today's competitive environment.[11]

Though I agree with their theses, to my mind this need is not a new one precipitated by the need for new organization structures in the face of changing competition. In the 1950s and 1960s, it was argued that the corporation needed to pay more attention to individualism because of the very success of its hierarchical bureaucracy. Now it is argued that the corporation needs to pay attention to individualism because of its failures. It seems more likely that individualism is quite simply an ever-present human need, independent of economic fortune. The society that is vital and moral must have individuals who are vital and moral. This is especially true for business.

It is important to note at the outset of this inquiry that the Covenantal Ethic suggested here is not a theoretical wishlist about the nation's corporate leadership, but a reality in many of the country's most successful organizations. Covenantal thinking has a proven economic and moral track record, as Herman Miller Company's legendary annualized earnings growth and product quality demonstrate, or J.C. Penney's continued and successful responsiveness to customers illustrates.

As its title suggests, this book poses the notion that it is possible for a manager to carry his or her moral concerns

[11]Tom Peters, *Thriving on Chaos* (New York: Harper & Row, 1987); Rosabeth Moss Kanter, *The Change Masters: Innovation and Entrepreneurship in the American Corporation* (New York: Simon & Schuster, 1983); and, more recently, *When Giants Learn to Dance* (New York: Simon & Schuster, 1989).

beyond the realm of good intentions into actual application in the achievement of economic success. The approach I suggest here conforms to what one would call "good business sense." It tries to enhance the way managers think about that concept by systematically analyzing the moral and humanistic dimension of good business judgment. This perspective is crucial if capitalism's moral objectives of social good and individual well-being are not to become obsolete. I firmly believe that there is a deep reservoir of decency in American management, but that too frequently the way in which managers set goals and measure success fails to tap that resource adequately. The number one American business challenge in the 1990s is to transform a manager's allegedly good intentions into a profound and enacted covenant with customers, employees, and the general public. None of these groups are limited to American shores. The global nature of this covenant only adds to its urgency, for how well it is fulfilled could either destroy or secure the tenuous foothold that democratic capitalism has in so many nations today.

2

Personal Morality and Business Ethics

There is no such thing as business ethics. There's only one kind—you have to adhere to the highest standards.*

While many corporate leaders are giving strong voice to the need for high ethical standards in business, it has been very difficult to find the right vocabulary and terms for describing the moral dimension of management. As Bower's statement implies, the term *business ethics* can be repulsive. To him and others it suggests the immoral idea of condoning a double standard—one ethic for private life, another for business decisions. To others, business ethics suggests a laughable contradiction in terms.

Thus, although many pundits express the need for strong moral standards in business, there have as yet been few successful verbal reconciliations of management and morality. What do we mean by the terms *integrity* and *highest standards of conduct*? Are these concepts, which are generally obvious, really so undeserving of remark when managers must daily confront the many gray areas of business behavior? Is it enough to outline what one shouldn't do and leave the rest to personal instinct?

*Marvin Bower, former managing partner, McKinsey & Co. Quoted in Walter Guzzardi, "Wisdom from the Giants of Business," *Fortune*, July 3, 1989, p. 81.

Obviously not, for as the thirty situations listed in Chapter 1 suggest, managers regularly face decisions that carry no obvious demarcation between right and wrong. Moral conduct in business deserves the same systematic attention any other aspect of management receives. So far, however, there has been little help in this area. Formal philosophical and theological analysis has not found a useful translation device for describing the concerns of the soul in the language of the pocketbook.

This failure should come as no surprise. Both fields have scorned the discussion of business for thousands of years. The Bible warns against serving mammon. Even Aristotle, writing over two thousand years ago, first considered the business person as a possible topic for his work on applied ethics, then rejected the proposition outright on the grounds that the purposes and mentality of the vulgar merchant or mechanic were not sufficiently well-minded for serious moral analysis. (*Eudemian Ethics* I.IV.2)

As for our instinctive responses, the idea of a business life of integrity simply does not compute for most people. In our culture it is easy to imagine a heroic doctor risking his or her own health to treat the sick. Or a heroic lawyer defending, at the expense of his or her own career, an unpopular client's right to a fair trial. Nor is the image of a teacher maintaining the search for truth at the risk of personal ridicule far-fetched.

It is far more difficult to idealize a stereotypical corporate executive nobly making money. And when doctors or teachers begin to reveal moneymaking motivations, they are firmly subjected to the same social cynicism. Philip Caldwell, former chairman of Ford Motor Company, commented on this terminally suspicious vision of business morality when he said, "Many people think that if you're a business person you must automatically be greedy and dishonest. I find that view to be repugnant."

The field of management science, while not as overtly cynical about executive morality as the media, has nevertheless exhibited a similar dearth of intellectual clarity on the specific application of ethical standards to solving the standard problems of business. Personal values are acknowledged to be important, but how do these translate into the substance of impersonal management systems? Most statements of business purpose are functional rather than ethical in nature. Drucker, for example, has described the overall purpose of business as "the productive utilization of wealth-producing resources."[1] Others assume that "producing greater and greater efficiency" is the overall purpose of business, at least in a democratic capitalistic system. Many other analysts of business describe essential business components either in overtly functional terms or in terms of "excellence" without ever defining the overall purpose to which such activities are aimed.[2]

Such statements are hardly a beacon for guiding a manager's personal integrity through the shoals of materialism and efficiency. Without an overarching understanding of how private values and institutional goals do or do not relate, the claim that business ethics is simply a matter of having a good conscience is rather useless and even misleading. On the other hand, the moral nature of business is not adequately addressed by bare descriptions of organizational or economic functions. We are taught that the corporation is a legal concept, defined as a legal entity, but in practice it is also a social entity. It is an organization of people whose actions have an effect upon each other's welfare and rights.[3]

---

[1]Peter F. Drucker, *Management* (New York: Harper's College Press, 1977), p. 62.

[2]See, for example, Tom Peters and Robert Waterman, *In Search of Excellence* (New York: Harper & Row, 1981), which is structured on the McKinsey 7S components of a business and eight attributes of excellence. Kenneth Andrews, in his classic business text on corporate strategy, begins his analysis with a definition not of business but of management which is overtly functional but not overtly social: "Management may be defined as the direction of informed, efficient, planned, and purposeful conduct of complex organized activity" (*The Concept of Corporate Strategy*, rev. ed. [Homewood, IL: Richard D. Irwin, 1980], p. 2.). Earlier, Chester Barnard (*The Functions of the Executive* [Cambridge, MA: Harvard University Press, 1938]) and Philip Selznick (*Leadership in Administration: A Sociological Interpretation* [Berkeley: University of California Press, 1984]) had already moved the definition of management from the impersonal definition of "the delegation of ownership" to a more social context. What they did not do, however, was describe purpose, but rather function. See, for example, Barnard, p. 18. "It [management responsibility] is responsibility for contribution. Function rather than power has to be the distinctive criterion and the organizing principle."

[3]Some have argued persuasively that the nature of an individual person is also essentially social, if for no other reason than that a person's very life is the product of a union of two. See, for example, F.H. Bradley, "My Station and Its Duty," in *Ethical Studies*, 2d ed. (Oxford: Clarendon Press, 1927). The point I am making here is that whereas individual people seem to have a mixture of privateness, separateness, and socialness, nothing in a business escapes the social context.

MOVING UP THE MORAL LEARNING CURVE

Difficult as it is to bridge the gaps between the traditional discussion of private conscience and the discussion of management science, the journey must be made. Morality is an inescapable fact of managerial life whose problems must be systematically analyzed.

Nearly every business decision and activity inherently has a moral aspect or significance. Many of these are variations on the quality of trust. A financial transaction, for example, cannot be obtained without the establishment of several mechanisms of trust: negotiators must be trusted to keep their word, prices quoted must bear some relation to prices charged, record-keepers must be relied upon to keep accurate records about what is done by whom and for how much. Product decisions require that people make assessments of quality and efficacy, which depend on the honesty and accuracy of those people. Complex service systems and transactions require efficient teamwork, which cannot be secured without cooperation, which in turn cannot be achieved, even when mandated by law, unless trust and mutual respect have been established between the players. If an employee does not trust that top management cares about him (or her), it is unlikely that he or she will care to deal meticulously on behalf of that management. If other business units cannot be trusted to tell a straight story and to take credit for only what they deserve, then why insist on personal standards of honesty unless they have a demonstrable payoff?

Amitai Etzioni has expressed the fundamentally moral aspect of business eloquently:

> Trust, of course, is pivotal to the economy, and not merely to social relations, as without it, currency will not be used, saving makes no sense, and transactions costs rise precipitously; in short, it is hard to conceive a modern economy without a strong element of trust running through it.[4]

[4]Amitai Etzioni, *The Moral Dimension: Toward a New Economics* (New York: Free Press, 1988), p. 8.

Moving beyond the ethics of trust on which managerial activities depend, it can be seen that managers also make decisions that engender moral *outcomes*. Most corporate activities have an impact on other people and are thereby inherently subject to consequentialist questions about their ultimate good or harm.

We know that such issues, far from being a trend of the 1980s, are at least as old as the Sumerians, who lived five thousand years ago. Writing itself, one of the most important inventions in the history of humankind, was developed in part as a response to a business ethics problem. The long distances and hazards of the great trade routes along the Tigris-Euphrates raised new difficulties in ensuring payment for and delivery of goods sold. The Sumerians developed the first crude forms of writing to record commercial activity on tablets so that distant transactions could be carried out in an environment of mutual trust and accountability. Once this environment was created, commercial enterprises and trade exploded. Clay tablets made possible taxation, inventory, and transactions, forming the economic and institutional basis of the first great Western civilization.

While the historical impact of "business ethics" is no doubt considerably less than that of the invention of writing, the current trendiness of business ethics is testimony to the fact that people are still plagued by the moral aspects of business life and still looking for appropriate responses to the practical challenges these problems raise. As the Sumerian example illustrates, there are no hard lines between the moral, economic, and social aspects of business. Business ethics tends to encompass all three areas of critical thought. It moves without constraint between the macroeconomic systems of capitalism to the organizational behavior issues of management to the very personal and private values that individuals hold dear.

What is more, despite the often-justified skepticism, there is reason to assume that these values and outcomes are capable of coherent analysis for the simple fact that they find coherent expression in actions every day. Even without Aristotle's help, business people manage to achieve ethical outcomes. Contractual obligations are fulfilled and accurate record-keeping is achieved daily. Many products serve the customer well. Many workplaces provide employees with a fair wage and a legitimate sense of self-worth. And there are many business leaders, from IBM's legendary Thomas Watson to J.C. Penney's Don Seibert, whose commitment to a business career has been marked by outstanding personal integrity, success for the company, and service to the general public.

TRADITIONAL RESPONSES TO ETHICAL RESPONSIBILITY IN BUSINESS

But how does the manager of good conscience address business ethics today? How do the heroic assertions of morality in business such as the resolution of the Tylenol crisis at Johnson & Johnson come about?

Response 1. Trusting in Gut Instinct

There are many ways in which managers respond to the pervasiveness of moral issues at work. One is to trust in "gut instinct" and not try to articulate the problem any further. In many ethics issues such a response is about as adequate as an aspirin in a car accident. Gut instinct alone hardly copes with the moral complexities of PACs, random drug testing, wage gaps, or environmental responsibility.

Nor does gut instinct equip a manager with an adequate voice for ethical leadership in a large organization. Everyone's guts do not rely on the same set of values and choices. One person's entrepreneurial pricing discount for a favored customer may be another person's definition of a kickback. Manager A may be repulsed by the suggestion that the company use the illegally obtained proprietary information of a competitor, while Manager B may feel this is simply a case of gaining the proverbial competitive edge. Merely appealing to one's guts as a guideline for the way a company does business will not ensure unanimity nor even sensitivity when the choices between integrity and easy profit become difficult.

Gut instinct also tends to lose its power as an individual becomes socialized into the value system of an organization. History has shown that individuals can make very different choices when they act together as a group. Some of the most admired individuals on Wall Street traded on insider information against their customers' accounts; managers who were presumably good parents systematically falsified accident reports at several nuclear plants across America; church-going executives at a major food processor not only failed to investigate clear indications that their "apple juice" concentrate was 100 percent chemical but later shipped cases of the chemical cocktail off to Puerto Rico in an effort to evade the FDA and sell the product anyway.

Fallibility is a human condition to which managers are as vulnerable as anyone else. As Kenneth Andrews notes in his preface to *Ethics in Practice*, business ethics is "a problem that snares not just a few mature criminals or crooks-in-the-making but also a host of apparently good people who lead exemplary private lives while concealing information about dangerous or lethal products or falsifying cost records."[5] If for no other reason than the frailty of human judgment—especially when confronted with the prospect of making lots of money—the gut instinct approach is not an adequate moral response to the ethical dilemmas and responsibilities of leadership in business.

Response 2. Defining the Shalt-Not's

A second approach to taming the moral issues of business is the commandment technique. Business activities are subjected to a series of how-not-to's on specific topics, often in the form of legislation or an ethics compliance code: No conflict of interest; Do not lie; Be honest and objective in keeping records; Avoid poisoning your customer; Do not pollute the environment; Do not oppress minorities; Do not harass females; Do not sell out the company to the short-term speculator; Do not put your hand in the till.

Such principles are a familiar component of most cor-

[5]Kenneth R. Andrews, ed., *Ethics in Practice: Managing the Moral Corporation* (Boston: Harvard Business School Press, 1989), p. 1.

porate policy statements. They contain important guidelines for groupwide behavior but are limited by their very topicality. For example, a strict guideline prohibiting company buyers from accepting gifts in excess of $25 may preclude out-and-out bribery, but it does not ensure that a buyer will exercise his or her procurement judgment with prudence rather than prejudice. No money may pass hands, and yet a buyer can still be seduced by all sorts of perks and sales incentives to purchase a product or service without an honest and responsible consideration of its ultimate appropriateness for the company. Moreover, no conflict-of-interest or record-keeping policy will prevent the same manager from massaging information in such a way as to make his or her purchasing decisions look better than they actually are.

The manager who develops a fine series of specific shalt-not's as a way of providing ethical leadership in the corporation quickly discovers that there is always someone else who can find a way around the rules, or that market conditions have developed that the rules never anticipated. This is not to say that rules are unimportant, but only that, on their own, they do not address the full range of ethical problems a manager confronts. As the saying goes, when it comes to personal integrity, the law is better understood as a floor than a ceiling.

Response 3. Explicitly Articulating a Business Philosophy

A third way of approaching the moral issues of business is to establish an overarching, explicit set of ethical *standards*—not just prohibitions—concerning the goals of the company and the means by which individuals are to carry them out. Here we can learn much from the Japanese business leader who considers the publication of a personal "business philosophy" to be an essential requirement of the top post. These statements do not address moral concerns in abstract isolation. Rather, they describe the company's business standards in integrated terms: they combine management's personal moral commitment with economic goals and cultural values. From the practical standpoint of how a manager really thinks, "being honest," "having fun," "being innovative," and "delivering a top-quartile return on equity" are all related.

Call such a mindset a philosophy, or an ethos, or just plain "the basics." What it expresses are the commitments managers feel are possible or impossible for themselves and their company to entertain. As stakeholders become more aggressive about what they expect from the corporation, and the workplace more diverse, the articulation of these commitments in advance becomes increasingly important.

Many of the CEOs quoted in this book feel that it is a fundamental responsibility of management to provide visible and direct leadership in articulating "what the company stands for" through a credo or mission statement. Others feel such values should be informally communicated. Whatever form it takes, the systematic exploration of those values, goals, and outcomes that describe "what the company stands for," or "who it is," is the first step in bringing the moral dilemmas of business to responsible solution.

TAKING THE FIRST STEP

Having argued for the application of one's personal sense of ethics to the problematic issues of business, an articulation of the general characteristics that define "ethical" and "responsible" management is helpful in grounding the discussion at the outset. John L. Casey, managing director of Scudder, Stevens & Clark, has written an excellent book on ethical issues for the financial manager.[6] At its outset he notes that the word *ethics* can itself be a "put-off." Many a manager seeking to discover an appealing title for a business ethics seminar would agree. Other words for morality in business are equally troublesome. In an echo of former grandeur, Chester Barnard's now-classic description of management, *The Functions of the Executive,* describes the morality of the effective manager with terms like *foresight, long purposes*, and *high ideals.*[7]

The term I find most useful for describing ethical decision making is not business ethics but *business integrity.* J.C. Penney's Don Seibert uses it in the title of his book on business

---

[6]John L. Casey, *Ethics in the Financial Marketplace* (New York: Scudder, Stevens & Clark, 1988).
[7]Barnard, *The Functions of the Executive*, p. 282.

ethics. Management professors Joseph Badaracco and Richard Ellsworth claim that integrity is the ultimate responsibility of corporate leadership; Tom Peters cites integrity as the final essential condition of managing change.[8] Nearly every business ethics document cites integrity as an essential component of good business practice.

What does integrity mean? What does it describe? In our pluralistic and individualistic society, is it a problematic, semimystical concept or is there a set of traditional values that people generally use to describe ethical behavior? Johnson & Johnson's former chairman James Burke has often claimed that the company's Credo describes "the common denominator" everyone can believe in. Is he right? Is there an uncontroversial agreement about moral ideals, or must a manager resort to tightly reasoned philosophical definitions in order to analyze ethics and management?

I have polled literally thousands of lower-, middle-, and top-level executives about their personal values, and I have discovered that Burke is indeed right. There are certain values that drive people's idealism with relentless regularity. What, I ask executives, drives *you*? What can't you live without and still be able to look at yourself in the mirror? The same set of values is voiced with little variation:

Honesty	Family
Integrity	Achievement
Trustworthiness	Reliability
Respect for other people	Fairness
Self-respect	Loyalty

Love, religion, and hard work are also cited with regularity if not unanimity.

With the exception perhaps of being clean and cheerful, the previous list sounds very much like the Boy Scout pledge, or Herbert R. Taylor's Four Way Test which was

---

[8]Donald V. Seibert and William Proctor, *The Ethical Executive* (New York: Cornerstone Library, 1984); Joseph L. Badaracco, Jr., and Richard R. Ellsworth, *Leadership and the Quest for Integrity* (Boston: Harvard Business School Press, 1989); and Tom Peters, *Thriving on Chaos* (New York: Harper & Row, 1987), pp. 45–46.

adopted by the Rotary Club.[9] And that is the point. These are not mystical concepts but part of our everyday commonsense descriptions of what makes up personal integrity. When I ask groups of college students the same question, the overwhelming majority cite the same values as ideals.[10]

On the other hand, agreement about ideals does not mean agreement about application. Abortion, for example, may or may not be considered an act of fairness, love, or respect for others. Hard work, when overdone, may be felt to harm the family even though it is intended as an expression of commitment. Honesty at the expense of career may seem an acceptable trade-off or not.

But it is important to note that, despite disagreement about specific applications, the terms are not meaningless. Ethical idealism is not totally relative even in pluralistic America. The many groups I polled have never suggested that their ethical ideals centered on, say, sadistic hedonism or uninhibited exploitation or rampant discrimination. Even though such values sometimes hold sway over management thinking, they are not hailed as acts of integrity.

HALLMARKS OF BUSINESS INTEGRITY

On this basis it is possible to use this list of values as a starting point for my discussion. Working from nearly two hundred corporate ethics codes gathered by the Business Roundtable, interviews with literally thousands of executives, and drawing on pro- and antibusiness articles in the general press, I would suggest that the generally same standards of decency drive our society's definitions of business integrity. Thus a general description of business integrity would comprise the following basic values.

[9]The Rotary's Four Way Test is:
    1. Is it the TRUTH?
    2. Is it FAIR to all concerned?
    3. Will it build GOOD WILL and BETTER FRIENDSHIPS?
    4. Will it be BENEFICIAL to all concerned?

[10]In my experience, despite much evidence to the contrary in terms of behavior, few people put making money and gaining material possessions on a list of ideal values. On the other hand, annual surveys by the Council of Higher Education have revealed that college students do not hesitate to cite materialism or career ambition as one of their chief *pragmatic* goals.

- *Honesty*—accuracy in assessing and representing the business and any activity relevant to a business.
- *Reliability*—being consistent in action with one's purported values. This can imply anything from consistently living up to product claims to not punishing employees who live out the standards you claim are integral to the business.
- *Fairness*—balancing the rights of various constituencies with consistency and goodwill. While companies differ strongly in terms of how far they will carry their sense of stakeholder responsibility in noncommercial relationships, there seems to be more agreement over the commercial manifestations of the ethic: fairness means adopting neither a totally buyer-beware nor seller-beware ethic. Rather than assume exclusive responsibility for every unforeseen outcome of a transaction, the seller accepts responsibility for keeping the specific promises that are made or implied to customers and employees.
- *Pragmatism*—making concrete contributions to the ongoing financial and organizational health of the business.

These four hallmarks of business integrity cover a wealth of ethical issues in a commonsense way. The first three preclude deception, intentional injury, favoritism, conflict of interest, and the abrogation of responsibility to pay for mistakes. The last precludes all forms of white-collar crime, inefficiency, and waste. It also precludes out-and-out philanthropy and, to my mind, implies high quality, in that there is not a company in the world that could market poor quality without compromising its honesty. Even if no injury is involved, a company that covers up or ignores poor quality has no choice but to lie in its representations to the public and shareholders, thus it automatically fails to fulfill the conditions of integrity.

Most important, *integrity is a condition that demands that you walk as you talk.* At its heart it means living up to what you imply is the right thing to do. It means that other people can depend on you to maintain standards of honesty, fairness, and financial prudence even when the going gets tough.

Another way of understanding the meaning of business integrity is put your choices and habits to two tests:

1. Do these decisions contribute to the good reputation of a company or a manager?
2. Do these decisions promote trust?

The two questions are obviously interrelated. Taken together they describe the bottom-line reference point for creating successful negotiations, successful cooperation, and successful investment mechanisms. When the exploration of ethical issues begins to create more heat than light, the two issues, reputation and trust-creation, can help put the discussion back on course.

Most important, the conditions described in the two questions and suggested as the hallmarks of business integrity do not run counter to values by which executives tend to define personal integrity. As such, their creation provides a first step in breaking out of the "business-ethics-is-a-contradiction-in-terms" mentality which has shackled so many attempts to advance managerial understanding in this area.

3

Setting a Leadership Standard

> Leaders owe a covenant to the corporation or institution which is, after all, a group of people. Leaders owe the organization a new reference point for what caring, purposeful, committed people can be in the institutional setting.*

With a general definition of business ethics established and the hallmarks of business integrity suggested in Chapter 2 serving as general guidelines for testing the meaning of the concept, it is possible to move on to the basic problem at hand: *How does the business leader successfully bring these values to bear on his or her own task?* Is integrity an ivory tower statement of idealism reserved for inspirational speeches but not strictly applied for fear it will be economically dysfunctional? Is it an automatic accompaniment to market success, in no need of separate analysis and attention? Or does business integrity represent a distinctive approach to management, not economically dysfunctional, but also not synonymous with purely economic reasoning?

I argue that business integrity falls into the last category. Managers of integrity do not make choices that are either-or in terms of pragmatism and idealism; rather, they

---

*Max DePree, *Leadership Is an Art* (Garden City, NY: Doubleday, 1989), pp. 32–33.

function in ways that are both economically healthy and morally sound. They are able to integrate (and inspire in others) excellent economic rationalism with the less-rational, other-oriented values' preferences which comprise most executives' private definitions of morality, as seen in Chapter 2. These values are not automatically operative if one applies only economic rationales.

A CASE OF MORAL BUSINESS LEADERSHIP

The Tylenol crisis is a good example of the kind of moral business thinking I am talking about. In 1982, executives at Johnson & Johnson received the shocking information that several poisonings had occurred in the Chicago area, apparently after the victims had taken Tylenol in capsule form. Lab tests confirmed that the capsules had been laced with cyanide. In the first twenty-four hours of the crisis, no one could identify the source of the poisoning: was it a disgruntled employee, a manufacturing mistake, or had someone contaminated the capsules outside the plant, either en route to or in the stores? Subsequent information overwhelmingly indicated that Johnson & Johnson's manufacturing process had not been at fault, and that the poisonings had most likely occurred after the capsules had left the plant. No one, however, could provide a definitive answer as to how the tragedy had been orchestrated, or how many other capsules might be contaminated.

Although the Tylenol market represented $100 million annually, and provided pain relief to many people, Johnson & Johnson recalled all Tylenol products. Experts thought it unlikely that other forms of the product were contaminated, but the company was taking no risk of a repeat or copycat poisoning.

Tylenol's reintroduction has become a marketing milestone. Having already won high marks from the public for the recall, Johnson & Johnson cemented that goodwill by widely publicizing its response to the crisis. Once Tylenol had been reintroduced to the market, consumers were given a toll-free hotline to call, and a certificate for a free replacement was offered to anyone who claimed to have destroyed the drug. Within eighteen months, Tylenol had regained nearly all of its lost market share.

Some outside managers have argued vehemently that there was nothing extraordinarily ethical or unusual about Johnson & Johnson's response. To them the problem was purely one of marketing, and the response a calculation of risk and reward. Supposedly any good marketer would have made the same decisions purely from the standpoint of self-interest.

I strongly disagree. Those who view the J&J response in these terms fail to account for and understand all the components of chairman James Burke's thought processes, not to mention those of the other managers who contributed to the two-hundred-plus decisions that had to be made in the first twenty-four hours of the crisis.

Having personally interviewed the three top officers involved, I am certain that no textbook marketing analysis could quantify or even identify the factors that informed their strategy. *From an economic and public relations standpoint one could have made a very reasonable argument for keeping the product on the shelves*: the contamination was not the company's fault and did not appear to have originated from a J&J facility; this was an isolated incident, the result of aberrant behavior; the benefits of the product to the majority of the public vastly outweighed the injuries that might occur if the product remained on the shelves. A savvy public relations person might have adorned this strategy with a limited gesture of goodwill by withdrawing the product from the Chicago area only. It would be difficult to argue against such a strategy on marketing grounds, were it well executed. Most likely, if measured by sales rather than opinion, it would have been seen to be convincing to most customers. After all, when glass was found in Gerber baby food jars several years later, that company was able to recover successfully by issuing only a limited product recall.

And yet a Gerber strategy would not have been morally indistinguishable from a total recall for Johnson & Johnson. As James Burke announced at the outset, Tylenol tested the very core of assumptions driving the firm's past success. Johnson & Johnson had always maintained explicitly in its Credo and implicitly in its advertising that its primary concern

was for its customers. Toward this end, J&J strongly empha-
sized product safety, quality, and reliability. Sterile dressings
could be relied upon to be sterile. Company revenues would
be distributed in such a way as to maintain strong research
and development. But Tylenol was no longer reliable. Any
strategy that hinted at a bias toward company profit over
user interest or at the expense of public safety would deny
these values. It would render the Credo claims dishonest and
top management itself unreliable. In Burke's own words,
their first priority was to remain true to the Credo (see
Exhibit 3-1).

Several aspects of Burke's Credo approach are noteworthy. Although he was obviously concerned about the financial implications of the crisis, his first commitment was to
the entire array of Credo values, which clearly defined profit
as a *result* of customer and public responsiveness rather than
the first goal and perspective for decision making.

Thus thinking about profit would not suffice as a substitute for thinking about Credo commitments in noneconomic terms such as trust, health, safety, and public satisfaction. In the end, this strategy was, from every point of view,
successful. Tylenol was again profitable and public confidence
as measured in a number of surveys and press coverage was
greatly increased. Trust was also increased inside the company. Burke had launched an extensive program to revitalize
the Credo throughout the company just prior to the first Tylenol crisis. His own commitment to the document's philosophy was clear, but the Tylenol crisis would test whether the
Credo really meant anything. Clearly it did. As one manager
later told me, "Tylenol was the tangible proof of what top management had said at the Credo challenge meetings. You came
away saying, 'My God! You're right. We really do believe this.
It's for real. *And we did what was right.*' "

Jim Burke's response to the Tylenol crisis integrated
economic reasoning with the hallmarks of business integrity.
As a leadership philosophy this way of thinking is difficult to
identify and analyze because of its qualitative nature and the
fact that it does indeed work in synergy with profitability goals.

If one is cynical or downright hostile to the proposition that ethics played a role, one could easily make the mis-

Exhibit 3-1
THE JOHNSON & JOHNSON CREDO

Our Credo

We believe our first responsibility is to the doctors, nurses and patients,
to mothers and fathers and all others who use our products and services.
In meeting their needs everything we do must be of high quality.
We must constantly strive to reduce our costs
in order to maintain reasonable prices.
Customers' orders must be serviced promptly and accurately.
Our suppliers and distributors must have an opportunity
to make a fair profit.

We are responsible to our employees,
the men and women who work with us throughout the world.
Everyone must be considered as an individual.
We must respect their dignity and recognize their merit.
They must have a sense of security in their jobs.
Compensation must be fair and adequate,
and working conditions clean, orderly and safe.
We must be mindful of ways to help our employees fulfill
their family responsibilities.
Employees must feel free to make suggestions and complaints.
There must be equal opportunity for employment, development
and advancement for those qualified.
We must provide competent management,
and their actions must be just and ethical.

We are responsible to the communities in which we live and work
and to the world community as well.
We must be good citizens — support good works and charities
and bear our fair share of taxes.
We must encourage civic improvements and better health and education.
We must maintain in good order
the property we are privileged to use,
protecting the environment and natural resources.

Our final responsibility is to our stockholders.
Business must make a sound profit.
We must experiment with new ideas.
Research must be carried on, innovative programs developed
and mistakes paid for.
New equipment must be purchased, new facilities provided
and new products launched.
Reserves must be created to provide for adverse times.
When we operate according to these principles,
the stockholders should realize a fair return.

Johnson & Johnson

take of dismissing the "soft" concepts that informed Burke's words and the Credo itself as merely voicing the company's long-term economic interests. One could rationally calculate that J&J *had* to be honest and self-sacrificing because that would pay in the long run. There really was no ethical issue, because the right ethical choices were obvious *from an economic standpoint.*

Such thinking basically dismisses the need to legitimize ethical discussion and denies ethical uncertainty. It is a comfortable approach to managerial integrity and ethical problem solving. It asserts as the primary value the one that is least controversial in business thinking, namely, that managers *must* think about a company's profit. It holds that the vocabulary of profit provides sufficient ethical guidance for the manager, and that asking what makes commercial sense will stimulate an ethical response. Anyone with good economic sense could have come to the same marketing decisions as Burke and his team without all the semimystical language about trust and Credos.

But to dismiss the Tylenol response as one of simple market sense is to fail to understand the full range of values that informed Jim Burke's leadership and caused Burke and his team to come to the conclusions they did as fast and unambiguously as they did. At the very least, the recall required an unequivocal commitment to public safety, even at the risk of heavy short-term penalties to the bottom line. This risk was real and its advisability controversial. By the company's own account, it was not automatically clear to anyone what would be the right thing to do. Even though in the end they were morally and economically sure of their decision, no one could guarantee that the company would recoup its losses in this heavily competitive industry. Nor could it be argued that *not* recalling the product would necessarily incur a costly drop in public confidence in the company.

The only way the managers could come to the conclusion *quickly* that a recall was right, given the extreme uncertainty of the situation, was if they had a point of view that respected public safety, valued product reliability, and recognized that good management must be measured in long-term calculations. These are a complex set of managerial assumptions which integrate rational economic concerns and nonrational ethical values in a synergistic way.

THE ETHICAL LEADERSHIP CHALLENGE

The ability of a James Burke to inspire this kind of thinking throughout a large organization rests on four essential character traits. Together they comprise a portrait of the kind of leadership that is critical to the fulfillment of ethical standards in large organizations today.

Quality 1. Ability to Recognize and Articulate the Ethics of a Problem

It is very easy to identify the ethical issues of a business situation in the hothouse environment of a case study or under the magnifying glass of a hostile press. It is far more difficult in the heat of the fray. Volvo's chairman Pehr Gyllenhammar asserted that understanding moral values "is really the thing leadership is about." Public opinion surveys in Sweden confirm Gyllenhammar's theory: his own repeated articulation of values in connection with Volvo's activities has made him a more trusted and recognized figure than the prime minister!

One of the comments I hear most frequently in corporate ethics seminars is: "Of course when you think about it, there's obviously an ethical issue here. I guess I just never thought about it that way before."

Jim Burke's up-front assertion that Tylenol was going to be the ultimate test of the Credo was an overt demonstration of moral sensitivity. He did not view the crisis as a tactically difficult marketing problem, but rather as a marketing problem that posed monumental ethical difficulties.

Moral leaders in the corporation have an unerring sense that the ethical stand, however commonplace from the standpoint of philosophical analysis, cannot be taken for granted or left to the interpretation of others. They recognize that without explicit signals from the top, other employees and managers are likely to ride a roller coaster of morality, high when it is to their advantage, low or passive when financial or career penalties threaten.

When Donald Melville became the top officer of Norton Company, his first act was to read the company's ethics code at a meeting of senior managers. Melville prefaced his remarks with the observation, "This is what I believe is the way to do business, and what I expect from all of us." Then-chief operating officer and current chairman David Nelson noted, "At first I thought with embarrassment, 'He's not really going to do this is he?' But then, after he went through it and added his own thoughts on what some of the problems might be or what the words might mean, it had a great impact on all of us. We knew there would be no nonsense on ethics. That made it easier for me to keep my people conscious of our business standards."

Quality 2. The Personal Courage Not to Rationalize Away Bad Ethics

As former Norton chairman Robert Cushman told his employees, "I've had to live by certain rules and so do you." When Colgate-Palmolive acquired a leading toothpaste manufacturer from Hong Kong whose top-selling product carried the brand Darkie, chairman and CEO Reuben Mark took an unambiguous stand: "It's just plain wrong," he said. For three years Mark continued to track the issue, urging Colgate executives to rename this important product. The new brand name and logo were similar enough to the old to retain customer loyalty but the racial content was entirely removed.

Ford Motor's former chairman Philip Caldwell reports that during the late 1970s the most difficult thing for him and the board at Ford was to ask, "What are we doing wrong?" Admitting that there was a problem was extremely threatening and contrary to the corporate culture. It took tremendous character and moral sensitivity to insist that the entire company, from boardroom on out, ask that question honestly, rather than cook up rationalizations for poor performance.

ITT's chairman Rand Araskog has had his share of unpleasant surprises over the years. One of the most painful was the discovery that an ITT general manager had illegally shipped embargoed trade goods under disguise to Iran during the 1979 hostage crisis. Araskog fired the manager and several people under him, and made it known throughout the company. Reflecting on the incident, Araskog felt that his most important task was to make sure that every employee was aware of top management's intention to monitor and punish ethical slipups. Araskog sums up his attitude as follows: "The most essential thing for us is integrity. The thing that has people in my office in five minutes in a rather intense meeting is any ethics or legal problem that would threaten the character of this company."

To appreciate the impact of Araskog or Caldwell's outlooks, one need only look at how many companies stonewall on employee wrongdoing, fudge product quality problems, and generally gloss over ethical dilemmas rather than risk spreading a tainted image. Harvard Business School professor Abraham Zaleznick, in commending General Dynamics chairman David S. Lewis for announcing his retirement one day after the Navy suspended the company from defense contracting, has said:

> We don't do enough of that [Lewis's acknowledgment of the problem] in American business. In Japan, it's common for the head person in the face of a disaster to publicly apologize. In America, there's a tendency to pass the blame on.

Zaleznick went on to say that he felt that a strong figure at the top who would acknowledge ethical problems in the company and take a stand alleviated employee anxiety and disloyalty. Stonewalling tended to make employees more anxious and likely to make worse decisions.[1]

Quality 3. An Innate Respect for Others

Call it street sense, high on people, or simply a good business nose, the foundation of good management is the busi-

[1]"When Scandal Haunts Company Corridors," *New York Times*, July 7, 1985.

ness leader's ability to step into the other person's shoes. An other-orientation that goes beyond a calculation of self-interest is implied in many of the values people list as most important to them. Honesty, love, fairness, being true to your word, caring for family are all commitments to other people. This sense of commitment is not a theoretical, rational calculation but a character trait psychologists and philosophers describe variously as empathy, self-sacrifice, or altruism. Whatever the label, such a capacity stands far removed from the self-serving image that cartoon stereotypes of business greed suggest and that some managerial approaches encourage.

Consider the bold phrase that often appears in sales recruiting: "Are you money-motivated?" Or the investment banking manager who unabashedly asserted that his business had to be run by greed. Compare these self-interested orientations with IBM's legendary attention to customer service and good employee relations. Ask yourself which companies respect other people. If the relationship of respect to current performance is not obvious, ask yourself which company you would expect to be in business ten years from now. Many analysts attribute Big Blue's past success to Tom Watson's nurturing respect for others. So, too, David Packard's outstanding leadership in the computer industry has been marked by an almost legendary concern for other people. Stories about his personal support of employees during economic recession and his fanatical concerns for customer satisfaction are a testimony to his consistent ability to respect the welfare of others in making business decisions.

Max DePree, chairman of Herman Miller, one of the consistently most profitable companies in America, described his innate sense of respect for others vividly when he commented, "I always try to make space to hear what others are saying. My people know that I don't look down on anyone, and conversely I hope that they have a sense of respect for me." Once, during the monthly brown-bag lunch with first-level managers, a supervisor somewhat evasively asked DePree about compensation. DePree embarked on a major analysis of how first-line managers and hourly employees regarded the company's wage scale. His genuine concern for their welfare and for fairness eventually led him to initiate a policy limiting the gap between the lowest and highest salaries in the company. (DePree has been listed by *Fortune* magazine as one of the nation's top CEOs.)

Quality 4. Personal Worth from Ethical Behavior

The ethical leader quite simply gets high on his or her own sense of personal integrity. Elmer Johnson, former executive vice president of General Motors and long-time partner at Chicago's prestigious law firm of Kirkland & Ellis, has frequently articulated the need for managers to take a strong and overt ethical stand. He believes that doing so usually results in better management decisions. He also feels that it has an intrinsic value. "In the end you don't take the ethical road because it makes money or makes sense from a company morale standpoint. You take it because you know it's right. At some point you have to feel that it's important for *you* to do the right thing." How different the attitude of the so-called yuppie manager, whose possession of material goods becomes the overriding indicator of personal worth.

These four character qualities of ethical leadership describe a person who confronts the issue of ethics and business deliberately and comes out strongly on the side of an overtly moral orientation, one motivated by more than a rational choice of management philosophies. Such values and personal courage hold up over time and ring true in an age of extreme self-aggrandizement. When ITT's chairman Rand Araskog was again faced with a contract fraud recently, he immediately ordered an internal investigation and six employees were fired. When Johnson & Johnson came through the Tylenol crisis with distinction, it had to turn right around and deal with a recall of another important product, Zomax. It would have been very tempting at that point to rely on the goodwill from the Tylenol recall to keep Zomax on the market while new labeling was being prepared. But as Burke said, "We knew we had to do the right thing again; and believe me, even though we were exhausted from Tylenol, that was no excuse not to do the right thing."

These biases and the patterns of thinking they engen-

der can be analyzed and emulated. There are also other familiar patterns of commercial thinking that tend to obstruct the
accomplishment of business with integrity. In the following
chapters I argue that one approach to management responsibility, namely, the ethic of enlightened self-interest as described by Milton Friedman and others, is actually suppressing
the kind of thinking it is intended to stimulate. James Burke
and many other successful corporate leaders seem to follow a
set of assumptions that in fact turns the Friedman ethic around
180 degrees. Not only is their approach commercially successful, it succeeds in integrating those moral values we purport
to hold dear. Such a prospect offers the revolutionary proposition that personal morality and the ethical norms of commerce
are inextricably linked.

Part II

Imperative for Change

4

Failures

It is not from the benevolence of the butcher, the brewer, or the baker that we expect our dinner, but from regard to their own self-interest.*

Drawing a lesson from the characteristics of ethical leadership outlined in Chapter 3, it can be concluded that the chief moral challenge that well-intentioned managers face is clear. It is not enough to hope that one's private values will not be compromised on the job. A manager needs to develop a business approach that *actively* brings standard moral norms to bear on economically sound decision making. This kind of problem-solving mindset, or business ethic, has three valuable advantages, first to the individual, second to the corporation, and ultimately to the community in which a business operates:

1. For the individual, an integration of private morality and managerial problem solving offers the prospect of fulfilling that deep-seated desire for self-respect. Financial success may provide the strokes at first, but few moguls are content with having money as their only notable feature when they look in the mirror. From Donald Trump to Lee Iacocca, corporate leaders desire to appear honest and of service to the community. It is an integral part of a manager's self-image. Even self-avowed S.O.B. Al Neuharth generously sprinkles his autobiography with vignettes of himself as the scrappy plainsayer who serves rather than exploits people.

*Adam Smith, *The Wealth of Nations.*

2. For the company, such an ethic provides access to a way of doing business that is directly consistent with the values it *claims* to hold. This consistency removes the need for the marketing contortions that are required in order to create a convincing image that is "better" than the company's real values. It also leads to clearer communication and implementation of internal efforts to improve standards of conduct. Many business ethics surveys document how confused or gratuitous an avowed commitment to ethics can be when the basic corporate culture assumes a totally different set of values.

3. For the community, an integrated business ethic creates a way of doing business that offers a greater contribution to the general welfare. A successful corporation that is also honest, fair, and in compliance with the law is on the whole of greater benefit to the general community than one that creates wealth by deception, cheating, and skirting the laws of the land.

How, then, can the goal and achievement of economic success be integrated with the basic moral concerns that inform one's sense of integrity? Do the management approaches and business rationales of today's top executives achieve this goal or not? In truth, there is no one business philosophy governing corporate leadership today, but of the many approaches to the problem of profits and morality that are possible, the ethic of enlightened self-interest, or to put it more crudely, the "do-good-to-do-well" ethic, has been among the most widely held.

In this chapter the theoretical and working assumptions of various forms of the self-interest business ethic are explored and found to be inherently unsatisfactory from the standpoint of motivating both integrity and competitive success. In brief, *it appears that a preoccupation with corporate self-interest runs a great risk of short-circuiting the enlightened awareness the ethic is intended to achieve.* Although it is well intended and often personally self-sacrificing, I argue that such thinking tends to stimulate the repeated rationalization and trivialization of moral concerns. The overwhelming self-centeredness of its assumptions has repeatedly worked to the destruction of the self-interest rationale. This ethic stimulates not enlightenment concerning the reality that all businesses—by their very socialness—share an identity of interests with others, but an avoidance of the extension-beyond-self that enlightenment demands.

Because justification for this failure most often rests on an appeal for company survival, I call this perversion of enlightened self-interest the survival ethic. Managers fail to recognize the need to treat others ethically because they fear putting the company (or themselves) out of business. Like individuals in life-threatening situations who will violate even the most basic moral tenets in order to survive, the manager or company with a survival ethic will justify actions whose moral implications run counter to their stated moral commitments based on a sense of "having had to do it."

Even the best managers fall prey to this mindset. When GM's legendary Alfred Sloan was presented with a new technological breakthrough called safety glass (already adopted by Ford), he simply dismissed the discovery out of hand. Complained Sloan in a letter to L. du Pont, "Accidents or no accidents, my concern in this problem is a matter of profit and loss. Somebody is always trying to add to the cost of the product."[1] Though Sloan was purportedly a very moral individual, his survival response in this case prevented him from framing an ethical answer to the safety glass issue. He did not, for example, entertain the idea of lobbying for an industrywide requirement for safety glass, a move that would have greatly reduced the risk of disfiguring wounds from automobile accidents without changing GM's relative competitiveness one whit. Fear of losing revenue excused him from thinking about the customer's welfare at all.

One can trace many unethical and poor business practices to the survival ethic. Managers will construct survival scenarios for themselves or for their subordinates to justify unethical behavior—from hesitating to investigate consumer complaints about product defects to reluctance to invest in new technology and training out of fear that anything other than cost-cutting would be suicidal. All such decisions

[1]Reported in Morton Mintz and Jerry S. Cohen, *America, Inc.* (New York: Dial Press, 1971), p. 259.

are fueled by the conviction that if you listened to ideas for change you'd soon be out of business.

Given the pervasiveness of survival appeals in times of economic downturn such as are being experienced in many industries today, it is helpful to explore how traditional enlightened self-interest philosophies and their survival ethics offspring have attempted to apply self-interested rationales to motivate responsible business behavior.

EVOLUTION OF THE SELF-INTEREST MODEL

The concept of enlightened self-interest has dominated business for a long time. Thomas Hobbes planted the seeds in the early seventeenth century. He argued that humankind was fundamentally egotistic and devoid of any genuine feelings for the needs of others. In the final analysis, every individual's primary objective could be seen to be self-preservation. As Hobbes put it, "The first foundation of natural right is this, that every man as much as in him lies endeavor to protect his life and members" (*Leviathan* V). Hobbes divided man's feelings and pursuits into two opposing characteristics: an appetite for good (or pleasure) and an aversion from evil (or harm). Though Hobbes meant many things by pleasure and harm, desire and aversion, these two characteristics roughly translated into activities of self-interest and self-preservation.

With self-interest and self-preservation as the ultimate regulators, all other constructs of society could be seen as logical extensions of the universality of self-interest. If, Hobbes argued, all people are primarily concerned with their own power to preserve themselves, then humankind is condemned by nature to a perpetual state of warfare, for each person has at hand some means to injure another in order to achieve his or her own end. Thus the personal costs of universal self-interestedness tend to outweigh the individual benefits that might be gained by living in this "natural state." Humankind's only logical response is to strike certain covenants with other human beings to suspend some liberties in order to achieve a better chance of self-preservation.

The moral rules and political constructs of society, then, were, in Hobbes's view, a pragmatic expression of self-interest and individual competition. For example, if individuals banded together collectively and imposed certain kinds of order on the group, they did so only insofar as it gained them protection in return for their forfeited liberties. The suspension of individual liberties to do as one pleased to whomever one pleased could only be justified in terms of the ultimate benefits that might be gained from such self-restraint.

Thus the idea of enlightened self-interest was planted. It rested not only on a fundamental assumption that unbridled egoism was a natural and not immoral state, but also on the belief that man had a rational capacity to reason his way to cooperation based on a calculation of self-advantage. Behind it all was a survival scenario.

The great utilitarians Jeremy Bentham and John Stuart Mill refined enlightened self-interest arguments further. Both felt that individual hedonism was a universal fact but that a concern for universal happiness *should* be the guiding moral standard for any legislative or social construct. Bentham, whose chief interest was social reform, constructed a relatively fixed calculus for determining the amount of pleasure or pain in a given piece of legislation. Mill directed his analysis toward a defense of the ethical principles underlying utilitarianism. His well-known prescription, "the greatest good for the greatest number," was established for the moral regulation of individual conduct and social reform. Mill was suggesting that the morality of an action must be measured not in terms of intentions or even means but in terms of ends. Wrote Mill:

> He who saves a fellow creature from drowning does what is morally right whether his motive be duty, or the hope of being paid for his trouble: he who betrays the friend that trusts him is guilty of a crime, even if his object be to serve another friend to whom he is under greater obligations.[2]

---

[2]John Stuart Mill, *Utilitarianism* (London: Longmans, Green, 1897), Chapter II.

In other words, if the ends were moral, the motivations were relatively unimportant from a moral standpoint. At the same time, Mill assumed that people would generally choose ethical means because it would be in their own interest to do so. Although he agreed with Hobbes that human beings were self-interested, he also believed that certain kinds of self-sacrifice or moral restraint were the logical actions of a self-interested person. Truth-telling, for example, was instrumental to achieving the majority's benefit, in that deviation from the truth "weakened the trustworthiness of human assertion" on which social well-being and human happiness depended.

Though both Hobbes and Mill believed unconditionally in the motivational power of self-interest, they were not justifying all-out self-gratification. Rather, they were advocating a set of social rules that could put individual liberty and social welfare *into balance*. One of the most concrete examples of this balance would be an injunction not to violate the rights of others in the pursuit of one's own happiness. Even the Golden Rule was understood to be an expression of self-interest. Hobbes called it nature's law for society. Mill made the famous assertion that, "In the golden rule of Jesus of Nazareth, we read the complete spirit of the ethics of utility." For both men other norms of morality such as truth-telling or property rights were necessary means to the self-preservation of as many individuals as possible in a society.

The primary assumptions of Hobbes and Mill have been repeated in the business philosophies of a number of economists and managers. Milton Friedman's work, sometimes called laissez-faire capitalism or the free-market point of view, is perhaps the outstanding example, but his arguments legitimizing an enlightened maximization of return have been reaffirmed or embellished by many other admired business thinkers such as Peter Drucker, Theodore Levitt, and a host of free-market economists in the Reagan administration.

Friedman posited his overarching ethic for business in his famous article, "The Social Responsibility of Business Is to Increase Profit."[3] He argued that the prime responsibility of

[3]Milton Friedman, *The New York Times Magazine*, September 13, 1970.

business was to maximize return. Placing a heavy faith in the beneficial powers of efficiency, Friedman felt that the pursuit of the greatest efficiency would ultimately benefit the greatest number of people. Like Hobbes and Mill, Friedman assumed that a rational appeal to self-interest, renamed "the profit motive," is the best motivator. Writes Friedman elsewhere:

> Few trends would so thoroughly undermine the very foundations of our free society as the acceptance by corporate officials of a social responsibility other than to make as much money for their stockholders as they possibly can."[4]

Ludwig Von Mises, an even stronger advocate of laissez-faire capitalism, has summed up the advantages of the process as follows:

> By the instrumentality of the profit-and-loss system, the most eminent members of society are prompted to serve to the best of their abilities the well-being of the masses of less gifted people. What pays under capitalism is satisfying the common man, the customer. The more people you satisfy, the better for you."[5]

While Hobbes was concerned with constraining the ultimately destructive pursuits of self-interest, Friedman has been concerned with refining them in order to achieve maximum efficiency. Hobbes regarded self-interest as a fact of life: "Of the voluntary acts of every man, the object is some good to himself." Friedman assumes that self-interest is not only a fact of life, but a powerful motivator leading to many socially desired consequences. For Friedman the best social construct for exploiting this truth is free-market capitalism. Like Mill, he is expressing a philosophy of ends: greatest good for the greatest number. The personal or psychological means by which such activities are conducted is left unexplored. To put

[4]Milton Friedman, *Capitalism and Freedom* (Chicago: University of Chicago Press, 1962), p. 134.
[5]Ludwig Von Mises, *The Ultimate Foundation of Economic Science: An Essay on Method* (Princeton: D. Van Nostrand, 1962), p. 108.

to rest any suspicion, however, that he is advocating a dog-eat-dog approach reminiscent of that of Hobbes's presocial human, Friedman makes a minimalist statement about the moral obligations of the manager: the act of maximizing return must "conform to the basic rules of the society, both those embodied in law and those embodied in ethical custom."[6] Perhaps Friedman assumes that people will naturally be as decent as he himself is reported to be, or that law will provide enough sanction to punish underhandedness in the marketplace.

In all fairness, Friedman's relative silence on the ethical issues of business can be attributed to the fact that his greatest moral concern is the potential constraint on individual freedom when so-called socially responsible laws are imposed on corporations. He is far less interested in the nuts-and-bolts behavioral questions, such as how to achieve ethical values like honesty in the marketplace, a topic he barely discusses and seems to take for granted.

Friedman's position is important to understand, for its basic suggestion that pursuit of profit is the most socially beneficial act a corporation can engage in *has in large part seduced many managers into thinking that the effective pursuit of profit—as long as it is legal—is in itself an assurance of high moral standards.* Those with good market instincts know that it can pay handsomely to serve the public well. There is a dollar advantage down the road if you develop a product people need or want, build a good reputation in the public's mind, or are perceived as a good employer. Thus anyone concerned with securing a maximized return must logically adopt a way of making decisions that has other people's interests in mind.

One can call such thinking an enlightened self-interest model of business ethics in that it solves the moral dilemmas of management through a complex calculation of how helping others helps oneself. This is the rationale on which Henry Mintzberg, for example, has based his arguments for expanding managerial social conscience through a variety of instruments.[7]

---

[6]Milton Friedman, "The Social Responsibility of Business Is to Increase Its Profits."
[7]Henry Mintzberg, *Power In and Around Organizations* (Englewood Cliffs, NJ: Prentice-Hall, 1983).

The "do-good-to-do-well" approach, though not precisely free market, is from an ethical standpoint a close variation of Friedman's. It recommends other-oriented behavior for ultimately enhancing one's own interests. Mill argued for self-sacrifice because in the long run serving the interests of others would serve you. Enlightened self-interest arguments today echo his reasoning, especially in speeches to the financial community concerning the allocation of corporate dollars to good corporate citizenship. One must think about others in order to do business efficiently.

To summarize, in a free market, or even in terms of an enlightened self-interest business ethic, the overriding moral calculus for the corporation is its own return. This is the star by which decisions can and should be guided. The pervasiveness of this ethic can be seen in the bottom-line, quantitative language most managers and the business press adopt in assessing corporate decision making.

There have been many theoretical criticisms and reaffirmations of Friedman's viewpoint. Adolph Berle and Gardiner C. Means, Thorstein Veblen, Peter Drucker, Herbert Simon, Kenneth Arrow, John Kenneth Galbraith, and other economists and social scientists have been suggesting for over forty years that successful corporate decision making is not based solely on a consideration of the owners' interest. Managers make decisions from a number of vantage points and with a number of purposes in mind, from perpetration of the current organizational power structure to establishment of noneconomic professional standards in the design and manufacturing of a product.

But despite the wealth of theoretical skepticism about the economic power and benefit of profit motivations, in practice, the idea that a form of self-interest translated into profit terms is the best motivator and purpose of business carries great legitimacy in corporate decision making today. Whether self-interest is unbridled or expressed in enlightened terms, it is assumed that it must be the predominant rationale informing managerial judgment. The continued diatribes against the profit mentality and the staggering number of exposés of profit-hungry predators in business are good evidence of just how strong these assumptions are.

The fundamental assumptions that define self-interest models of business ethics can be schematized as follows:

The Self-Interest Model of Business Ethics

Purpose: Maximize return

Contract: Act within laws and customs of the land

Driving assumption: Corporate self-interest provides greatest return to greatest number

Primary means: Tangible efficiency measures

What of ethics in this model? In a self-interest model, two important assumptions are made about ethical issues in business: 1) *Laws and traditional ethical values such as honesty and fairness are viewed either as imposed constraints upon efficiency or as practical means to a profitable end; and 2) in neither case are they integrated into the primary assumptions governing managerial priorities and decision making.* In practice these values frequently are left implied rather than expressed in the language executives adopt for defining incentives and in assessments of managerial judgment. Even when ethical standards are made explicit, the motivation to obey ethical norms is firmly couched in arguments of self-interest rather than an absolute sense of things being right or wrong simply for their own sake or society's welfare.

Under such a rubric, ethics tends to suffer a conversion into dollar terms. A typical explanation of the role of honesty, for example, would run as follows: "We're meticulously honest with our customers because it pays to be so in the long run." Similarly, people are understood primarily in terms of their instrumental dollar value: "It's important to treat your people right because a happier work force is a more productive work force." A ghoulish twist on this philosophy is Robert Goodin's view of most economists: they tend to assume that you can do anything to people as long as you make it in their financial interest to tolerate such treatment.[8]

If ethics is not seen as being of immediate dollar benefit, then it is viewed in terms of financial cost, i.e., as a constraint on the bottom line. Thus a conscientious company obeys the law not because of any assessment of the law's justice but because of society's ability to impose profit-reducing punishments. This is the "stick" method of ensuring ethical behavior and an extremely weak basis for motivating serious attention to ethical responsibilities. It establishes an inherent contradiction between what the business person would ideally "like" to do and what he or she must do.

Even executives who do not necessarily agree with the self-interest model in theory nevertheless succumb to its influence in the language and strategies they adopt. As one particularly sensitive and upright senior executive said after we worked together on an ethics seminar: "Look, you're not going to surprise me are you? I mean, I want my people to understand the need for honesty and all that, but I also need you to understand that this business runs on greed. I don't want them to feel bad about themselves." While this man was being consciously self-mocking, his words held a familiar ring: talk ethics but assume self-interest and the idea of maximized return as the ultimate responsibility and motivation for success.

When moral values are viewed only as costs or benefits within a basic world view that judges all activities in terms of their capacity to promote self-interest, then the felt immediacy of moral commitments quickly diminishes. A sage executive, responding to his company's stakeholder ethics statement, thus remarked candidly: "I'm given four balls to balance: the customer's, the employees', the community's, and the stockholders' by which I mean profit. It's never made clear how I am to keep them all going, but I know for certain that there's one I'd better not drop, and that's profit."[9]

[8]Robert E. Goodin, *Two Kinds of Compensation*, Conference on Ethical Approaches to Public Choice, University of York, September 1985.

[9]A very interesting survey conducted by Brenner and Molander for the *Harvard Business Review* in 1976 seems to contradict this assertion. When asked to identify primary responsibility, executives

In this approach to establishing standards of business conduct, the reality of ethics is reduced to a dry document itemizing the costs and benefits of moral behavior. The results of such thinking are about as imaginative and motivating as the ethics code of a former *Fortune* 500 company—ironically now out of business. (See Exhibit 4-1.) This code attempts to legislate ethical standards by constraint. Couched in quasi-legal terms, essentially it equates the moral issues of management with compliance with the law. There is absolutely no clarification of how any of the sanctions fit into the competitive thinking of managers other than as shalt-not's. There is no exploration of the positive moral issues on which competitiveness depends, such as trust and sensitivity to others. Neither is there any indication that ethics is more than a function of law. By way of contrast, one thinks of retail chain Nordstrom's extraordinary ethics code as most exemplary: "You are expected to use your own best judgment."

DRAWBACKS OF THE SELF-INTEREST MODEL

One cannot bring empirical data to bear that would demonstrate *decisively* that the self-interest model motivates unethical behavior in X amount of cases and poor commercial judgment in Y situations. It would be more accurate to say that it is empirically untested in a convincing way. Executives who believe strongly that it is important to demonstrate to the junior managers of the world that good ethics does indeed pay have sponsored research in this area, but the jury is still out. There has yet to be a statistically valid study showing that

---

ranked "maximizing long-run profits" third after "being an efficient user of energy" and "assessing potential environmental effects of the company's technological advances." When asked to rank their company's responsibility to various stakeholder groups, the executives chose customers over stockholders. But the extensive attention currently being developed to address managerial failure to think about the customer seems to indicate that although managers theoretically understand that this is where the bread and butter come from, attention to others does not in fact appear to be their primary mindset. Interestingly, the survey did not include responsibility to the long-term interests of the company in the list of choices. Steven N. Brenner and Earl A. Molander, "Is the Ethics of Business Changing?" *Harvard Business Review* (January-February 1977), pp. 57–71.

Exhibit 4-1
WIDGET CORPORATION
Statement of Mission

A. The mission of Widget Corporation is to consistently earn superior financial returns through the pursuit of a leadership position in the Company's businesses.

   This means, simply, that our shareholders will get a return on the money they've invested in this company equal to, or better than, the return on any investment of comparable risk. We don't know of any consistent way to achieve this other than being out front of our competitors.

B. This mission is based on the belief that Widget must provide the potential for long-term profitability at or above the market-required rate of return, the cost of equity, to create value for the Company's shareholders. Expressed in real terms, Widget's cost of equity is approximately 10 percent.

   In today's double-digit inflation environment worldwide, we must achieve a rate of return on shareholders' equity of approximately 20 percent.

C. To accomplish this mission, Widget has become a diversified worldwide manufacturer and marketer of quality products. The businesses within the Company are expected to achieve and maintain a *leadership position in attractive industries*. A true leadership position means having a significant and well-defined advantage over all competitors. This can be achieved through continuous, single-minded determination to achieve one or both of the following positions within an industry:

   Strange as it may seem, many have difficulty in grasping this fundamental idea of leadership. Sales volume is not leadership; lack of competition may not be leadership; backlog is not leadership. One leads competitors in a market or industry by having an acknowledged edge—a "competitive advantage" fairly achieved and consistently held.

corporations with good ethics have on the whole achieved a performance rate superior to those without.[10]

Nor is the self-interest ethic totally illogical: there is indeed a commercial payback on such ethical values as honesty or fairness or compliance with the law. Companies that fail to comply with these conditions are often severely punished when found out.

The problem, then, is not one of logic but of priorities. Although the mix of values in an enlightened self-interest model is theoretically sound, *it fails to achieve this mix in practice*. The failure is both moral and economic. The legitimization of a self-interested approach to business that emphasizes return and efficiency is

1. dysfunctional, in that it fails to motivate in others the complex ethical values it claims to represent; and
2. unpragmatic, in that the priorities it defines are not the first building blocks of competitive excellence.

Drawback 1. Self-Interest Ethically Dysfunctional

The intentions of the self-interest ethic are to facilitate efficiency and channel a variety of ethical considerations to the purpose of making a profit.[11] The moral outcome of efficiency will be the greatest good for the greatest number. In practice, however, it has a tendency to stimulate a far more limited perspective.

The self-interest ethic deliberately validates self-

---

[10]One of the reasons for this ignorance is that no one can agree on a stable standard for measuring goodness, and few agree on a stable measurement for performance. One of the most frequently cited studies is that of the Ethics Resource Center, commissioned by Johnson & Johnson chairman James Burke. The center's president, Gary Edwards, is adamant in asserting that the center claimed no statistical validity in its study, which it decided not to publish.

[11]I have deliberately chosen not to address Berle and Means's arguments concerning the theoretical impossibilities of a maximized profit orientation for managers. Most of their arguments, though correct in positing that there are other motivations governing managerial decisions, are grounded in the same self-interest orientation. For a very good critique of the motivational power of profit maximization, see Kenneth J. Arrow, "Why Profits Are Challenged," in *New Challenges to the Role of Profit*, ed., D. Friedman (Lexington, MA: Lexington Books, 1978), pp. 49–64.

aggrandizement (personal or corporate self). It indirectly validates ethical responsibility to others: you do something for others because it is in your interests to do so. It is actively helpful only where benefits are demonstrable. But where moral norms require a suspension of self-oriented considerations, it does not strongly motivate commitment to others. One might say that the model is theoretically right and attitudinally wrong.

In theory, the moral reference point of enlightened self-interest should be a complex set of problem-solving perspectives. In practice, managers tend to reduce the issues of self-interest to simple terms of self-preservation, admittedly a sign of interest served, but not a very good moral guidepost. Management may seem to value honesty, integrity, the customers' best interests, ecological viability, and long-term health of the company; but when it must choose among what *will* make a profit (as long as you don't get caught), what *might* make a profit, and what is definitely a short-term sacrifice of profit, only a tedious and highly rational calculation of risk to the bottom line will succeed in overcoming the immediate attraction of the first alternative. Such calculation rarely takes place. Rather, one rationalizes the unethical choice by enlarging the specter of personal or corporate risk, falling back on the old thought, "What do you want to do, put me out of business?" Or as one junior manager told me: "It's a dog-eat-dog world out there. That's a fact. You have to do what's necessary, even if it goes against your scruples. If you don't, you'll be out of business."

There are many good reasons why survival should be a concern today. But a total preoccupation with a survival mindset can make ethical obligations to others seem like a decency the drowning person cannot afford.

By imposing a survival mindset, managers fail to anticipate mutually beneficial approaches to other constituencies even when the long-term consequences of self-centeredness will ultimately have a negative effect on their own return. In most cases, the payoff of self-sacrifice and service to others is down the road, not guaranteed, and frequently not obvious in many corporate environments. Charles Kelly's prototypical manager, the Destructive Achiever, is a good example of how survival scenarios are used to reinforce exploitative, self-centered ethics. According to Kelly:

> [The Destructive Achiever] has an exaggerated sense
> of urgency. To the DA, any high-visibility short-term
> objective is a crisis . . . . The DA doesn't motivate
> subordinates, he threatens them. The project you are
> on at the time is the most important one, and if you
> fail at it, it could mean the end of your career. But he
> says this on almost every project.[12]

Needless to say, like Michael Macoby's "Gamesman" or Harry Levinson's "Abrasive Personality," the DA's values are not rock solid on such issues as honesty, trust, compliance with the law, or the welfare of the team.

As I pointed out earlier, enlightened self-interest is inherently biased toward a product or results orientation, a perspective reinforced by the corporation's strong reliance on quantitative measurements. This in itself limits managerial understanding of the purpose of business. It also tends to diminish the felt importance of ethical means, of doing business a certain way.

Thus if one is dealing with a gray-area problem where the unethical course is not shatteringly obvious, or where ethical values or compliance with the law are not directly seen to be consonant with maximizing return, ethical choices have little impact on a manager's thinking except as artificially imposed constraints. Many important business problems fall into this gray area, from choice of product and advertising content to choice of words in communicating with subordinates. Many exploitations of people's trust, degrading assumptions about their inherent laziness or ignorance, and controversial products are legal and profitable. What in an enlightened self-interest model will sensitize managers to the importance of not adopting such strategies and tactics?

Some of the most pervasive management systems are built on self-interest orientations which frequently distort a

---

[12]Charles M. Kelly, *The Destructive Achiever: Power and Ethics in the American Corporation* (Reading, MA: Addison-Wesley, 1988), p. 35.

manager's moral barometer in favor of immediate self-gratification. Many traditional incentive systems and approaches to problem solving exaggerate the distortion even further. Or, as the unnamed manager in Charles Kelly's book said to his subordinates, "Cooperate if you feel it's needed, but you're still going to be judged on the basis of present production schedules."[13] Such language is guaranteed to send a "get-the-job-done-any-way-you-can" message.

A supervisor firmly announces a performance target for sales in order to motivate greater effort from the sales group. Top management escalates the importance of return even further by creating an incentive system that makes both the sales and the division's bonuses dependent on meeting target. Everyone in top management, if pressed, would profess that the business should be "honest." Yet nothing in their language articulates even a dim awareness of the dilemmas that "being honest" might pose for the sales force, given the product and the target goals. The supervisor's habitual question to his or her salespeople is, "How are sales?" The first question of his or her VP in turn is usually, "How are we doing?" Neither question stimulates an exploration of whether that return is based on honest performance.

Logically, a salesperson should be able to reason that on the whole long-term sales success is ultimately a function of serving the customer, and that honesty and fairness are important factors in gaining a customer's trust. But given the self-centered nature of the incentive system, chances are that the salesperson will not be focused on these values. Rather, his or her attention is on the company, on its product, on its track record, on its policies, and on its targets. If product and service are in market terms mediocre, and return not as good as hoped, managers feel no constraint in resorting to devious corner-cutting to improve their own results record or to meet the expectations of the financial community. Should there be signs of customer dissatisfaction or public outrage, well, what do they know anyway? This attitude holds true even when the customer is a member of the same organization, as in internal purchasing or training departments.

---

[13]Kelly, *Destructive Achiever,* p. 8.

In other words, self-interest has a sneaky habit of turning into self-centeredness, which in turn muffles the conscience. A classic case in point is the falsification of quarterly expense reports at H.J. Heinz in the late 1970s, an event that eventually forced the company to revise its annual earnings statement upward by 29.4 percent.[14] Heinz managers at several divisions repeatedly revised quarterly sales figures or delayed receivables to bring their performance into close conformity with their targets. Most of the time the revisions were downward, a way of buying time and getting a leg up on the next quarter. It was also a way of ensuring that next year's targets were not set uncomfortably high. A lot rode on the figures: the individual manager's compensation and that of his or her division. The internal auditor's evaluation and compensation were determined by the division head. Later the SEC described Heinz's way of doing business as displaying a "lack of control consciousness." The board of directors instituted an independent internal auditing team. No one was fired, however, because, according to top management, "This company doesn't believe in this sort of thing philosophically or morally. But nobody got hurt and nobody benefited, except some guys who got a leg up [on their incentive goals] for the next year. The amount of money involved was peanuts."

The Heinz managers were well intentioned. They wanted to produce a steady earnings flow for shareholders. They did not believe in dishonesty and cooking the books. They had good products and no cash flow problems. Yet they failed to motivate even the simple basics of accounting honesty. Division managers had an insufficient sensitivity to both the overall interests of the firm and the ethical concerns that are purportedly a condition of market success. Instead of enlightened self-interest they achieved short-sighted self-centeredness out of fear of failing to perform.

One can generalize from Heinz's experience. The *intent* of enlightened self-interest may be to stimulate awareness of the rights of the business community, but in fact it provokes a "me-first" attitude. Self-oriented efficiency measures only exacerbate the problem. That intangible quality of character

[14]Kenneth Goodpaster, "The H.J. Heinz Company: The Administration of Policy," #382-035. Boston: Harvard Business School, 1981.

we call "drive" is reduced to expressions that ultimately condone predatory greed and exploitation: "lean-and-mean," "quick-and-dirty," "killer competitors," "sharks," "toughness." Practical translation: walk on whomever you can to get ahead. Squeeze your suppliers dry, manipulate your customers into accepting second-best, waste shareholder dollars on the maintenance of status in an effort to establish your image—oh yes, and stay within the laws and customs of the land.

Today's marketplace is not so naive or meek as to accept such behavior without resistance. Suppliers become overnight competitors, customers move on, and shareholders are much more aggressive in demanding an honest accounting. Consumer and environmental groups, somewhat dormant during the last Reagan administration, have recently increased their activism.

Thus others are provoked to impose heavy legal or quasi-legal constraints on managers' exploitative tendencies. Laws on fairness and honesty become the only practical ethical controls. This approach to motivating ethical behavior is both inefficient and ineffective. The current litigiousness of our nation threatens to bring many areas of business activity to a halt while we argue about the rules of the game in court or threaten untold punitive damages on the corporation for its failure to stay within the laws and customs of the land. Such legally oriented systems of moral control rarely stand the test of hard or unpredictable times. Either the law falls behind life-threatening technological advances or desperate executives will knowingly break the laws that do apply.

Equally inadequate is the ability to stimulate managers to adopt the kind of ethical values that help hold an organization together. When simplistically applied, as they usually are in practice, appeals to self-interest do not in the end motivate self-sacrifice and delayed gratification, both of which threaten to be in particularly short supply these days. Every corporation has a need for trust, loyalty, and cooperation. Rapidly changing competitive environments demand a new efficiency of communication and decision making. There is no time or organizational capacity to check on every manager's decision and transaction. Top management and other executives have to trust each other to conduct business in accord-

ance with the high standards of honesty, fairness, and cooperation they profess to expect from the team. Loyalty and cooperation depend on trust, but self-interest rarely favors
a vocabulary and an ethic that acknowledge such things
directly.

The costs of such failure are heavy. Currently there
is rampant cynicism about business behavior at all levels of
the firm. Studies at several universities and survey firms show
that people are not convinced that their peers value honesty
above getting ahead or that their bosses will punish such behavior.[15] Such mistrust is particularly destructive during periods when job mobility is high, or in periods of recession, as is
now the case for many industries. Moreover, today's disgruntled employee, feeling betrayed and abandoned, has the ability
in many cases to commit massive fraud or sabotage against
the company.

As Hobbes noted, a me-first attitude creates a perpetual state of social warfare unless there is some constraint on
individual liberty for the sake of securing group power. At first
glance the company-first orientation of the enlightened self-
interest model appears to be a successful modification. It requires a degree of personal self-sacrifice to create a social
group powerful enough to advance the interests of the entire
corporate entity. The same assumptions concerning self-
interest are made as in Hobbes. Self-interest is the natural
goal while the only justification for personal sacrifice from
employees is the promise of a reward down the road, based
on the company's achievement of *its* self-interest.

Economically rational but behaviorally and intellectually flawed, this focus on the interests of the company irresponsibly limits the playing field of managerial morality. Ethical norms are reserved for the company, where its interests
in having such a value system in-house are obvious. But these
same values do not seem to include anyone else. Like the
religious fanatic who is meticulously honest and generous

---

[15]For example, according to a University of Pittsburgh survey, when executives were asked
whether they thought honesty paid, 25 percent said honesty did not pay, and 56 percent said they
believed that managers they knew would bend the rules to get ahead. Fifty-one percent said they
trusted people less than they used to. A number of surveys confirm what I like to call the cynicism
factor in business. See, for example, D.L. Lincoln, M.M. Pressley, and T. Little, "Ethical Beliefs and
Personal Values of Top-Level Executives," *Journal of Business Research* 10 (1982), pp. 475–487.

with the brethren, but lies and cheats the rest of the world in order to gain riches for the church, the manager who uses company self-interest as the sole effective moral beacon runs the danger of constructing a hallowed cage around his or her ethical obligations. Secure in the belief that he or she is doing the right thing toward the company, the manager can be an S.O.B. to the rest of the world without compunction. Thus it is that Al Neuharth, former chief of Gannett, could win acclaim by boldly recommending an ethic of devious calculation as long as it makes a company money.[16] So, too, many Wall Street executives are said to have tolerated the obvious hyperbole of an Ivan Boesky or Jeff "Mad Dog" Beck because these men routinely made millions for their partners.

Obviously business integrity is more complex than this. You are not necessarily behaving ethically just because you did not cheat the company. But if a manager's perceptual faculties are constantly turned toward profit, it is very difficult to notice that such ethical lapses are occurring and are significant.

What gives the self-interest ethos such tremendous power to seduce managerial morals is that at face value the manager who puts company return first *seems* to be very noble. His or her self-denial and loyalty are obviously voluntary suspensions of individual liberty for the sake of the group's welfare. One can feel very good about such nobility, especially if the corporate culture reinforces lockstep obedience and unflagging focus on immediate return.

But eventually such behavior takes its toll in-house as well. The habitual double-talker and double-dealer in the marketplace has few moral brakes at hand to stop him or her from doing the same thing in the firm when it can be gotten away with or when it seems expedient. What is more, often the manager who steps on everyone else on the way to the top is rewarded for such behavior as long as it is generally perceived that that person was instrumental in increasing the company's size and profit.

The lesson is clear: once you impose self-aggrandizing goals as the primary managerial obligation, everyday ethi-

---

[16]Al Neuharth, *Confessions of an S.O.B.* (Garden City, NY: Doubleday, 1989).

cal norms go out the window. In short, "every-person-for-him-or-herself" is an ethos that belongs out in the fever swamps. In practical terms it is destructive, insensitive, and inappropriate for a profession in which the single most secure fact is that it takes two people to complete an act of commerce or carry out a process of delegation. It is out of date in a world where global markets and global problems require new partnerships and long-term commitments. "More!" was the slogan attributed to Samuel Gompers. As a higher purpose it has been seen to fail the test of time and social cooperation. In just the same way, a business ethic of personal aggrandizement and profit maximization fails to capture the critical factors of business and organizational success. We need a managerial mindset that can get to ethical decisions faster and more often.

Drawback 2. Self-Interest Competitively Counterproductive

When Sony co-founder Akio Morita was recently interviewed by *Fortune* magazine, he remarked that he was most disturbed by the American trend away from manufacturing. He described the typical American business person as taking pleasure only in making profits from moving money around.[17] One could reduce Morita's analysis even further: many Americans have adopted a value system that only takes pleasure in making profits. The extreme materialism of today's college students, as documented in national surveys, is only one manifestation. The widespread adoption of self-serving motivational language is another, to the degree that it creates a rationale for an extreme orientation on return.

Not only does this orientation impose severe restrictions on a manager's capacity to approach the job ethically, it also affects an executive's commercial judgment, as Morita noted. When your own welfare is the primary concern, you tend to adjust your antennae in such a way as to filter out the rest of the world.

This limit on perception has many dysfunctional fallouts in terms of commercial judgment. Customers, suppliers,

[17]"A Japanese View: Why America Has Fallen Behind," *Fortune,* September 25, 1989, p. 52.

even one's own employees, pale in importance when compared to meeting a financial target as quickly and efficiently as possible. The chief causes of business failure have traditionally been either cash flow or ignoring the customer. Competent management of cash flow is a relatively mechanical exercise which requires few ethical conditions other than accurate bookkeeping and competent finance officers. But listening to customers, or gaining the organizational cooperation required to meet their needs, requires a host of other-oriented moral values. These values do not automatically spring from an ethical standard that has self as the primary focal point. *One cannot achieve market sensitivity or organizational cooperation by working off the assumption that your own way of doing things and your profit are necessarily more compelling than anything else.*

Unfortunately, this is precisely the message that many authoritarian corporate bureaucracies and authoritarian financial analysts love to deliver. If the subject is a business plan, the only articulated goal is growth, or size. Totally legitimized by the expressed purpose of the self-interest ethos, such an approach is a fast track to forgetting about the customer.

Take the former fiascos in American automobile manufacturing in the 1970s. When the Japanese compacts first began to make a significant entry into the American market, by many accounts the American automobile manufacturers were so wedded to the idea that their own competitiveness was invulnerable that they dismissed the new compacts as a limited niche. When market share of midsize American cars picked up after a temporary decline during the Mideast oil crisis, the bottom line convinced them of their earlier judgment.

In-house and outsider accusations of poor quality and dinosaur design strategies were summarily dismissed. As David Halberstam put it so eloquently in describing Japan's victorious entry into the American automobile market, "Detroit was Detroit, and more than most business centers, it was a city that listened only to its own voice."[18] Ford was being "run by the numbers" and GM had an unshakable confidence

---

[18]David Halberstam, *The Reckoning* (New York: Avon Books, 1986), p. 9.

that size guaranteed intelligence. Both companies focused on the bottom line, but in such a self-oriented way as to render the focus commercially dysfunctional. They were able neither to acknowledge quality problems nor assess public taste. What is more, they made the terrible mistake of thinking that their own interest was synonymous with high ethical standards and service to the public. Thus could "Engine Charlie" Wilson assert a decade earlier with a straight and patriotic face, "What's good for General Motors is good for the country."

A self-interest ethos can profess to be enlightened. But in truth, it limits a manager's capacity to entertain complex moral commitments to multiconstituencies and ultimately the landscape of competitive imagination. Such a focal point has never been a formula for competitive success since the days of the buggy whip's demise.

Unfortunately, many managers are afraid to think about anything beside their own company or product for fear that if they are not constantly attentive to the scorecard the game will be lost. Such thinking is analogous to the idea that you have to think solely about breathing because humans cannot live without air. In fact breathing is an automatic result of many other conditions. So too is profit. These other matters are the rightful focus of a manager's attention, but in a survival scenario breathing is the first preoccupation.

The performance fallout of survival reasoning is as inevitable as it is tragic. By limiting one's sense of purpose to survival, one limits one's performance as a person or a company. In most cases this translates into an acceptance of the status quo. Marketing expert Regis McKenna has called this phenomenon a "market share mentality." A manager or management team identifies an existing market and then puts all resources and efficiency measures into carving out a piece of that pie. He or she motivates others to carry out this strategy by fixating on familiar quantitative expressions of self-interest: one's own share of market, one's own return on sales.

In so doing one runs the risk of motivating mediocrity. A self-interest ethic solves problems through efficiency. Should performance be mediocre, managers will tend to look to their own inefficiencies rather than to the customer. Translation: cut costs. While cost-cutting is a generally sound economic principle, as a market strategy it has limited power. It does not guarantee adequate financial and creative commitment to product development or even to efficient manufacturing. Nor does it provide access to the assumptions that might be working against effective performance. No cost-cutting measures or appeals to the need for return would have caused Detroit managers to question their own extreme arrogance in thinking their cars were the only game in town.

In the end, a self-directed ethos motivates not excellence and innovation, but the construction of artificial barriers between managers and the marketplace. A returned order is seen not as a source of information about the marketplace but as a financial setback from some crank who doesn't know what's what.

Managers construct such barriers constantly. How many market surveys assume that the company's product is the central topic rather than the customer's total experience in buying and using the product? Today many marketing organizations are shifting away from self-oriented survey questions to open-format interviews to profile the factors that cause customers to "bond" with a certain company. The success of this latter approach depends on having a felt immediacy about the needs and desires of *others,* not one's own expectation of a return.

Without this sensitivity, even the soundest management advice can get morally and functionally perverted. For example, Harvard Business School professor Michael Porter's work on competitive strategy systematically analyzes ways to identify the business relationships that can be the key to competitive advantage. Identifying and putting to work such factors as supplier conditions or distribution channels makes good sense and is not inherently unethical. But when a management's ethical assumptions focus on primary obligations of corporate self-interest, there is a tendency to exploit rather than build business relationships in an ethical and mutually helpful way. In order to motivate a winning attitude, competitors are viewed as personal assassins of one's own bottom line. Thus they are open to exploitation in an ethical sense. With such a mindset it is very difficult to adjust to the need for new alliances, including among former competitors, as has occurred in as disparate industries as copiers and automobiles. Nor does it encourage trustworthy supplier relationships. He who is exploited tends to exploit back.

The "me-first-and-last" mindset runs the risk of undermining the spirit of partnership that today's competitive conditions require. If you understand other people simply as instrumental to the advancement of yourself or your company, you will tend to destroy the basis on which their cooperation can be gained. Customers are valuable only insofar as they can do you good. Employees are valuable only insofar as they can make a profit. Such an evaluation of people encourages exploitation and most people are sophisticated enough to recognize such treatment.

Whether or not one adopts Tom Peters's tactical recommendations, his widely accepted ABCs for competitive success speak to the same issues. Among the needed skills which he lists in *Thriving on Chaos* are flexibility, high value-added service, responsiveness, listening to the customer, quality consciousness, willingness to discard established systems, partnership mentality, and innovation. The final characteristic is integrity, by which he means giving people a fair deal and empowering them to assume more authority.

But appeals to enlightened self-interest do not *directly* motivate any of these characteristics. The best they can do is motivate such other-oriented feelings indirectly. Self-centeredness, the all-too-frequent expression of self-interest, positively obstructs these characteristics of managerial excellence. It seduces a GM not to think, "What's good for the public is good for General Motors," but just the opposite.

CONCLUSION

A self-interest business ethic pragmatically fails to motivate the other-oriented values essential to responsible behavior and business success or it attempts to motivate them through a twisted logic which is all but dysfunctional. A survival ethic is not a success ethic. It stops at self-preservation rather than moving ahead to value-creation. At its most extreme, it cultivates an ethic of greed and entitlement. More frequently and less extreme, it tends to construct barriers between a management team and the outside world.

Moreover, because the self-interest ethic historically evolved out of a perception of universal competitiveness, managers mistakenly assume that this standard can automatically be equated with market competitiveness today. Nothing is further from the truth. As the success of globalization indicates, today's marketplace will require new partnerships rather than outdated enmities.

To attempt to share a world view responsive to the needs and expectations of others—admittedly difficult for every person—by appealing to thoughts of self is to construct a basically weak and inherently inefficient ethical motivation. It is vulnerable to survival ethics excuses for managerial insensitivity to the marketplace or unwillingness to accept short-term, bottom-line penalties for the sake of moral values. When reinforced by corporate incentive and reward systems, a self-interest ethic magically holds a manager's moral values in bondage. It makes the idea that business and ethics are a contradiction in terms very persuasive. With this impossible view of business integrity, it is very easy to feel not responsible for unethical acts.

Corporate self-interest benchmarks such as increased size and profit do not inherently motivate anything except megalomania. In the models of the classic tragedians, whose lessons are frequently relearned in today's marketplace, a preoccupation with size and self-confidence leads to delusion and delusion to downfall. As the mainframe computer companies learned from Apple, just because you got it right today doesn't mean you'll get it right tomorrow, even if you are bigger.

There is one final objection to the self-interest business ethic and that is its extreme dependency on logic for ethical behavior and competitive judgment. It assumes that humankind is by nature supremely rational and constantly self-interested. It has already been noted that the standards of enlightened self-interest rest on the assumption that other-oriented impulses are functionally based: they are important inasmuch as they facilitate maximization of return.

I would argue that this is too limited a view of the nature of moral impulses. People's tendencies to prefer "ethical" behavior are far more deep-seated than our limited abilities to demonstrate their logic. Though moral standards have functional roles, they often arise irrationally.

The eighteenth-century philosopher David Hume is perhaps the most adamant supporter of the theory that although reason is essential in carrying out moral decisions, the *source* of morality is sentiment. He even went so far as to suggest that it was misguided to rely upon reason to regulate moral standards because people essentially greet reason with indifference rather than action:

> What is honorable, what is fair, what is becoming, what is noble, what is generous, takes possession of the *heart* [my emphasis], and animates us to embrace and maintain it. What is intelligible, what is evident, what is probable, what is true, procures only the cool assent of the understanding. (*An Enquiry Concerning the Principles of Morals,* iii)

Professor Amitai Etzioni agrees with the nonrationalist view of morality and, in applying it to economic choices, calls this phenomenon "the irreducibility of moral behavior."[19] By this he means that people will choose courses of action based on values that are not demonstrably more efficient from an economic standpoint. For example, it is clear that honesty does not always pay in economic terms, especially in a marketplace so complex as to be virtually unpoliceable. And yet one can find scores of executives who would respond to the possibility of getting away with a deceptive practice with the simple statement, "We don't do business that way."

Whether the source of such impulses is religion or culture or the preferences of one's parents, the irrationality of moral reasoning and behavior is a fact. To construct a business ethic that works only on commercial logic to motivate ethical behavior is to fail to draw on that deep reservoir of spontaneous decency. As one senior executive told me during

---

[19] Amitai Etzioni, *The Moral Dimension: Toward a New Economics* (New York: Free Press, 1988), pp. 67–87.

an ethics course, "I want to be able to say at the end of my career that I stood for something."

Such are the sentiments that stimulate great self-sacrifice and long-term commitment to larger goals. Undoubtedly self-interest models have at times made a lot of money for people. But they have also failed to motivate change and responsiveness and long-term financial health in many corporations when times got rough.

It must be concluded that the choice of an overarching standard for business behavior, while it should not contradict business logic, *must ultimately maximize the motivation of irrational preferences for other-oriented values.* Such a construction will have commercial logic and will establish problem-solving attitudes that are conducive to honesty and responsible business behavior, as will be demonstrated in the next chapter. Such a replacement of self-interest ethics is sorely needed. It is the only possibility for achieving profit not out of self-interest, but out of self-respect.

5

Striking a New Bargain

What bothers me is how management thinks. There's nothing wrong with wanting to make money—except that it should not become the sole objective.*

The top manager of a well-known consumer food products company was recounting how he and his senior management group had been trying to write a statement of the company's values. He found the exercise very frustrating. "I mean, look," he confidently asserted, "you have to admit that the first value in any company is profit. It has to be. And I guess the second value is not killing anyone. After that, what do you say?"

Not killing people was the *second* value? I doubt that in his private thoughts the manager would ever condone *deliberately* making a profit from a product that could kill someone. But his unquestioned prioritization of profit, though well-intended, showed a complete insensitivity to the ethical aspects of decision making. This manager needs to be freed from the "corporate embeddedness" that legitimizes his definition of responsibility totally in financial terms. Unless he adopts a different framework for problem solving, his own ethical impulses will be sluggish, and he will set goals and reward systems that stimulate the same insensitivity in others.

*William Batten, former chairman of J.C. Penney and former chairman of the New York Stock Exchange. Quoted in Walter Guzzardi, "Wisdom from the Giants of Business," *Fortune*, July 3, 1989, p. 86.

Meanwhile, he is setting himself and the company up for a potentially disastrous mistake. It was just such insensitivity that led Beech-Nut executives to fail to see the full implications of not stringently checking their apple juice concentrate supplier. These failures eventually resulted in the conviction of the company's president (now under appeal on a legal technicality) and a major blight on their reputation in the marketplace.

A BETTER ETHICAL ROAD MAP

It is imperative from the public's point of view and the point of view of the conscientious manager to replace the enlightened self-interest framework for business problem solving. The chief problems of the self-interest models of business behavior were the failure to integrate ethical constructs into managerial decisions, the provocation of a psychological bias toward self-centeredness, and the results of such an orientation, the chief being market insensitivity, poor employee relations, and failure to uphold basic ethical norms even when they would make market sense in the long run.

A new analytical framework for problem solving must, at a minimum, be more responsive to the challenges of business by encouraging the following conditions:

1. the *integration* of a full range of ethical norms and "business"-directed decisions;
2. a psychological bias that moves beyond personal and corporate self-centeredness to *motivate responsiveness to others*; and
3. the capacity to motivate pragmatic and sound business decisions from the point of view of *organizational health and economic success.*

With these three factors in place, the likelihood that a well-intentioned manager or corporation will actually do the right thing for the right reasons is greatly enhanced. Further, the driving assumptions of capitalism, namely, voluntary exchange, are more likely to be fulfilled with success and integrity.

Such a framework does not have to be knit totally from theory. As William Batten's remark at the opening of the chapter indicates, there are already many respected corporate leaders who effect an integration of moral values and economic concerns. Much of the so-called excellence literature today and the actual decisions of many ethical companies reflect this approach and rest on similar moral assumptions about the purpose of business and role of profit, assumptions I call a Covenantal Business Ethic.

In examining this business approach it is helpful to start with two examples of important business decisions which had high ethical and financial stakes. These incidents actually occurred and were resolved with a covenantal approach.

Decision 1. Marketing Baby Oil at Johnson & Johnson

The Tylenol crisis was an extraordinary nightmare in which Johnson & Johnson's corporate heroism was highly evident and has frequently been praised. But I find that the less publicized decisions at J&J, when the public was not especially watching, provide more insight into how a Credo-type business philosophy influences managerial ethics. The following story is one such case.

> About twenty years ago, J&J's baby oil was very successful as a tanning product. At that time there was little public awareness of the sun's potentially harmful effects on the skin.
>
> Young Carl Spalding, who had recently been promoted to product manager of baby oil, walked into his first presentation to the executive committee full of confidence and excitement. He had what he felt was a creative new set of ideas for promoting the already profitable product.
>
> But shortly into the presentation, president David Clare interrupted Spalding with a question: What did he mean by "healthy tan" (a phrase which

has been used for years in connection with the product)? Could he prove tanning was healthy? Clare's
question had been prompted by a recent conversation
he had had with a medical friend, who happened to
have seen an article suggesting that tanning might
have long-term harmful effects.

Taken by surprise, Spalding said he hadn't
heard of any such evidence from his own medical advisers. It was suggested that he look into the issue
before proceeding with the campaign.

Sure enough, evidence was emerging suggesting that tans might be harmful. What should
Spalding do? The evidence was not conclusive. The
product was a J&J classic and one worth $10 million
in annual sales.

A manager who operated from an enlightened self-
interest approach would most likely tackle this problem by
assessing the potential *costs* of responding to the health issue
now or later. The first concern would be that the company
could not afford to lose $10 million, even though in absolute
terms this would not be true. All ethical concerns would be
tailored (and ultimately subordinated) to sustaining this profit.
Thus the manager would approach the health issue from a
defensive standpoint, in terms of the bottom line, by asking:
Can you prove tans are harmful? Given the uncertainties of
the health issue, the answer would have been no.

Most likely he or she would recommend doing nothing until the medical evidence and political climate were more
certain, at which point the potential penalties or rewards for
responding would have to be assessed again. In this approach,
ethical concerns are minimized and/or indefinitely deferred.

Carl Spalding did not think this way, nor did the executive committee. Their informing question was: Can you
prove tanning is *not* harmful? There was no way around the
fact that the jury was still out but there were reasonable medical uncertainties of which the marketplace was still unaware.
On this basis, Spalding made the very difficult decision to recommend to the executive committee that J&J "pull the plug"
on this product position. The committee agreed. There was no

way the company could ethically continue to promote baby oil as a tanning product, if by speeding up the tanning process, the product could cause future injury to the consumer's health.

Sales immediately fell from $10 million to $5 million. While this did not put the company out of business, it was a life-or-death decision for that particular product at that time, and thus highly vulnerable to survival scenario reasoning. The managers in question did not succumb to such reasoning precisely because they did not try to separate ethical obligations and commercial activity. Continued marketing of baby oil as a tanning product was unambiguously unethical. The company was willing and able to absorb the immediate costs of taking an ethical stand, and it has always been willing to take a hit on the balance sheet for the sake of such issues.

But if Spalding was expected not to drop the ethics ball, he was also expected not to quit competing in the marketplace simply because the current strategy was not viable. After extensive research he came up with a new product position for baby oil: cosmetics remover. This campaign turned out to be even more profitable than tanning lotion.

When asked to summarize his thinking on this decision, David Clare later told me that the committee's view was quite clear: "It would simply be wrong to entice people to harm themselves." Spalding, who is now president of the entire Dental Care group, feels that the incident was highly significant for his own understanding of business values. "It told me that the Credo meant something to the people at the top and that it should mean something to a product manager too."[1]

Decision 2. Repairing Cars at Lex Service

Lex Service PLC is a diversified multinational based in the United Kingdom and the United States. Its chief products are in automotive distribution, leasing, and service, and electronic components distribution. At chairman Trevor Chinn's

---

[1] Quotations are from personal interviews conducted for the Business Roundtable's Task Force on Corporate Ethics. See Laura L. Nash, "Johnson & Johnson's Credo" in *Corporate Ethics: A Prime Business Asset* (New York: The Business Roundtable, February 1988), pp. 97–98.

initiative, senior management addressed the ethical and competitive issues that faced the firm in the 1980s. The following story was told to me by the president of the motor division as an example of how his own awareness of ethical responsibility had changed his way of doing business.

> For years I had tried unsuccessfully to improve quality in our service garages. This is a very difficult area to change. Complaints with auto servicing are notoriously common. Our own record of satisfactory completions of the job was unsatisfactory. Customers were constantly coming back claiming that the mechanics had said the problems were fixed when they weren't.
>
> I tried everything to ensure that the mechanics would do what they said they were doing. We put on more stringent supervision and imposed penalties for jobs done wrong. Nothing helped and it was a mess.
>
> But after our top management discussions of ethics I think we all agreed that it was imperative that we develop a more sympathetic view of customers and just as importantly of our own employees at all levels of the firm.
>
> In the end I decided to try putting the customer and mechanic in direct contact. I dismantled the entire structure of the service system. No longer was an order filled by a clerk to be processed by a service supervisor to be assigned a mechanic to be checked by another supervisor before a clerk saw that the car and owner were reunited at the end of the day. Mechanics met directly with the customer whom they would service and they discussed the repair problems face-to-face. Customer satisfaction rates went way up and completed repair times improved dramatically. Not only were mechanics better able to diagnose the problem, it was discovered that they seemed to care more about getting the job done right.

The president explained what had occurred not in complicated mechanical descriptions of organizational structure but quite simply in terms of the commonsense values which he in fact brought to bear on the problem:

> It's very easy to feel indifferent about the welfare of some bloke who can afford a forty-five thousand dollar car. But when you actually meet the owner of the Jaguar whose blood will be spilled on the highways if you make a mistake, you care more about the job you're doing.

In both cases the managers fulfilled the three conditions for ethical decision making which were outlined at the beginning of the chapter. These three facets of their thinking stand out in sharp relief to an enlightened self-interest ethic, and are hallmarks of business approaches like Johnson & Johnson's, which has deservedly earned the company an outstanding reputation.

1. Integrated ethics. First of all, *basic ethical issues were an integral part of their problem-solving calculus.* Baby oil was not "simply a marketing problem" with ethical fallout; the health of the customer was an essential component of management reasoning. In the Lex example, the long-term, potentially disastrous effects of a mismanaged repair to a Jaguar were a reality, a motivator, a normative concept. The fact that the customer was not getting the service the company claimed to stand for was a morally unacceptable breakdown of the contract between them.

2. Other orientation. *These managers centered their focus not on the company's bottom line nor its own way of doing business, but on other people, in this case their customers.* Managers had what I would call an "automatic sympathy" with others which influenced the way they defined the problem and led to a more immediate response. Their working definition was not how to increase the bottom line preferably by serving the customer well, but rather, how to serve the customer well. They were very sensitive to the customer's point of view, to the prospect of injury, or to promise-keeping. This sensitivity freed them to check their moral barometer openly and with other managers rather than hold such values in check out of fear for corporate survival.

     3. Economic success. *The other-oriented values which were dominant in their reasoning generated action, and specifically action of a commercially successful nature.* It was a specific way of perceiving the problem which contained an absolute imperative for instituting change. This encouraged extreme risk-taking from a personal and corporate standpoint, and led to innovation. Because their ethics were integrated, the managers did not abandon an appropriate and pragmatic sense of economics. They were well aware of the financial implications of the problem. Although J&J chose a short-term sacrifice of revenue, management did not try to turn the company into a philanthropic organization in order to salve its conscience. It looked for solutions in a market context.

     Thus these managers were successful in making their moral impulses a positive and active contribution to the company's financial success. But to achieve this result, they did not start with the conceptual framework of a self-oriented, neoclassical model.

THE THREE CONDITIONS OF ETHICAL PROBLEM SOLVING

     These three facets of ethical management decision making engage a complex set of ethical and cognitive assumptions about the purpose of business and the ways in which to carry out the purpose most productively. These components of ethical decision making are analyzed in detail below. I argue that the kind of successful and ethical leadership that many corporate leaders are calling for has and must rest on these characteristics if the general conditions for achieving business integrity are to be fulfilled.

Condition 1. Integrating Ethical Norms with the Pursuit of Economic Success

     An integrated model of ethics and profit-making is a must, as many corporate leaders have indicated. According to John Casey, managing director at Scudder, Stevens & Clark and author of the excellent book entitled *Ethics in the Financial Marketplace,* it combines knowledge-worker experience with personal insight and moral imagination.[2]

But such an integration is no small task even from a theoretical point of view, for in both the casual stereotypes and formal philosophies about business, ethical values, and money have traditionally been assigned opposing moral meanings. The great pragmatist John Dewey pointed out that the idea of integrating material success with ethical values was a needed but revolutionary proposal. Moral commitments are typically regarded as high pursuits and the pursuit of the dollar as a base or low occupation. In Dewey's opinion, the results of this dialectic were more destructive than they appeared. He wrote:

> Carried into practice, this dialectic has an import that is tragic. Historically, it has been the source and justification of a hard and fast difference between ideal goods on one side and material goods on the other.[3]

In the personal values poll mentioned in Chapter 2, it was evident that many executives tend to think in precisely these categories. Moral abstractions are the things they personally idealize while money is rarely mentioned. Neoclassical models of problem solving try to resolve the dichotomy by suggesting a prioritization of values: return is the first purpose, and complying with the law and moral custom an accompanying constraint. Thus ethics is only relevant when it poses an either/or choice, in which case you either choose to forego profit for your moral scruples or not.

Such a dialectic is indeed as pragmatically destructive as Dewey suggested. If you separate moral ideals and material goods, you banish idealism from the workplace. Moral idealism is an essential aspect of leadership in a field where the ethical dilemmas are tough and require breaking out of either/or trade-offs between ethics and profit. From a personal standpoint, if you begin with a business approach that as-

---

[2]John L. Casey, *Ethics in the Financial Marketplace* (New York: Scudder, Stevens & Clark, 1988).
[3]John Dewey, *Reconstruction in Philosophy* (Boston: Beacon Press, 1948), p. I.vi.

sumes that money and ethics have opposite moral values, you then close the door to ethical business behavior. Your only choices are to be morally indifferent, or hypocritical, or engaged in not-for-profit activities.

If a business ethic is to put good intentions to work, it must not forego consideration of profit, but it also must not create priorities that effectively create a profit-only context for morality. The ethic must develop a framework for allowing a host of self and other-oriented values to work in complementary ways. For highly ethical companies the connection between integrity and profit is never lost. As David Collins, former vice chairman of J&J, has noted:

> We are *not* an eleemosynary organization. I would not want anyone to think that just because we believe in the Credo's values that we are not competitive. Our managers are *very* competitive. The Credo is about competitiveness. As Jim Burke points out, if you follow all the tenets of the Credo your business will prosper.

Champion International chairman Andrew Sigler makes a similar point about "the Champion Way," his company's statement of business ethics:

> We're not a hollering sawmill operation. The Champion Way is an attitude that overrides differences between our business styles in different markets. It talks about competence and adding a people dimension to our managers' qualifications. Of course there is a morality in this, but there is no distinction being made between morality and performance.

Here is a brief example of just how difficult it can be for people to sustain the concept of profit and ethics in the same equation. Early in this century the American Medical Association launched a campaign against advertising patent medicines in the popular press. Such ads, which were used by quacks and legitimate pharmaceutical companies alike, had duped many people out of their money and in some cases destroyed user health. Such practices were giving the health profession a bad name.

Was the AMA's campaign against such ads ethical or not? Pulitzer-Prize winner Paul Starr has pointed out that the campaign was not simply an act of public service but the first step in rechanneling the purchase of drugs away from the general public and through doctors. The move carried its own financial and status premiums.[4] The implication for many is that to the degree that the AMA's decision was self-serving, its integrity was tainted. To the degree that money was to be made, there must surely have been an accompanying exploitation of the sick or at best an indifference to their welfare. So, too, as the medical profession has become more of a business, the credibility level of the profession has dropped.

Such attitudes place ethics and money in classic disalignment, but their theoretical assumptions must be questioned. How does one account for and accurately assess the protection of public health, which also accompanied the move toward prescriptions, if profit motives preclude service? Today these same protections are part of federal law.

Rather than adopt an irresolvable dichotomy of ethics and money, the AMA's integrity must be tested by a more integrated ethical construct, one that measures how well it avoids dishonesty, injury, and exploitation in conducting the successful business of getting helpful medicines to the public. The key to this approach can be found in the concepts of *value-creation* and *mutually beneficial relationships*. These are the commitments and conditions that have been the foundation of honest business in America for a long time. If you understand the informing concepts of business to be about relationships of mutual benefit and the creation of value, then personal morals and making money become more compatible. It is precisely the Confucian ethic of mutual obligation that has so successfully informed Japanese approaches to the marketplace and employee relations. Describing the chief differences between Japanese and American corporations, Peter Drucker

[4]Paul Starr, *The Social Transformation of American Medicine* (New York: Basic Books, 1982), pp. 127–134.

notes that the Japanese conception of ownership is based on what is essentially "a relationship of mutual obligations rather than a right."[5]

I call this departure from the self-oriented assumptions of neoclassical models the Covenantal Business Ethic. This approach to ethical problem solving is a covenant because it involves values and attitudes which cannot be totally accounted for in legal contracts. Rather, this ethic represents the promises and tokens a capitalistic community makes with its business agents, and vice versa. It is at heart about mutual obligation. Like the covenants of early New England communities, it is intended to be simultaneously beneficial to individual and community well-being. The moral values on which it draws are coincident with standard definitions of private morality. In Puritan times these were the values of the Protestant work ethic. Today these values are less religiously oriented, but nonetheless consistent with individual integrity as defined in a Judeo-Christian context.

The highlights of this conceptual approach can be stated as follows:

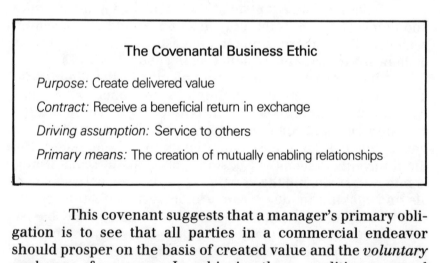

The Covenantal Business Ethic

Purpose: Create delivered value

Contract: Receive a beneficial return in exchange

Driving assumption: Service to others

Primary means: The creation of mutually enabling relationships

This covenant suggests that a manager's primary obligation is to see that all parties in a commercial endeavor should prosper on the basis of created value and the *voluntary* exchange of resources. In achieving these conditions, several of the assumptions of the neoclassical model are reversed. Whereas the self-interest ethic focuses on profit as the first

[5]Peter F. Drucker, *Managing in Turbulent Times* (New York: Harper & Row, 1980), p. 183.

purpose and other-oriented values as a secondary contractual condition, the covenantal approach has as its first purpose the welfare of others, and views profit as a secondary contractual condition. Whereas the neoclassical model regards efficiency measures as a primary focus of problem solving and benefit to others (greatest good for greatest number) as an assumed result, the Covenantal Ethic sees the creation of mutually enabling *relationships* as the assumed result and servicing relationships as the primary vehicle for problem solving.

Under this covenant, return is acknowledged to be an essential component of business, but the receipt of a legitimate return *is absolutely conditional on the creation and provision of value in other people's terms.* One's own return is transformed from being a primary purpose to a secondary result. Says American Express's Lou Gerstner: "We almost view financial results as the by-product of the other measures of performance. We are only satisfied if we get profits in ways that are innovative and unique in some instances."[6]

From an ethical standpoint the Covenantal Ethic draws on very different values to motivate and guide decision making. It is not enough to rearrange the pieces on the financial playing board so as to win more for oneself, one must create something of perceived value for others. A *commitment to service*, rather than the egotistical pursuit of one's own interest, is the spark that ignites managerial problem solving. By fixating on this commitment a manager begins to see business as a *series of enabling relationships* rather than a set of efficiency measures. Note how the Johnson & Johnson Credo, for example, is constructed around four relationships in the company's business. So, too, Andrew Sigler spoke of the "people values" which the Champion Way of managing unleashes.

The effect of this change in purpose on managerial problem definition is profound. Instead of asking, How big are we getting? How can I arrange my resources to grow? a manager asks, What does the other person need? How can I gather my resources to provide it? Instead of chaining one's outlook to milking the status quo, one tries to build upon it. Service and value-creation become intrinsically important on

---

[6]Quoted in John Junkerman, "Miss Liberty Meets the Corporate Entrepreneur," *Harvard Business School Bulletin* (Spring 1984), p. 73.

their own. *As a building block of quality, such assumptions are far stronger than an appeal to profit.*

I am reminded somewhat archaically of the first occurrence of the word *integrity* in a business context, as reported in the Oxford English Dictionary. One F. Junius, writing in 1638, was bemoaning the fact that "an integrity of workmanship had been put down by false and adulterate ways." Junius saw an unbreakable connection between product quality and moral health. The decline of one was a devaluation of the other as well.

Today's fascination in some business quarters with the deal itself, rather than the created value or quality of service, has heralded a parade of moral abominations which Junius could have predicted. It also stands in sharp contrast to covenantal thinking, which draws heavily on private moral norms to fulfill its primary assumptions of business purpose. Many standard commonsense indicators of integrity such as honest representation, accuracy, and caring about others are all essentials of successful value-creation. These are also consonant with some of the most frequently prescribed recipes for success: innovation, listening to the customer, making it happen for others. Many of the ethical norms contributing to trust (honesty, fairness, concern for others) are consistent with and crucial to the establishment of mutually enabling relationships.

Thus a covenantal approach to business succeeds in establishing at the outset a purpose and method of problem solving that integrates standard ethical norms and economically productive thinking. It does not preclude efficiency, which provides its own kind of value for both the provider and the receiver, but it refocuses efficiency and every other business activity to the creation of value and establishment of mutually enabling relationships. The Covenantal Ethic draws together in one theoretical framework the values assumptions that inform such classic models of creative strategic thinking as Kenneth Andrews's concept of corporate strategy, where he suggested that strategy was a four-part process of looking both inward and outward to assess resources (self), recognize opportunity (other people's perceptions of value), consider environment (expectations of outside community), and bring to bear irrational management values (both self- and other-oriented preferences).[7]

As a road map for cooperation and voluntary exchange the covenantal approach to problem solving draws a more compatible connection between business purpose and the social conditions on which business depends. This is precisely the conceptual foundation needed for the fulfillment of stakeholder business missions. Two excerpts from NCR's mission statement are a good illustration of this reasoning:

> STAKEHOLDERS: We believe in building mutually beneficial and enduring relationships with all of our stakeholders, based on conducting business activities with integrity and respect.
> CUSTOMERS: We take customer satisfaction personally: we are committed to providing superior values in our products and services on a continuing basis.

Or as General Robert Wood Johnson stated in his preface to the first publication of the J&J Credo: "Accept attainment of a decent living for all as the fundamental goal of business."

Condition 2. An Other-Directed Attitude

A Covenantal Ethic pulls many values beside self-aggrandizement into the manager's universe of active concerns. But if variety were the only factor, it would look very much like an enlightened self-interest approach. A Covenantal Ethic does not just respect other people's needs, it takes them to be the *first* purpose of business thinking. In so doing, the Covenantal Ethic prompts a different set of psychological attitudes or character traits than do the self-interest assumptions.

To be fully realized, the cultivation of a covenantal mindset requires a manager to break through the psychological boundaries of a self-interested orientation. This is a particularly challenging proposition at a time when the suspicion that nobody cares for anyone but him- or herself is being

---

[7]Kenneth Andrews, *The Concept of Corporate Strategy,* rev. ed. (Homewood, IL: Richard D. Irwin, 1980).

loudly voiced among managers and the public alike. Recently
Judge Lasker, in passing sentence on convicted stock manipu-
lator Boyd Jeffries, told the audience that it was "important
for the court to send a message to the financial community."
His message was: "It may be that it was appropriate and accepted to cut corners and skirt the edges until recently. This
country is beginning to awake, I hope, to the morally corrupting effect of thinking of oneself only."

Even if Lasker's assessment of the nation's commer-
cial *zeitgeist* is not universally true, it is a perceptive insight
into the psychology of many corporate scandals today. Wall
Street has repeatedly displayed a me-first climate of greed and
dishonesty at every level of its ranks. Defense Department officials and the companies that woo them have continually held
their own return above the moral and legal constraints of fair
play and accurate bookkeeping. Recent disclosures of unau-
thorized ingredient substitutions in the generic drug business
have revealed a shocking disregard of both public health and
other competitors in that industry. In short, the pervasiveness
of greed and exploitative self-centeredness is no small reality.
It must be reckoned with by a management team that seeks
to conduct a business with integrity. The motivation system
and definition of business purpose that seeks to stimulate market responsiveness through an appeal to individual advancement only feeds this self-centeredness.

Many business leaders, recognizing the moral frailty
that unbridled self-interest invites, reject a me-first or even
company-first approach to problem solving in favor of a
stronger emphasis on "the other guy" such as a Covenantal
Ethic suggests. *BusinessWeek* and the Boston Consulting
Group talk about "caring" as the new competitive weapon.
Tom Peters urges managers to keep close to the customer, and
respect each and every employee. Japanese sales and service
guidelines regularly begin with greeting the customer and listening to him or her before taking an order. J.C. Penney begins
its business guidelines, which have fueled the company's success since 1913, with the statement, "To serve the public, as
nearly as we can, to *its* complete satisfaction."

So, too, on the inevitable field of interoffice combat or
interbusiness negotiations, an understanding of the other

side's point of view is essential if one is to succeed in securing its cooperation. Harvard Law School professor Roger Fisher, in his widely acclaimed books on negotiation, argues that a skilled negotiator must understand clearly his or her interests *and the interests of the other parties* in a negotiation. He writes: "If you want to influence them [other people in a negotiation], you also need to *understand empathetically* the power of their point of view and to feel the emotional force with which they believe in it"[8] (emphasis added). Fisher, who bases his analysis on extensive observation of political and transactional negotiations, feels that a coldly rational calculation of probable responses is rarely a sufficient basis for a productive relationship when two parties are in conflict. A felt understanding of the other person's point of view is a must.

Is all this talk about felt understanding, serving, caring, listening, and keeping close to the customer and respecting employees so much soft stuff? Or does it have a fundamental commercial and psychological truth? Many experts have suggested that a self-oriented world view is characteristic of an immature stage of personal development.[9] The psychological transition of growth is generally described as moving from the view that one's own needs are the only regulator of attitude and action, to a perception and acceptance of the *validity of other people's needs and points of view.*

In other words, a mature person feels others deserve respect simply for their intrinsic worth as people. From a self-interest business viewpoint, however, a manager's psychological orientation is stunted at the start. Other people's needs and interests are perceived only in terms of their capacity to enhance or inhibit one's own interests. After conducting a kind of self-enhancing cost-benefit analysis, one responds to these needs because it "pays." Psychologist H.S. Sullivan described this way of thinking as basically a "morality of cooperation."[10]

But mature human beings generally hatch out of this

---

[8]Roger Fisher and Scott Brown, *Getting Together: Building a Relationship That Gets to Yes* (Boston: Houghton Mifflin, 1988), p. 24.

[9]For a very good summary of the literature, see Robert Kegan, *The Evolving Self: Problem and Process in Human Development* (Cambridge, MA: Harvard University Press, 1982).

[10]H.S. Sullivan, *The Interpersonal Theory of Psychiatry* (New York: Norton, 1953), cited in Kegan, *The Evolving Self,* p. 57. In moral psychology terms, the corporate covenant suggested here uses the concept of mutual benefit as a mediating principle.

self-oriented approach to arrive at a more balanced consideration of self and others. Such growth is not fully logical. It draws its strength on emotional capacities as well: on empathy, literally "being in another's feeling," caring, and respect. Out of such capacities one develops a collaborative mindset. One's involvement in another is for another; in other words, it is other-enhancing.

Though difficult to prove, it is possible to distinguish between caring, other-orientations, and self-enhancing logics of cooperation, which distinguish a Covenantal Ethic and an enlightened self-interest approach. They are differences of attitude, much like the differences between manipulation and love. Do you try to meet your spouse's needs primarily because it is in your interest to do so, or do you service them because you care? Which marriage is likelier to prosper and be a mutually beneficial relationship: the one based on self-interest or the one based on genuine caring?

Many of today's admonitions for business success, from closeness to the customer to empowering employees, rest on an other-enhancing point of view. If you understand the admonitions only in mechanistic terms, they will never be achieved. As one manager put it, "I can establish an open door policy until the cows come home, but if I don't respect my employees, no one will willingly walk through that door."

The Covenantal Ethic rests on and seeks to motivate an other-enhancing attitude. Its need in management is only too clear. Consider the time-honored dictum, "The customer is always right." This maxim is not some crazy observation that customers never make mistaken claims, but that the spirit in which a manager deals with customers must always be founded on respect and consideration for the customer's needs. Such empathy makes sense. How can you meet a market need unless you have a "feel" for the market's point of view? How can you cultivate such a "feel" in yourself and others unless you draw on an ethical foundation of respect and service?

The relationship orientation of the Covenantal Ethic is particularly suited for motivating an other-enhancing, collaborative approach to problem solving. Business is inescapably dependent on social interactions and often social conflict.

Every business activity, from a simple transaction to managing complex compensations systems, involves at least two people, often with overtly different goals, but whose interests are inescapably connected. Most ethical concepts are also deeply embedded in a self- and other-orientation, which Amitai Etzioni has eloquently described by the phrase "I&We orientation."[11] By this he means that a person defines his or her highest purposes and practical value system with a paradoxical acknowledgment of personal autonomy and of being part of a larger community whose welfare and values are inextricably tied to one's own identity. From this orientation many ethical norms follow. Such concepts as honesty and fairness, inherently dependent on a relationship between two or more people for their fulfillment, become motivated by the sense that all people have intrinsic value. Many ethical norms take their power from this viewpoint. When people have an intrinsic value, you cannot tolerate the violation of their well-being through deceit, injury, or exploitation, *even if you could get away with it.*

Etzioni's paradox can be productively extended to the ethos of successful capitalism. As Max Weber noted, the distinguishing feature of capitalism is voluntary exchange. Exchange requires two people. Voluntary exchange rests on mutually enabling conditions unless one party resorts to deception or exploitation. The Covenantal Ethic describes these conditions as the provision of value and receipt of a fair return. The mature moral world view of "self-in-community" is complementary to this ethic and a sustaining assumption. Corporate egoism, on the other hand, in its orientation on self sets up blinders between a company and its own dependency on the other people's welfare. Thus it fails in the marketplace. As Knight-Ridder chairman Alvah Chapman quipped, "You can't sell peanuts at a funeral."

The reason for this blindness is, again, the prioritizing aspect of self-interest models. By prioritizing self-concerns, one constructs an insurmountable barrier to the paradoxical viewpoint of self-and-others. Examples of this barrier are the products by which corporate egoism measures success: share

---

[11] Amitai Etzioni, *The Moral Dimension: Toward a New Economics* (New York: Free Press, 1988), p. 8.

of market, number of sales, size of assets, reduction of manufacturing errors. These are all self-enhancing concepts with
the marketplace as a secondary beneficiary. By contrast, a
Covenantal Ethic tests success through quality of service as
defined in other people's terms: customer satisfaction, community health, team welfare.

But however obvious the need to think about the other
point of view in a transaction or communication problem, the
question remains, how does one cultivate an other-directed
orientation in a way that brings commercial success? A service
attitude is the ignition key to this orientation. It is the primary
problem orientation of a Covenantal Ethic and an informing
concept of many excellence theories, including those of Tom
Peters, Peter Drucker, Max DePree, Thomas Watson, and
Robert Greenleaf. The attitude of service has informed some
of the most spectacular successes in the marketplace. IBM's
legendary awareness that it was service, and not the specific
hardware, that gave it its competitive edge is perhaps the best
example.

Or take Tom Peters's account of the extremely successful Elgin box company in Elgin, Illinois, which operates
in what is generally regarded as a "dying" industry. In Peters's
words:

> Elgin's competitive edge are service and responsive-
> ness to its customers' needs. Elgin has not been late
> in shipping an order for over six years. *Elgin's attitude
> has been to serve customer needs first.* [my emphasis]
> If a hard special order comes in, they'll take it and
> run at the risk of lower profit. Because down the road
> the small custom orders often lead to bigger ones.
> According to one customer, "If they'll do the tough
> stuff for us, then we'll give them the bread-and-butter
> orders too." In a commodity type business like card-
> board boxes, it is very hard to give value-added, but
> it is Elgin's mindset of service which leads them to
> find this distinctive edge.[12]

The distinctive edge created by good service has been

---

[12]Tom Peters, *Thriving on Chaos* (New York: Harper & Row, 1987), p. 69.

observed time and again in the most successful companies: the personalization of a Nordstrom shopping experience, the reliability and flexibility of Federal Express, the special responsiveness of ServiceMaster in the difficult business of industrial cleaning. When you're waiting for the ServiceMaster truck after a fire, your house won't just be cleaned competently, you'll be treated with respect. You'll even get a phone call by the supervisor if the truck is going to be more than ten minutes late out of respect for *your* schedule. Ever wait around all day for a repair service that never showed up and when you complained the company told you its scheduling problems? That's the difference between a service mentality and a self-centered approach to the marketplace.

The concept of service has a strong foundation in Judeo-Christian values. New Testament passages in Matthew on Love Thy Neighbor and Do Unto Others are good examples. From Jewish tradition there is the wonderful proverb from "Lives of the Fathers" which reads: "Who is to be honored? He who honors others." This was the leadership theory on which this nation was founded. George Washington, good soul of the Enlightenment that he was, recognized that the true source of legitimate power was service, which required both personal denial and risk. Nowhere was this theory more apparent than in his two great acts: his voluntary rescindment of his commission as commander in chief after the war, and his surrender of the presidency.

A covenantal psychology is neither "buyer beware" nor "seller beware," but the empathetic maxim, "seller must care." But the concept of service as an essential covenantal psychology extends well beyond customer relationships into every aspect of the management function. Any business relationship can and should be subjected to a Covenantal Ethic. Most business leaders describe the universe of relevant relationships in very wide terms. Korn/Ferry International's most recent attitude survey of corporate directors has suggested that 90 percent of outside directors felt they represented a range of constituents beyond shareholders.[13] Some of the most admired managers in America have expressed a strong identi-

---

[13] Korn/Ferry International, *Board of Directors, Sixteenth Annual Study* (Los Angeles, March 1989).

fication with the larger community in which they work and fashion their company's community relations accordingly. IBM's Thomas Watson, Chase Manhattan's David Rockefeller, or Xerox's chairman David Kearns devoted considerable leadership to promoting the notion that the business person should be servant of the public and an innovator in helping society create solutions to its problems. At the policy-making level, such prestigious business organizations as the Business Roundtable have put themselves on record as believing the corporation has a long-term responsibility to both the economic and noneconomic aspects of the society (or societies) in which it operates.[14]

In practical terms this responsibility may be played out in the form of charitable giving, public-private partnerships, educational assistance, or compliance with environmental legislation. Once again, such responses can be rationally justified in either an enlightened self-interest ethos or a Covenantal Ethic. It is easy to see how compliance with the law sometimes pays (though sometimes not), or how contributions to the local charity can be demonstrated to have a strategic return on local image and goodwill. But no rational assessment of enlightened self-interest could fully justify the innovative and extensive contribution an Electrolux makes in initiating a $6 million program to help its employees find local jobs when it closed down its plant in Greenwich, Connecticut. Nor does it explain the reasoning behind the considerable sums (over $1 billion annually) spent by business on underwriting local sports events. These decisions illustrate the strong sense of linkage to the community which is one manifestation of the covenantal capacity for empathy and a service orientation. They are yet another indication of how the other-oriented basis of a covenant provides an appropriate expression of basic values in the business community.

At the same time, it should be remembered that this other-orientation is not synonymous with philanthropy. The covenant suggested here rests on a condition of mutual bene-

---

[14] *The Business Roundtable Statement on Corporate Responsibility* (New York: The Business Roundtable, January 1982).

fit. The adoption of an other-orientation as a primary attitude does not demand a total denial of self. Rather, *it demands that the needs of self be balanced with an attitude of service to others.* Thus while the Covenantal Ethic clearly puts customer need as a first purpose, a management's strategic choice of market niches must be complementary to the advancement of the company.

In short, the Covenantal Ethic is neither disinterested nor self-interested. It defines an ethic of mutual benefit. The Goldman Sachs statement of business philosophy is one such example. It begins with "client first" and continues as follows: "Our experience shows that if we serve our clients well, our own success will follow." J.C. Penney's second "idea" is "to expect for the service we render a fair remuneration and not all the profit the traffic will bear."

To summarize, although the Covenantal Ethic describes an ethic of mutual benefit, it invites mutual benefit through a different set of assumptions and psychological orientations than in an enlightened self-interest model. Although service has many concrete and mechanical expressions, the underlying psychological attitude that informs all such activities is the "other-orientation" with which this discussion began. While a must for covenantal thinking, there is still a final part of the ethic to be identified, and that is the conceptual vehicle through which the attitudes, purposes, and contracts which have already been described will be translated into action.

Condition 3. A Business Ethic Must Be Capable of Motivating Pragmatic and Competitive Behavior

Psychologist Rollo May once observed that "Will follows from caring." In the previous section, I suggested that the psychological quality of caring, and its ethical equivalent in the form of respect for other people and a service attitude, can create a will to market responsiveness which the self-interest ethic inherently fails to motivate. Charles Garfield, in his best-selling management book *Peak Performers*, has called the caring-service-performance relationship a "creative loop."[15] This attitude of universal concern for others can even overcome some of the most deeply seated enmities in business relationships, such as the "dump-on-the-competitor" attitude. The manager who concentrates not on how competitors take away company profit but rather on how they serve the customer can gain a great competitive edge. Such an attitude is fueled by respect, not denigration.

THE LENSPIECE OF RELATIONSHIP

The Covenantal Ethic further extends the pragmatic power of a manager's ethics by having a problem-solving focus on *relationships*. It suggests that the goal of the manager is not so much a specific product but the maintenance of that process by which service attitudes are translated into value-creation. *This is a mindset on people and relationships over concrete products or measurements.* Unlike the self-interest ethic, which directs business judgment through the lens of efficiency and technique, the Covenantal Ethic channels judgment through the lenspiece of relationship. A manager's understanding of problems will not be in terms of concrete products, specific cost reductions, or even balance sheets (though obviously these will be secondary results and scorecards), but in terms of *the quality of the relationships that are inevitably created by any business activity.* An appropriate term for this quality in a covenantal context is "enabling relationship" (as always with the covenantal understanding of mutual benefit).

All sorts of business activities can be analyzed through this lenspiece. A value-providing service enables a customer to better meet his or her needs. Even the most trivial product establishes a relationship between producer, seller, and customer. These relationships can be deceptive, exploitative, oppressing, and injurious, or conversely, informative, empowering, beneficial, and constructive. All of the latter qualities rest on ethical norms such as honesty, respect, and not hurting others.

---

[15] Charles Garfield, *Peak Performers: The New Heroes of American Business* (New York: Avon Books, 1986), p. 104.

The relationship reasoning of a Covenantal Ethic can provide immediate insight into these values as well as market responsiveness. An ice-cream cone may not seem to require ethical values until one surveys the relationships required to make it an economic success. Then the relevant values and obligations become clear: the quality of the product must be good enough to ensure trust between customer and producer concerning that quality. The relationship with the middle agents who deliver and sell the product must be fair, i.e., financially enabling. The production process must thrive on an environmental strategy that enables the community's viability. And so on. All of these relationship outcomes rest on trust, honesty, and mutual benefit. If these are enabling relationships, i.e., ones that result in an improvement in the receiver's quality of life, then value will have been created and return legitimately received. The covenant will be fulfilled.

Even a company's quality assurance can be subjected to relationship analysis. Many managers see quality as cost reduction. But when quality becomes an expression of the covenantal relationships, then innovative products, good prices, and reliability are the focus of quality programs. This is the difference between using a cheaper brand of ink in a fountain pen and developing the first Bic ballpoint for 19 cents and selling it in supermarkets. At the heart of such innovations is an ethic of service and respect for others, which makes issues of quality and honesty a matter of course as a management assesses market opportunities.

The idea of assessing problems and measuring success in terms of relationships can seem revolutionary and "soft" in the face of bottom-line pressures. But in today's marketplace of fickle customers and investors, exploding technological breakthroughs, and ever-new competitors, products and quarterly earnings reports have a new kind of obsolescence. They are not necessarily a basis for predicting future success. The only base—and even it is in no way secure—is the relationship you establish with others—customers, suppliers, employees, community. James Burke's ringing refrain after the Tylenol crisis has special relevance here: "We got through Tylenol by drawing on ninety years of public trust in the bank." Looking once again at IBM's legendary success in the marketplace, it is clear that a relationship orientation has always driven the company's management philosophy. What an IBM manager does so well is establish and maintain good relationships with customers and employees.

While the importance of relationships in business is obvious, the absence of relationship reasoning in so many statements of strategic purpose or assessments of problems—whether they include ethical components or not—is a strong indication that many managers must become more sensitive to the relevance of good relationships. Attempts to establish high ethical standards of conduct must also cultivate a strong sense of relationship in order to bring ethical standards into the marketplace.

Assume that Manager X has an "average" sense of right and wrong. Theoretically he (or she) does not condone lying, cheating, or injuring others. One day his contractor solicits an "agent's fee"—off the books, of course. The chances of getting caught are remote. What should the manager do? Theoretically an enlightened self-interest ethic would forbid acquiescing. It is illegal even if it may be general custom, and lying is definitely a moral no-no. In practice, however, the vocabulary of self-interest which Manager X would bring to this dilemma would not have much power to constrain him from acting unethically. Manager X might reason as follows: my private self doesn't *like* this, but I have to do it for the sake of the job. In other words, ethics are decorative, a function of taste, and the significant factor is whether payment is likely to cost or benefit the company.

Obviously several relationships of trust are threatened if Manager X acquiesces to the contractor's demand: public trust that the company will obey the law, shareholder trust concerning prudent management, company trust of Manager X's bookkeeping practices. The client-contractor relationship is also being destroyed. Should Manager X pay the fee, he or she will have become a captive to further demands in exchange for the contractor's silence. A self-interest approach would perceive these consequences only to the degree that they could impose tangible costs on the bottom line. Compared to the benefits, these considerations would be weak. A covenantal approach, however, would take the destruction of relationships into account for their own sake. This would throw the consequences into sharper relief, and thereby increase the likelihood that Manager X could apply moral brakes. Thus relationship reasoning would facilitate the application of Manager X's private ethical norms to competitive thinking. A covenantal approach would give a manager a more useful perspective for constraining unethical behavior. It would also, by linking value and enabling relationships, aid in more positive ethical decisions such as producing a beneficial product or marketing honestly or keeping costs down in creative rather than destructive ways.

This kind of reasoning cannot be taken for granted. Recent research in moral development suggests that women reason and act in terms of relationships and caring much more frequently than men, who think much more in terms of rules and justice. The seminal work on this is Harvard professor Carol Gilligan's book *In a Different Voice.* Professor Gilligan suggests that by adopting a standard of "relationship, caring and nurturance," women tend to adopt less-hierarchical moral frameworks than most males.[16]

Whether or not one accepts her notion of gender bias, it is instructive to consider Gilligan's distinction when thinking about a manager's ethical interpretation of commerical competition and managing other people. In a self-interest model, one tends to approach questions of managerial obligation to other constituencies in terms of hierarchical priorities: Who can hurt the company most? Which person, group, or moral value will make the greatest contribution to the bottom line? One can even mistakenly associate the right moral judgment with the person higher up in the organization: ethics is what the boss says, even if someone lower down has more knowledge of the facts and probable outcomes. A relationship-oriented ethos, inherently less hierarchical, is a battering ram for breaking out of the hierarchies which an enlightened self-interest model tends to encourage. It facilitates a competitive and honest execution of company claims to "care about the customer."

Take the case told to me by a former employee of the

---

[16]Carol Gilligan, *In a Different Voice* (Cambridge, MA: Harvard University Press, 1982), pp. 62–63.

Bell system. Now an upper-level manager, she began her days as an operator. The old Bell system—like many other larger corporations—was notoriously rule-oriented, bureaucratic, and authoritarian. One day a rule came down from on high. After every call, operators were instructed to say, "Have a nice day." Sounded great on paper, except that operators frequently receive calls from people in distress. Their houses are on fire or they have a medical emergency. It is obviously absurd to tell someone to have a nice day when they've just shouted into the phone, "Help, my house is burning, call the fire department!" It flies in the face of logic and compassion. It sees customers as interchangeable parts rather than as individuals to be dealt with individually. Had upper management been less bound by its emphasis on rules and hierarchical authority, it would have recognized the distinction and never suggested so inflexible an approach. Had it respected the lowly operator, it would have trusted him or her to use a close relationship with the customer to best advantage.

Though the success of every business activity depends on the maintenance of good relationships, many management theories and systems frequently fail to integrate relationship reasoning in their planning and execution. Bill Johnson, a vice president at Digital Equipment Corporation, relates with relish how he learned this lesson the hard way. Digital, IBM, and many other companies had cemented a historic, new joint collaborative venture in which the downstream benefits of cooperation around communications standards were quite clear. The lawyers established the ground rules and the engineers set to work. After a few months, it was clear to Bill that the project was foundering and Digital's engineers were frustrated. Relationships, not technology or bureaucracy, were the culprit. His group could not put aside its conventional mindset about being "competitors." To express the problem in terms of a Covenantal Ethic, it could not put the creation of value, servicing of the market, and contribution to mutually enabling relationships before a consideration of its immediate and traditional interests. Neither group *cared* to provide value for the other side and there were no rules in place which could substitute for caring. Are there ever?

Johnson and his counterparts in the new organization still personally manage the new relationship. Johnson reports that he now trains all of his people in "the three Cs," which summarize his view of the three most important things to think about based on the circumstances. They are three relationships: customers, collaborators, and competitors. All three depend for their maintenance on the strong ethical value system which DEC's top management has encouraged over the years.

One can see the same neglect of relationship reasoning in the way people define value-creation. Take the definition of a business. A management team often shapes a definition of the business from the standpoint of the product or the product's function, as in the mission statement, "We are in the business of transporting people." A relationship definition of a business, however, is much more closely tied to the customer. The proverbial buggy whip manufacturer is no longer a buggy whip manufacturer, not even a transportation equipment producer. It is an ongoing servicer of people on the go. This changed definition opens the way to addressing any aspect of the delivered product or service, not just the manufacturing process. It puts the focus back on what the customer is doing. Business strength becomes a function not only of the product, which is obviously important, but also of the relationship the company has established with the market. The stronger that relationship, the more sensitive the company can be to change and the more credibility it will have as it creates new responses to change. The phenomenally versatile and successful Honda Corporation, for example, builds its business approach on the assumption that it should be cultivating a life-long relationship with a customer rather than a one-time purchase. This relationship attitude influences every aspect of the company from car design to after-purchase service systems.

It was precisely this approach that fueled the success of such upstarts as Fidelity in the investment field. Fidelity's managers saw customer needs rather than existing brokerage products as the launching pad for decision making. As Fidelity has grown it has continued to invent new vehicles for strengthening customer bonds to the company.

A good rule of thumb: the more your business leans toward being a service, the more relationship reasoning counts. Given the many arguments today that service will be the number one competitive distinction for most companies, relationship reasoning will play an increasingly important role in management thinking. If you are relationship-oriented, *you automatically measure and motivate yourself with reference to the state of affairs between you and the other person, be it customer, employee, shareholder, supplier, distributor, or the public.*

The ethical implications of this attitude are significant. Because relationships are ongoing and procedural in focus, one tends to be more aware of the long-term perspective. It becomes easier to draw on values that support not just the short-term sale, but also the long-term well-being of both parties. These include honesty, empathy, caring, respect, trustworthiness, fairness, and developing the competency to deliver on one's stated or implied promises in the marketplace. In other words, in a covenantal perspective, private ethical norms are integrated into managerial thinking.

The difference can also be seen in how a manager defines success. If you operate from enlightened self-interest, you will probably judge success in terms of money and size. You then run the risk of being preoccupied with quarterly earnings, or EPS, or standing in the *Fortune* 500. Your mission statement may even state growth rate or size of market share as the first objective. Preoccupations like these do not invite responsiveness to the marketplace.

Moreover, enlightened self-interest can bolster a belief that ethical values are functional constraints: Oh yes, and we can't afford a front-page scandal, so be good kids. J.C. Penney's chairman Donald Seibert concluded that one of the biggest risks managers run is becoming so obsessed with creating "winners" that they will inadvertently adopt an ethic of lying not only to others in the company and to the public, but even to themselves.

I cannot think of a single ethical problem in business that does not rest on a breakdown of the Covenantal Ethic and consequent betrayal of trust. Most legal and institutional remedies to unethical practices in business are an attempt to reinstate a condition of trust between the parties and redefine the terms of value and return. This cannot be done by concentrating solely on rules and results; it must also be applied to relationships. As Exxon learned after the Valdez incident, no legal posture or technological expertise could change the fact that a relationship with the public had been damaged. Most of the company's effort will have to go into repairing that relationship if the company wants to maintain market competitiveness and the public goodwill on which it depends.

One must first caution against oversimplification. It is rarely sufficient to be oriented toward one relationship. The nature of business requires a manager to service multiple relationships, multiple responsibilities, and, when things go wrong, multiple victims. Setting up a fair and balanced concern for all relevant relationships is an ongoing process. At the very least, the relationships that must be included in a manager's thinking are the following:

1. Customers
2. Suppliers, advertisers, and distributors
3. Community
4. Competitors
5. Subordinates and the "boss"
6. Shareholders
7. Peers competing for career advancement
8. Top management and the board of directors, whose world view may not be the same as that of one's immediate superior

While these constituencies are important, nowhere is the need for respect and trust more evident than in relationships with employees. Both employer and employee should be able to expect a spirit of service and mutuality from the other, or in covenantal terms, the relationship should be enabling. The corporation has the same right to a Covenantal Ethic from its employees as does the public: employees should be ready to give value not only to the customer but also to the company—i.e., competency, creativity, and a willingness to put corporate interests before their own gratification. As well, employees have the right to expect covenantal approaches to work in their interests: they should receive benefit in return for their provision of value.

Unfortunately, such concepts get undermined every day, especially by the gargantuan bureaucracies and status systems American companies construct. I think here of Tom Peters's cautionary advice to dehumiliate the work environment, i.e., to destroy those roadblocks to respect that we create in a large bureaucracy: the two-tiered status symbols, the heated and unheated parking garages, the elaborate perks for top management while layoffs are rampant at the first-line level. Writes Peters:

> If we are to depend increasingly on people's wholesale involvement, then integrity is more of an issue than ever—integrity, as I've come to see it, means that if there are no employee bonuses there are no executive bonuses. It means trusting first-line employees to do all the quality control after providing them with the tools and training required to execute.[17]

Such conditions cannot be met without an assumption about the equal dignity of every person. Consider the legendary innovativeness and customer service at 3M. Its influential mission statement, which is claimed to be an accurate description of the company culture and ethic, bases its definition of purpose on a variety of ethical principles related to the maintenance of self-respect for every individual in the company. The first principle mentions entrepreneurship and freedom in the workplace to pursue innovative ideas. These conditions rest on values of "mutual trust and cooperation" and "preservation of individual identity." The Post-It pad attests to the value-creativity that is possible.

The second caution in relationship thinking is to remember that relationships are not a static product but a dynamic process. Relationships suffer constant change, especially in today's marketplace. Today's captive supplier is tomorrow's new corporate parent, today's captive customer is tomorrow's cut-rate discount purchaser. Today's competitor

---

[17]Peters, *Thriving on Chaos*, p. 46.

is tomorrow's colleague. To assume that relationships are static and that you can continue to treat captives as such long after you've lost your monopoly is both disrespectful and economically unwise.

In their analysis of Xerox's phenomenal comeback to beat the Japanese at the copier game, authors Gary Jacobsen and John Hillkirk point out that one of the major changes in Xerox's strategy was its recognition that it needed outsiders to gain a technological edge. Its historic licensing agreement with Savin for the Landa process and current executive exchanges with Landa are perfect examples of how mutually beneficial relationships provided the vehicle for competitive excellence.[18]

While relationship reasoning can have macro effects on a global scale in business, a relationship-oriented, empathetic manager, no matter what rank, never stops caring about the micro details of the end-user's experience (nor does the end-user). I recently had the opportunity to watch Norm Sanju, general manager of the Dallas Mavericks, firsthand during a home game. As soon as we sat down in the stands, his eyes wandered upward to the scoreboard. They stayed there longer than was necessary to check the score. It turned out he was counting the number of bulbs out (not many) so that he could remind his staff to fix them before the next game. Fixing bulbs is a major project, costly in terms of time. To do it less frequently gives a certain economy of scale, as it were. But as Sanju's assistant later told me, every Maverick employee understands that the quality of the scoreboard is part of their pact with the customers.

Relationship, service-oriented managers count the light bulbs; they get ulcers when a promised delivery is late and will even deliver it themselves if necessary. They won't respond to a customer's complaint by expecting the customer to understand their problems back at the office or plant. Most of all they don't lie. As Immanuel Kant noted, once one accepts the possibility of lying, all social discourse becomes impossible. Words become meaningless, promises untrustworthy. So,

---

[18] Gary Jacobsen and John Hillkirk, *Xerox: American Samurai* (New York: Collier Books, 1986).

too, a relationship orientation admits no violation of ethical norms which strengthen rather than defeat relationships.

CONCLUSION

To sum up, the Covenantal Ethic is a necessary approach to business from both a competitive and moral standpoint. It requires a fundamental realignment of thinking which moves beyond self-interest to the seemingly paradoxical concept of a self-and-other orientation. It is neither maximization of return nor philanthropy.

Although the Covenantal Ethic disagrees with Hobbes's assumptions about universal selfishness, Hobbes's remarks are here to the point. A covenant, he pointed out, is an instance where two parties agree to terms of performance in which one or both trust that the other will carry out an obligation in time to come. Whenever someone fails to keep a promise, or violates the faith of the other party, he or she commits an act of injustice. (*Leviathan* XV)

Covenants must be binding; the receipt of return for the provision of value must be an absolute standard for the business manager. Whenever it is broken, it should be viewed as an act of injustice against all others who participate in this system. That includes the entire business community, all customers, and the nations whose social and political organization make voluntary commercial enterprise possible.

In practical experience this is precisely what occurs. Sell a customer a rum piece of goods, perpetrate a not-very-beneficial benefits package, abuse the local environment, or dramatically reduce the value of corporate bonds through a new leveraged buyout strategy, and outsiders will tend to pronounce the corporation and its managers unjust.

Broken covenants destroy community trust. To trust in anything other than this covenant as a guide to corporate conscience is to lay the foundation for a community at war with itself. In war one party forcibly takes that which the other party has not agreed to give up. So, too, when managers fail to keep the corporate covenant, they make war on their customers, or their communities, or their own people. They seek a return without the provision of value.

In emphasizing the importance of value provision, an other-orientation, service psychology, and relationship reasoning, a Covenantal Ethic offers the welcome possibility of *directly* integrating important ethical considerations into managerial thinking. This is a morally emancipating concept for a manager. It frees personal morality from the constraining prioritization of profit. One begins to take the risk of allowing profit to become the result of one's effort to create these other conditions. Once again, this is not to say that profit is not desirable, only that other values must precede its achievement and direct one's thinking.

The Covenantal Ethic rests on the assumption that a typical manager's personal definitions of self-worth and preferred ethical commitments are precisely the best motivation for commercial thinking. *This integration of ethics and economics is particularly compelling as a competitive mindset when one contemplates the values that people claim count most to them in their private lives.*

Were every manager morally invulnerable, it would make no difference from the standpoint of moral consequences whether a self-interest or covenantal approach were adopted. But given the pressures of business, the daily examples of fallibility, and the limitation of vision that most managerial environments present, it is crucial to have a habitual way of reasoning that will increase your ability to see the moral issues in such a way that they *matter* in your economic decisions. The purposes and assumptions of a covenantal approach are more likely to stimulate such a commitment.

To review the strengths of the corporate covenant as a beacon for sound business behavior, they are that

- It is oriented on a social relationship rather than on individual interest, reflecting the fact that business activity is a social activity involving multiple relationships.
- It is pragmatic in several ways. It describes what is generally agreed to be good business practice. It is not tipped too far toward a buyer-beware or seller-take-care ethic.

- It recognizes that a logical appeal to self-interest is insufficient to motivate maintenance of ethical values in the marketplace.
- It gives courage. By moving beyond thinking about oneself, it opens up a manager's moral dialogue to consider more than the weighing of personal risk and reward.

We tend to think of ethics in terms of limits and getting caught. This thinking in turn tends to generate personal injunctions of restraint—the shalt-not's. Such reasoning is fine insofar as it provides the moral brakes for certain obvious kinds of misbehavior such as falsifying records or cheating on taxes. But managers also need intellectual tools for more positive thinking, for opening up the moral choices they perceive. The covenant is not fulfilled simply because you do not lie to a customer; you must provide value to the customer, which requires infinitely more managerial creativity. It is not enough in searching for competitive excellence to, say, stay close to the customer, or be technologically innovative, or be people-oriented. One has to adopt a moral framework and psychological attitude that put other's interests first in order to transform the attributes of excellence into productive actions.

In view of the tremendous need for change, flexibility, and partnership in today's marketplace, the assumptions of the Covenantal Ethic increasingly make economic sense. They are commercially imperative to the degree that they enable a manager to use the ethical and practical mindset that motivates the kind of attributes that are generally understood to be the key to success for the future. They are morally imperative in view of the demonstrated destructiveness that a me-first attitude can and has introduced into many American companies. The need for a realignment of traditional managerial priorities has become urgent. This process has already been established at many companies. As one of the CEOs on the Business Roundtable's 1988 Task Force on Corporate Ethics put it: "What we're trying to get across is quite simple to express, but hard to make believable: You *can* make money by acting with integrity."

Part III

The Covenantal Ethic at Work

6

Endemic Roadblocks to Ethical Behavior in Business

There is only one way to achieve happiness
On this terrestrial ball,
And that is to have a clear conscience,
—Or none at all!*

Ethicist Sissela Bok in her analysis of lying wrote that a person gains true moral wisdom not so much by looking at those cases where lying is unconscionable, but where there seem to be *good reasons to lie.*[1] It is through an examination of the lapses from idealism that one gains transforming moral insight. A hitherto unexamined practice, in which wrongdoing is excused, trivialized with a euphemism, or simply denied, may on further reflection be a case of having caved in to other pressures, some of which are morally justifiable, and some not.

Given the human tendency to think of oneself as a good person, and given most managers' generally sound intentions to be good, unethical results can easily be overlooked

---

*Ogden Nash, *I'm a Stranger Here Myself.*
[1]Sissela Bok, *Lying: Moral Choice in Public and Private Life* (New York: Vintage Books, 1979), p. xxii.

or rationalized away. In one study, for example, managers described unacceptable accounting procedures as "professional compromises," but they did not feel that such compromises were indicative of a personal lapse of integrity.[2]

In practice, and despite good intentions, managers, corporations, and people in general have a tendency to deny those activities and decisions that would be damaging to their self-image if examined dispassionately. Rather than judge ourselves by our actions, as others usually do, we tend to judge ourselves by our good intentions even when the facts are otherwise. The fallout from such behavior has destructive consequences in nearly every aspect of life, consequences that are all the more serious since, in many cases, they could have been avoided. For the person of integrity, it is imperative to understand the whys and wherefores of moral rationalization.

Gaining this understanding is particularly challenging for a manager. The business environment seems to cultivate a condition of moral schizophrenia in which the boundary lines between an acceptable sense of dilemma and an unacceptable compromise of standards are constantly blurred. Too many factors in the culture of the marketplace, financial pressures, and one's own role-playing conspire to turn what would seem to be ordinary, clear-cut offenses into problematic, gray-area difficulties or excusable departures from normal moral standards.

It is crucial that the well-intentioned manager intend not only to uphold high standards. He or she must also develop a sensitivity and understanding of why these standards might be compromised in practice. An ideal way to achieve this skill is to explore the systemic reasons, organizational or personal, for typical breakdowns of common standards of integrity in business.

In Part II a set of moral and business assumptions for informing ideal business conduct was suggested under the title Covenantal Ethic. As a framework most managers can believe in, and one many leading business people already adopt, it has two great advantages:

---

[2]Kathy E. Kram, Peter C. Yeager, and Gary E. Reed, "Decisions and Dilemmas: The Ethical Dimension in the Corporate Context," *Research in Corporate Social Performance and Policy,* vol. 11 (1989), pp. 21–34.

1. It draws on typical private moral norms for a definition of business purpose and standards of integrity.
2. It stimulates a commitment and sensitivity to others, which is a crucial factor in maintaining most ethical norms and achieving economic and organizational success.

The chief question at this point, to paraphrase Bok, is not whether one should believe in a Covenantal Ethic, but rather, What are the circumstances in business under which it seems justifiable or inevitable to compromise moral values that are held to be important in this model and by most individuals?

Why do failures of conscience occur in business? When a company begins with a strategic goal of providing a customer-oriented product or service of quality, why does it end up creating a mediocre, unresponsive product and engaging in unfair, deceptive, and potentially injurious activities? How do well-intentioned executives with a theoretical respect for business integrity end up straying so far from their original standards?

Many aspects of the large organization tend to undermine the managerial perspectives needed for a covenantal viewpoint and ethical business performance. The incentive systems we create, the goals we set, the language we speak, the way in which information is gathered, and the channels through which it can be communicated all contribute to an individual's ability to distinguish right from wrong. Four systemic factors in particular appear to be major contributing causes to unethical business behavior. These are:

1. The inarguable importance of the bottom line;
2. An overemphasis on short-term efficiency or expediency;
3. The seductive power of ego incentives; and
4. The difficulties of personally representing the corporate polity (wearing two hats).

All four factors have psychological, intellectual, organizational, and chronological components. Each imposes a limitation on managerial perspective, a condition of not seeing beyond: 1) the quantitative goals of the firm, 2) the immediate consequences of a decision or action, 3) one's own immediate interests, and 4) the institution's viewpoint and needs. There are good reasons for their existence, but they have often been criticized for inciting bad management decisions. When carried too far, they also create major intellectual and psychological barriers to ethical behavior.

Such moral failures are not exclusively limited to the criminal mind. In Chapters 7 through 10 more than thirty familiar business dilemmas are analyzed for their vulnerability to these four factors. Each problem is tested for how one or more of the factors influences the ethical and competitive decisions which must be made. Questions are suggested within each example to help a manager overcome these barriers and introduce a covenantal perspective into his or her problem solving. Actual examples of covenantal solutions are frequently included.

DESCRIBING ETHICAL FAILURES

It is helpful, however, before turning to specific cases and causes, to distinguish between two general types of ethical problems in business. In my experience, most failures of managerial conscience fall into the following two very different kinds of categories.

Problem Type A. The Acute Dilemma

The acute dilemma represents a problem of ethical uncertainty; it describes those cases where *managers do not collectively know or agree on what constitutes right and wrong*. These are problems for which, despite a decent upbringing, good intentions, and general confidence in one's own moral judgment, the best application of one's highest standards remains problematic. Most top-level, policy formulation issues of ethical content fall into this category.

Random drug testing in the workplace is a good example. Nothing in one's childhood, one's philosophical under-pinnings, or common experience is going to offer a solution a manager can recognize as absolutely the right thing to do in response to the problem of drugs in the workplace. He or she must confront important trade-offs between moral values which, in the solutions offered so far are mutually exclusive: invasion of private rights and the potential for self-incrimination versus the public safety or financial stewardship. There are no ethical entrails to tell a manager what to do about this issue. Plant closures are another case. No matter how pressing the need, many managers will never feel totally secure that a closure was the "right thing to do" from a moral standpoint. Type A problems fall into the gray area of ethical judgment where the alternatives do not automatically suggest a clear-cut boundary between right and wrong. The acute dilemma presents a manager with choices that are morally ambiguous and sometimes painful, as in the case of layoffs.

Successful resolution of Type A problems usually requires a manager to give as much attention to the *creation of a moral process* for decision making and implementation as to the ethics of the decision itself. No matter how long a Type A issue is contemplated, there will never be a definitive standard of right and wrong. A Covenantal Ethic, however, can provide a moral baseline and standards against which one can frame and measure the choices involved. Value-creation, enabling all constituencies, service provision, and financial return provide the focal point on which to fix shifting perceptions of right and wrong.

Type A problems can also be resolved more ethically by establishing a *process of evaluation* which maximizes careful consideration of the trade-offs involved. To return to random drug testing, for example, an ethical resolution of this issue clearly depends on creative cooperation and communication between affected constituencies. Not only must representatives of the tested people be consulted, federal representatives of the public safety and the judicial process must help resolve this problem.

Equally important, because Type A problems are heavily weighted toward policy formulation, they must be considered in the wider context of their execution. Morally responsible considerations of a random drug testing policy at top levels of management must also take into account pragmatic considerations of its implementation: is it really possible to establish a fair and accurate testing program? If not, what level of imperfection is acceptable at the expense of individual rights and reputation? What policies concerning safeguards against unfairly administered tests are essential? The only way that such decisions can be said to be morally acceptable is if the policy formulator has also anticipated and responded to the ethical problems likely to be raised in the policy's execution.

Such questions about execution are often overlooked in the face of uncertainty concerning the basic grayness of Type A decisions. They must, however, be faced, for as I have said before, moral leadership requires not only being above reproach in one's own behavior, but also accepting responsibility for the behavior of others. If, for example, you have set your subordinates an ambitious deadline and performance requirement for a product strategy, you must also provide them with realistic training, resources, and a time frame for execution. Otherwise they are likely to cut corners in order to get the job done, at the expense of quality, perhaps also of safety, and ultimately at the expense of honesty toward the customer. Thus, in Type A ethics dilemmas, questions of process, execution, and business competence are inextricable from a determination of the ethical principles involved.

Problem Type B. The Acute Rationalization

Unlike the acute dilemma, where right and wrong are always ambiguous, the acute rationalization describes ethical failures where *a manager knows what is right and wrong, but fails to do the right thing.* Examples abound: cheating on vouchers, creating misleading marketing vehicles, stretching the truth about product quality or probable delivery dates in order to make a sale, failing to keep promises to other employees or suppliers, neglecting important maintenance procedures and then covering up product failures or operator accidents. A more seductive extension of this type of problem are those cases where deliberate role-playing causes one to look the other way on private rules of behavior. An ambassador, that fellow who lies for his country, would be an example. Closer to home would be the manager who lies to a trusted colleague about impending layoffs in order to keep up morale.

If the first kind of business ethics problem is one of moral uncertainty, the second is often one of denial. Lying about layoffs isn't *really* lying. At its most deliberate, this is a problem of hypocrisy. Such behavior is clearly not restricted to psychopaths and villains. Everyone finds him- or herself looking the other way on moral lapses. To quote American humorist Don Marquis, "A hypocrite is someone who . . . but who isn't?"[3]

The greatest difficulty with the Type B business ethics problem lies not in being able to distinguish right from wrong in a theoretical situation, but rather in *recognizing* that ideal values are being violated in practice. Say someone has stretched the truth on a voucher, or claims to have changed a part when he or she did not. If you ask whether he (or she) believes it is ethical to lie and cheat, the answer will be negative unless that person is pathologically deceitful. But if you question the specific practice mentioned, the perpetuator will most likely fail to see any ethical issue at all.

In Type B ethics problems, then, satisfactory resolution depends first on developing a heightened recognition of unethical practices. One needs to have in mind clear boundary lines between right and wrong and the perspicacity to recognize when the boundaries are being violated. I have found the following questions to be particularly useful in recalling these values:

> Is it right?
> Is it fair?
> Am I hurting anyone?
> Could I disclose this to the public or a respected mentor?
> Would I tell my child to do this?
> Does it pass the stink test?

---

[3]From *The Cynic's Lexicon*, ed., Jonathan Green (New York: St. Martin's Press, 1984), p. 131.

Second, a manager needs to develop a sense of moral power, the ability to bring the ethical course of action to actual conclusion. Both of the necessary faculties can be extremely constrained in managerial situations. The ethical course of action may seem so impossible to execute that it becomes impossible even to entertain it. Implementation may depend on the cooperation of people who do not agree with your priorities or on other factors beyond your control.

The more these factors occur, the more habitual it becomes to look the other way on all occasions of unethical behavior of a Type B nature. Every slipup is unimportant or not your fault. There is not a manager or human being alive who has not offered one of the following excuses for failure to act with integrity:

> "Nobody's getting hurt."
> "Everybody does it. That's just the way things are done."
> "Everybody understands what's really going on."
> "I can't afford to do otherwise."
> "Nobody cares about this anyway."
> "That's not really an ethical issue."

Whenever such rationalizations are voiced, it's time to take a second look at your behavior or that of your company. Nine times out of ten you are in a Type B situation.

Problems in Business Ethics

Type A (The Acute Dilemma): Situations where you do not know what is the right or wrong thing to do.

Type B (The Acute Rationalization): Situations where you know what is right, but fail to do it.

It must be recognized that although top management tends to deal predominantly with Type A decisions, and mid-to first-level management with Type B, most managers face both kinds of moral challenges. The thirty familiar ethical quandaries listed in Chapter 1 describe a well-stirred mix of dilemmas. In some of them, such as drawing a line between a misleading versus a fantasy-based advertising claim, deciding the right thing to do from a theoretical standpoint is difficult (e.g., a Type A dilemma). In others, such as making a clearly unsafe design decision, the practice may be theoretically wrong and clear, but executionally fraught with problems (Problem Type B).

Top managers often fail to achieve moral results, despite their good intentions, because they have thought only in terms of a Type A dilemma. Mid-level managers can wrongly assume that top management is unethical and condone unethical behavior because they themselves are judging a situation in terms of Type B difficulties in policy execution. In short, executives in the same company can fail to understand and acknowledge each other's ethical concerns because they are used to thinking primarily in terms of one kind of problem and not the other. Out of this failure at problem recognition in the ethical arena, a number of unintended ethical consequences can result.

For example, a CEO who is extremely sensitive to macro issues of fairness can be totally insensitive to the people problems subordinates face in carrying out his or her policies. Say a CEO and board have wrestled long and hard with the formulation of a restructuring policy. They conclude that the fairest and best decision for shareholders, customers, and employees is to redirect resources in certain new businesses and cut back in others. To further this end, they offer as generous a retirement incentive as possible to all officers with fifteen years' seniority. From the CEO's standpoint, a highly ethical choice has been made between painful alternatives. From the subordinates' standpoint, however, things look different. Product managers in the businesses that are being cut back suddenly find themselves unable to deliver the same level of service to the customer. Do they cover up? Do they exploit the customer's trust and hope he or she won't notice the difference? Other managers face the painful task of forcing some managers into a retirement decision they would not otherwise make. What is more, some of the more heartless bosses will use the program to summarily get rid of people who they feel do not fit in, whether or not a more objective review has occurred. Thus from the mid-level manager's perspective, the new restructuring policy seems unethical.

Both top- and mid-level managers need to judge such situations with both perspectives in mind. The morally sensitive manager must recognize that a problem such as downsizing will have acute dilemmas (i.e., unresolvable conflicts or trade-offs between desirable goods) and will also give probable cause for acute denials (doing the wrong thing from an impersonal, theoretical standpoint) unless action is taken to preclude such events from occurring. One way to keep these differences in mind is to think in terms of macro versus micro issues, e.g., overall justice versus individual welfare, systems versus people. Another way is to think in terms of policy formulation and execution. Type A and Type B problems will generally correspond to these two aspects of a single problem.

RESOLVING ETHICAL PROBLEMS

Thus it is necessary, in adopting a covenantal approach to business, to develop a way of thinking about business that arms managers against both types of problems. In addition to keeping the assumptions of the Covenantal Ethic in hand, managers must be morally sensitive, able to recognize moral complexity and trade-offs, aware of both the macro policy and micro execution aspects of a moral dilemma, and armed with the moral and economic competency to do something about these things.

The Covenantal Ethic represents a problem-solving orientation that positions a manager's judgment beyond the potential roadblocks to morality, which were defined earlier: bottom-line pressures, short-term thinking, ego image, and role-playing. With a covenantal approach, a manager's orientation *starts* at a point already beyond the demands of his or her own ego, beyond hierarchical power structures, and beyond immediate gratification at the expense of long-term value-creation. By addressing problems in terms of relationships as well as results, it applies such desired values as honesty and fairness directly to the assessment of problems and measures of success. These relationship and value-creation perspectives stimulate thinking about problems in ways that supplement or, when necessary, override quantitative and materialistic goals.

By contrast, a self-interest management approach plays right into the four factors which seem to undermine standard personal moral norms. Its appeal to personal and corporate self-aggrandizement motivates ego and cuts off other-oriented outlooks. Its emphasis on efficiency tends to favor short-term expediency and to suppress sustained moral commitment to solving long-term, complex problems. Its focus on return reinforces an already extremely results-oriented approach to problem solving and an overemphasis on quantitative measurements and motivators. This in turn invites an "ends-justifies-the-means" mentality and overlooks the "softer," more qualitative factors that motivate people to adopt a strict integrity able to stand independent of short-term economic consequences.

In the end, the self-interest ethic imposes a restricted set of vocabularies on managerial problem solving which fails to meet the moral challenges of business problems. It motivates by ego, arranges by impersonal rule-oriented hierarchies, and measures by the bottom line. Carried too far, which is often the case, it is indifferent to others, scornful of individualism, incapable of appreciating the nonquantifiable managerial qualities that hold team and organization together, and detrimental to the financial health of the company.

But while the theoretical soundness of a Covenantal Ethic is capable of theoretical expression and demonstrable through the examples of covenantal leaders such as James Burke, there must be tools for putting the ethic into action. A combination of responses, both external and internal, is required. Timely laws, strong monitoring and detection systems for wrongdoing, punishments for the same, and reward systems for ethical behavior are the most obvious external methods of control, but on their own these measures cannot be depended upon even when well formulated and executed. Many occasions of business wrongdoing have repeatedly demonstrated that *even when detection is almost guaranteed in the long run, knowledge of this will not necessarily deter managers from engaging in fraud in the short term.* Moreover, many of the ethical issues a manager faces will never be detected by the legal system, the public, or even others in the company.

To ensure a covenantal response to business problems, it is necessary not only to have in mind what should not be done (which is the focus of most external measures). A manager must also know what needs to be thought about to ensure moral decision making. No matter how effective the external methods for influencing managerial integrity, every manager also needs an internal regulating system to keep his or her private moral vision active in the pursuit of business. I am reminded of H.L. Mencken's comment: "The difference between a moral man and a man of honor is that the latter regrets a discreditable act, even when it has worked and he has not been caught." (*Sententiae,* 1916)

The challenge, then, is to develop in advance a personal capacity for surmounting common obstacles to ethical decision making in the face of Type A and Type B problems, *whether or not there are strong institutional mechanisms to reinforce this viewpoint.* Einstein said that he first gained insight into relativity by imagining himself to be a proton circling 300,000 miles out in space. Managers need a similar mental transportation device, a way of taking their moral vision beyond the incapacitating factors of ego, corporate image,

---

Six Questions to Heighten Moral Sensitivity

Is it right?

Is it fair?

Am I hurting anyone?

Could I disclose this to the public or a respected mentor?

Would I tell my child to do this?

Does it pass the stink test?

role-playing, bottom-line pressures, and expediently short-ened time frames.

The result will be a broader moral vision of business life to which both managers and the public are entitled. The questions raised in the following chapters offer managers a powerful tool kit of perspectives for effectively carrying out this challenge. With these perspectives it is possible to break through many of the destructive roadblocks to moral behavior in management, and reignite the creative sense of responsibility on which sound and honest business thinking is based.

7

The Inexorable Bottom Line

Winning isn't everything. It's the only thing.*

Whether the arena is sports or the marketplace, preoccupation with winning is a familiar facet of the competitive mindset. The single-minded desire to win can focus effort, reenergize a faltering team, and drive success. The plainer the scorecard, the easier it is to encourage a winning attitude. And in business there is no plainer scorecard than the bottom line. Managers and shareholders are driven by profit, and they use it to drive others.

Every business person understands the power of profit to motivate, measure, and reward successful competitive behavior. Short-term performance goals are the predominant feature of most management incentive systems. But both the economic and managerial effects of America's bottom-line bias are being widely debated today. While it is an inarguable duty to keep an eye on profit, an incentive system that tries to stimulate winning through a one-dimensional motivation scheme is bound to work against some of the other dynamics on which success depends.

Business is not as simple as a football game. The bottom line is only a crude indicator of the multiple successes on which a thriving organization depends. Reconciliations be-

*Attributed to Vince Lombardi.

tween customer satisfaction, an adequate research strategy, acceptable return to shareholders, good community relationships, individual incentive, and teamwork cannot be boiled down to one figure.

In short, while profit is undeniably important, a fixation on profit is a poor analytical tool and an inaccurate measuring stick for the many crucial aspects of a manager's work, most especially the ethical aspects.

ETHICAL IMPLICATIONS OF A BOTTOM-LINE ORIENTATION

Taken in isolation, the bottom line is morally neutral. You cannot tell how the game was played or to what purpose simply by how much money was made. And yet in many companies, profit is the only well-articulated purpose on the block. High standards of conduct, when discussed at all, are linked to the bottom line for motivational and assessment purposes. The "do-good-to-do-well" axiom applies. Ethical conduct is motivated through the promise of a dollar reward.

As discussed at length in Chapter 4, this appeal to self-interest for moral behavior can sound legitimate in theory, for in an enlightened scheme it argues for a variety of ethical considerations. What is more, it offers management a secure baseline of responsibility for relentlessly "soft" moral considerations, in keeping with most managers' bias toward tangible goal setting. Bottom-line ethics can be a felicitous kind of "power ethics" for efficiently solving the knotty moral dilemmas of management.

But, in practice, when profit becomes the dominant purpose it is not just prioritized, it is "exclusified." Profit is so concrete and "strong" a claim and ethics so abstract and process-oriented that the former can easily gain dominion over one's decision making.

Former Morgan Stanley executive "Buzz" McCoy wrote a moving and insightful article for the *Harvard Business Review* about a mountain-climbing incident, in which the ethical fallout of adopting rigidly superordinate goals was brought home to him in a very personal way. He and his group encountered an Indian holy man, half-clothed and very ill, during a grueling, long-awaited hike in the Himalayas. None of the sherpa guides would take the man back to a village, nor was it clear that he would receive help there anyway. After doing all they could to relieve his physical distress, the expedition moved on up the mountain.

In reflecting on the experience, which left him profoundly uncomfortable, McCoy noted that the conditions of the hike were very much like the conditions of business—high stress, high adrenaline, a superordinate goal, and a sense of a once-in-a-lifetime opportunity. He wondered how often these conditions caused executives to hike right by serious moral dilemmas.[1]

The truth of his observation is profound. Superordinate profit goals and high-stress, exciting, bet-your-company scenarios are powerful motivators. But they also tend to suppress the capacity for articulate moral reasoning. Marshall Clinard's surveys on illegal corporate behavior have reported profit and cost pressure to be the number one work pressure cited by middle managers. Nine out of ten of the respondents felt that such a pressure does lead to unethical behavior in a corporation.[2]

The suppressive power of profit on individual morality is magnified in a large organization. As McCoy pointed out, the fact that the members of the group, from all over the world and previously unacquainted with each other, had no shared set of values beside mountain climbing severely stymied their capacity to develop a consensus about anything besides their determination to scale the peak.

The potential moral limitations of adopting a superordinate bottom-line orientation and managerial vocabulary can be summarized in two parts: it leads to a restriction of a manager's definition of goals, and to an indifference to the means by which these goals are pursued. In the words of the manager who defended doing nothing about dealing with organized crime to get a job completed: "I would never buy a stolen car

[1]Bowen McCoy, "The Parable of the Sadhu," *Harvard Business Review* (September–October 1983), pp. 103–108.
[2]Marshall B. Clinard, *Corporate Ethics and Crime: The Role of Middle Management* (Beverly Hills: Sage Publications, 1983), pp. 91–95.

or cheat on my own taxes, but, hey! I wouldn't be having to make a buck either, would I?"

EFFECT ON GOAL SETTING

Kenneth Andrews wrote that "the rational examination of alternatives and the determination of purpose are among the most important and most neglected of all human activities."[3] When a superior invokes the bottom line as the single most important performance goal, other goals such as value-creation and integrity have about as much lasting power as a snowflake on a hot rock.

For example, many investment managers adopted a single-minded profit orientation in the 1980s. The profit mentality blurred the already ambiguous distinctions between investing, speculating, and gambling still further, as managers mistook financial success as an indication of superior service. By failing to explore what was precisely of value in the acquisitions game or any other financing and investment services, and what was simply a high-stakes product in a temporarily unbalanced marketplace, they had few resources for responding when the market turned downward. It turned out that some people could only make profits by cheating, and others could not keep integrity coincident with high performance when the easy deals turned sour. This industry showed how vulnerable bottom-line goal setting is to market fluctuations from both a performance and ethical standpoint. Some managers invoke a survival scenario to motivate a more urgent winning attitude, but in so doing, they dig an even bigger profit-dominated hole for employees to fall into. When the bottom line is the overriding goal, the needs of others, including customers, are lost and the rules bent. Other vocabularies of problem solving which could lead to ethical and creative solutions are suppressed in favor of blunt statements about the bottom line.

---

[3]Kenneth Andrews, *The Concept of Corporate Strategy*, rev. ed. (Homewood, IL: Richard D. Irwin, 1980), p. 104.

EFFECT ON THE MEANS BY WHICH GOALS ARE ACHIEVED

In the study of corporate crime, many organizational factors—from position in the hierarchy to inadequate forums for voicing ethical concerns—have been demonstrated to have an effect on managerial moral behavior.[4] No factor is stronger or less subtle a diversion to moral norms than too strong a focus on the bottom line. A study of 3,000 managers by the American Management Association revealed that a majority "felt under pressure to compromise personal standards to meet company goals [by which they meant profit]."[5]

This bottom-line preoccupation not only emphasizes the achievement of economic success to the suppression of other important goals, it also undermines the moral norms regulating the *means* to success. When a company operates with a strong bottom-line framework in a shark-infested, lean-and-mean environment, a manager's moral muscle may end up under the knife of a cost-cutting agenda. Moral obligations such as honesty or reliability are excised for the sake of success. It becomes very comfortable to adopt Plato's classic justification of a lie as being "sometimes necessary to the welfare of the state." Or as a business cartoon by Saxon once put it, "Honesty is one of the better policies." The moral fallout from such rationalization can be as small as tampering with the taste of a brand-name product or as deadly as the failure to correct defects in brake design.

Marshall Clinard's interviews in his study of white-collar crime revealed a telling correspondence between the bottom line and managerial sensitivity to unethical practices. In many cases, the correlation was undetected even by those who recognized the pressures of the bottom line. For example, although 70 percent of those executives interviewed favored reporting serious safety violations to the government, only 25 percent said they would report price-fixing or illegal kick-

---

[4]See especially, Kathy E. Kram, Peter C. Yeager, and Gary E. Reed, "Decisions and Dilemmas: The Ethical Dimension in the Corporate Context," *Research in Corporate Social Performance and Policy,* vol. 11 (1989), pp. 21–54; see also, J.A. Waters and P.D. Chant, "The Moral Dimension of Organizational Crime," *Journal of Business Ethics,* vol. 6 (1987), pp. 15–22.

[5]Fred Luthans and Richard M. Hodgetts, eds., *Social Issues in Business: A Text with Current Readings and Cases* (New York: Macmillan, 1976), p. 53; see also, Barbara Toffler, *Tough Choices: Managers Talk Ethics* (New York: John Wiley, 1986).

backs. Explained one executive, apparently without a qualm, "We might lose business if we didn't give illegal rebates and kickbacks."[6]

A business approach that uses profit—even enlightened profit—as its guiding star invites a weakening of other values, however strong they may be in private life. Bottom-line blindness, though intended to provoke only a clean competitive spirit, is inherently fraught with moral problems.

In my experience, the bottom line is the most effective ethical conversation stopper known to business. Whenever a moral question is raised, all someone has to do is say, "Of course, we have to think about profit." Thus endeth any second thoughts on what the company is doing or how it is doing it. Managers use profit to stop themselves and others from opening up shadowy avenues of moral inquiry. "I had to do it, our profit was on the line and I had to get the job done." And yet, if outside critics charge business with "only thinking about profit," managers will deny it vehemently, citing many good examples to the contrary.

The problem, then, is to develop ways of recognizing when profit considerations are erecting barriers between your understanding of the problem and the complexities of judgment which are needed to bring it to responsible and productive resolution. F. Scott Fitzgerald's statement that the mark of a first-class intelligence is the ability to sustain in one's mind two opposing ideas simultaneously is to the point. Bottom-line thinking can only operate constructively if it is balanced by an intelligent reference to the qualitative, ethical values on which responsible decision making is based.

WHERE BOTTOM-LINE THINKING AND PRIVATE CONSCIENCE CONFLICT

The following cases illustrate typical business problems in which the emphasis on profit poses a real threat to managerial morality. The dilemmas posed here are not the macro ethics problems of institutional responsibility vis-à-vis

---

[6]Clinard, *Corporate Ethics and Crime*, p. 123.

other institutions, but rather the nuts-and-bolts issues which put the business person on the moral line every day. The questions provide a mental handle for grappling with the perceptual roadblocks which bottom-line blindness can create.

Bottom-line thinking traps managers into seeing every ethical dilemma as a choice between morality and profitability. Many of the questions that accompany the examples change the definition of the problem to highlight other matters beside the costs or benefits associated with an ethical response. These questions are not restricted to the examples they illustrate but are meant to expand the general problem-solving vocabulary of a manager to help illuminate many kinds of ethical dilemmas of management.

Problem 1. Responding to Unethical Practices in an Industry

While it is easy to see how a person whose only concern is to make money will inevitably resort to lying and cheating others, the moral pressures from the bottom line are usually more subtle. Take the very difficult situation of widespread wrongdoing in an industry. How does the moral manager respond with integrity to the problem of industry-wide corruption? Not participating can be a costly decision for a company, but a relatively easy decision for a morally strict person. Much more difficult, however, is the question of whether or not to take a more active stand by cooperating with law enforcement agencies to expose the corruption.

Bottom-line reasoning is frequently the wrong avenue to take in exploring such a question because it is so widely accepted as an excuse for doing nothing. Consider the recent frauds on the Chicago Futures exchanges. One conscientious CEO, Dwayne Andreas of ADM, bucked the system by allowing the FBI to plant two moles in his organization. ADM hired and trained the men as traders and introduced them to the network in the Board of Trade's pits. This sting led to the discovery and substantiation of widespread fraud in several of the exchanges, and sparked a long-needed internal investigation into the exchanges' oversight procedures. No one yet knows the full extent of the problem.

It is instructive to look at the ways in which you could frame the moral dilemma the ADM executives faced. The decision to cooperate with the FBI could be described as a painful choice between two kinds of betrayal. By taking no action on what it knew was wrong, ADM was betraying the public's trust. By agreeing to harbor undercover agents, however, it was betraying trader trust on the exchange. Success in the marketplace required maintenance of both kinds of relationships, but corruption in the marketplace had made the conditions contradictory. ADM's decision to help the FBI with its sting operation could be seen as a restoration of integrity in the marketplace. It could be viewed as an act of personal courage and honesty.

Many of the people quoted in a *Wall Street Journal* article on the sting, however, *tended to explore the rightness or wrongness of Andreas's decision solely in bottom-line terms.* Some pointed out that it could be good for business because customers would be attracted to a firm with Andreas's integrity. Others sourly suggested that he was irresponsible not to consider the effects of his own bottom line more seriously. After the first round of indictments, ADM traders experienced widespread ostracism on the trading floor. Remarked one trader:

> If I were a stockholder in ADM, I would go to the annual meeting and say, "Did any of you clowns think about the long-term ramifications of doing this?" The guys in the pit have a long memory. ADM will never be able to buy at the bid again, or sell at the offer . . . that's going to cost them millions of dollars.[7]

What is so poignant about the remark is how the assumed legitimacy of a bottom-line orientation binds the trader's ethical beliefs to a self-serving frame of reference. An automatic filtering device screens out even the most obvious moral qualms, such as condoning substantial cheating.

One way to reenergize an awareness of ethical con-

---

[7]"Grain Maverick: Dwayne Andreas Plays Hardball as Head of ADM," *The Wall Street Journal*, February 9, 1989, p. 1.

cerns when corporate financial obligations threaten to restrict or silence your sense of duty is to ask,

Who might get hurt beside ourselves?

Many applied ethicists have suggested that the avoidance of injury is a moral minimum beyond which no one should willingly step. The Hippocratic oath which in part states "Never willingly do injury" was the first professional credo, adopted by physicians in the fifth century B.C. Deliberate assessments of injury to others can provide great insight into otherwise condoned wrongdoings. People inside the futures industry excused their own passivity by arguing that as long as they were not personally promoting such practices, they could not be expected to do more. Their own financial dependency on the existing system was really on their minds. They did not want to alienate the traders even if it meant condoning an uneven playing field. A view to the public damage they were perpetrating would have shown such passivity to be inexcusable.

Adopting a least-injury ethic, though not foolproof, is a good way to trigger an ethical response quickly. Thus are high marks due to General Mills when it immediately issued a total recall of one of its toys which had caused several deaths by choking. The company did this in spite of the irrefutable evidence that the toy had been misused, according to the unbiased Consumer Products Safety Commission. The decision came at a particularly costly time, during the peak of the winter holiday shopping season. General Mills did not perform endless cost-benefit analyses of which action would be better for the bottom line. It kept to its mission, which was—in founder James Ford Bell's words—to obtain a record that was "clean and fine." When such missions are in place, a potential or real-injury situation prompts immediate action.

And yet there are bottom-line rationales for silencing moral scruples being offered, not only by managers, but by the business press as well. Take, for instance, the notorious case several years ago of a money manager who bilked his clients of millions of dollars. He had not invested their money in the stock market, as he had claimed, but had diverted it to his own use. Most of the funds were spent on luxury items, which the manager still had when he was finally caught. The press reports about the incident were curiously mixed. Clearly the man was an out-and-out cad, whose capacity for fraud was large. And yet, by not being in the market on the October 19 crash, he had avoided a major loss of capital. In the meantime the luxury items, many of them antiques, had appreciated, and were reappropriated by the courts to recover part of his customers' losses. Even after deducting other little peccadillos like a few luxury trips, his clients most likely ended up with more money than had their accounts been fully invested. With the bottom line relatively unscathed, the story became a joke. Could you really get excited about the ethics of the case when nobody got hurt? You could, but only if you pried your eyes off the bottom line.

Am I perpetuating a dishonest and fraudulent relationship?

When consequentialist reasoning says that "nobody is getting hurt" in terms of the bottom line or physical injury, one way of sharpening the moral sonar by which you steer through business problems is to refocus problem solving on the relationships involved. Is bottom-line success being gained at the expense of honesty and trust? If so, it is wrong, whether or not the bottom line (including that of other people) remains intact.

Problem 2. Listening to the Customer

In most managers' minds there is a tacit connection between customer service, profit, and competitiveness. If you get out there with a good product, price it for a reasonable or even excellent return, and compete like a madman, you and the company will do all right. Assuming that the first condition of this triad is true, i.e., that the production, sale, and distribution of the product is of quality and service to the customer, then the second two fall into place without too many ethical problems. The bottom line will raise a tactical problem of pricing, financing, and controlling costs, not a moral dilemma concerning deception or injury to others.

But when a manager becomes preoccupied with the

bottom line, he or she can overlook that first condition of ethical business. Subsequent quality problems and misleading marketing practices can result, not out of a deliberate desire to cheat, but out of insensitivity and fear. Thus the ethical trap is laid: exclusive focus on the bottom line invites the disregard of outsiders' interests.

Take the classic experience of Hogan Systems, an up-and-coming producer of mainframe software for banks. In three years Hogan's value rocketed from $1.3 million in revenues to a market value of $296 million. Two years later it carried a $13.8 million loss on revenues of $28 million.

It was generally agreed that the cause of the spectacular disaster was forgetting about the customer. On management's own account, when the company went public it became fixated on analyst expectations to grow very quickly. It prematurely introduced a new program with serious flaws and before setting up an after-service program. It filled rush orders based on claims of outstanding product and service. Did Hogan have an ethical problem? You bet it did. Its failure to achieve quality and take orders anyway was both deceptive and exploiting customers' trust. Hardly competitive ethical behavior, and yet no one expressed moral reservations about such practices. Nor was it a winning strategy. When the program's failures became apparent, the company began to see delays in its accounts receivable, and orders were being canceled.

When George McTavish was brought in from Martin-Marietta as Hogan's new CEO, the first thing he did was shatter management's bottom-line bias. He adopted an others-first attitude. He informally polled the customers. This turned out to be the first such survey ever to be conducted! In his words, he discovered that clients "didn't perceive us as dependable, didn't think we could relate to their problems, and they felt abandoned."[8]

These are emotional, empathetic words, based on a vocabulary that goes beyond rational calculation to the realm of good human relationships. McTavish's attitude was a vivid example of covenantal thinking and it saved the company.

[8]Lisa M. Keefe, "We Forgot About the Clients," *Forbes*, July 14, 1986, p. 54.

Losses were cut in half within a year, the stock rebounded from $3\frac{1}{2}$ to $10\frac{1}{2}$, and the firm was rewarded with a five-year licensing agreement with IBM.

Whose needs am I considering in my definition of the problem?

A great way to put your own thinking back on the customer track, especially when profit considerations seem to dictate bending a few ethical corners, is to examine how strongly profit goals are coloring your definition of the problem. A quick examination of the language in which you are couching a problem or communicating goals to others can often spot when bottom-line bias is preventing an ethical solution to the problem. In Hogan's case, analyst expectations were creating an earning-growth approach to every problem to the exclusion of even a simple poll of customer satisfaction. McTavish reversed this bottom-line focus by considering customer needs as the first solution to the company's business concerns. McTavish was not unconcerned about the bottom line, but he drew on a set of standards and problem-solving vocabulary which broke through the bottom-line bias of the financial markets to reestablish the first condition of business success, customer responsiveness.

Have I tested the other person's needs directly?

Following up the first question with a reality test is another way to free yourself from the tyranny of a self-enhancing orientation in the marketplace. Often a marketer or designer will assume he or she knows the market without ever testing these assumptions outside the paraphernalia of corporate communications channels. Look at how many marketing surveys focus on the company—its product, its pricing, its quality—without ever directly determining customer needs independently of the company's existing product line.

Directly testing how the customer feels, as did McTavish at Hogan, requires a more imaginative set of people skills than many managerial mindsets would like to entertain. The classic example is American Express's successful restructuring of its customer service business in the mid-1980s. At that time, the conventional wisdom was that you could not measure quality in a service organization in a meaningful way. AmEx failed to succumb to this "concentrate-on-the-bottom-line" wisdom. It developed two hundred tangible ways to measure customer service, including how many people hang up while waiting for their phone calls to be answered.

Problem 3. Cost Pressures

Nothing raises more bottom-line barriers to ethical problem solving than cost pressures. Even the manager who normally draws on skills and values that sensitize him or her to the customer's point of view cannot escape ethical dilemmas when a company is under a cost-cutting program. How can a firm honestly maintain and meet a customer's expectation of value when cutting costs? How can it be fair to suppliers, who also deserve respect and a fair return for their services?

Casting these problems into a risk analysis in reference to the bottom line will not provide a responsible answer to the conundrum. It will only constrain your ability to find responsible solutions in the marketplace. And yet many managers, preoccupied with the bottom line in cost-cutting, survival periods, inadvertently create such constraints on their ethical reasoning. Further, those who motivate efficiency with a cost-cutting strategy need to be aware of how seriously it can undermine ethical thinking in others.

William Smithburg, chairman and CEO of Quaker Oats Company, ruefully tells one such story on himself. Smithburg has long been admired for his leadership and has been very open about a values-oriented management responsibility. His extraordinary marketing savvy became well established when, as a fledgling product manager, he created the "Mikey Likes It" campaign for LIFE cereal. When he became chairman, one of his first concerns was to instill a higher marketing consciousness in newer Quaker managers. He devised eleven rules for good marketing and constantly drummed them into new managers' ears. Rule number one was never jeopardize the brand franchise.

One day Smithburg was reviewing market share figures for a cereal product and noticed a slight erosion. The product manager dismissed the number as insignificant. It turned out that he had approved certain ingredient substitutions even though there had been some indication in trial tests that consumers detected a taste difference. Smithburg wondered aloud how the manager could forget marketing rule number one. "Well," wailed the manager, "you *said* to cut costs!"

Such incidents form the basic lessons of Marketing 101, but they cannot be divorced from their ethical implications and a manager's ability to balance superficially conflicting claims. One way to revive the ethical side of the conflict between cost and the implied promises of a brand franchise is to ask yourself the following question:

Is this decision consistent with the values we wish to convey by the brand or company name?

To tamper with the quality of a brand franchise for the sake of costs while keeping prices up is a betrayal of consumer trust. It is a lie. A brand franchise is a promise from a company that value will be consistent over time. One box of strawberry Jell-O, for example, should taste like another; new products under the same corporate name should be of similar quality. To use cheaper ingredients in a franchise brand without indication to the consumer—or worse, to call it "new and improved" on the basis of a wish rather than objective evidence—is a fraud. It is important, therefore, for every manager to be aware of the values that are implied in a brand or corporate image and then live up to them, or alter the claims. Rarely can this be accomplished by boiling down decisions to a simple cost calculation.

What language am I using to set targets for other people?

As Smithburg discovered, no amount of personal integrity can on its own stimulate consideration of consumer trust in a brand franchise if the language used to motivate competitive decisions in others is tied to the bottom line. A cost-cutting strategy is particularly vulnerable to being understood in only the most limiting terms because it is so often communicated in survival language. Customer rights seem inconsequential in comparison to the bottom-line imperative.

Commonsense marketing would want to avoid giving a consumer the feeling he or she was being ignored. But such common sense is constantly being subverted by marketing strategies that have immediate profit rather than long-term customer relationships as a frame of reference. Dissatisfied customers become enemies of the firm rather than legitimate indications of its responsiveness. The long-term results of such a mindset can be product or service shoddiness or stonewalling on problems. A bottom-line approach can set a tone of general unconcern about health issues and customer satisfaction, unless the dollar costs of such a concern are very obvious and immediate (which they usually are not). This is a weak baseline for establishing credibility about a company's alleged customer responsiveness.

Problem 4. Balancing Different Stakeholder Expectations

In many cases, however, it is difficult for a manager to know what is "the right thing to do" because a consumer constituency is not homogeneous. This condition poses a Type A ethics problem, where definitions of right and wrong are not generally agreed upon even by people of above-average moral integrity. Such problems arise frequently for unspecialized or diversified consumer goods and service companies, which by definition serve a broad range of tastes and values. Given the diversity and relativism of today's society, it is inevitable that such companies will become embroiled in public controversies. On these occasions a manager may be presented with equally attractive or compelling responses which simply cannot be reconciled. It is very tempting when this happens to fall back on the one secure fact, that the bottom line counts.

But as Sissela Bok points out, when people are confronted with genuinely intractable moral dilemmas, it is important that they examine the morality of the *process* by which the dilemma is resolved and not restrict themselves to an analysis of the specific outcome of either choice.[9] A bottom-line orientation, however, confines the analysis of problems to outcomes and runs the danger of rejecting process concerns out of hand.

Consider the grape boycotts which occurred at many grocery stores in the late 1960s and early 1970s on behalf of the United Farm Workers and their efforts to improve the lot of the grape pickers. UFW sympathizers across the nation held a long and bitter series of secondary boycotts against major grocery store chains that stocked nonunion grapes. In many areas local church leaders backed the boycotts, which presented a difficult choice to some managers loyal to church and company. At Jewel Foods, the targeted chain in the Chicago area, the protests were so intense that a group of nuns held a sit-in in the hallways of the company's executive headquarters.

In the late 1960s, Jewel agreed with the UFW's demands that workers be allowed collective bargaining representation and backed up its belief by refusing to stock nonunion grapes. But four years later, after the UFW had joined the AFL-CIO, the rival Teamsters charged them with some of the same abuses they were claiming to fight. As *Time* magazine put it, the controversy now looked more like a battle between two major unions than a substantive effort to improve the farm workers' lot. The ethical course of action was a lot less clear.

The manager who would decide such a controversy in terms of the bottom line would be sorely underequipped to handle this problem in ethical or any other terms. First, no one could accurately assess the relative costs of capitulating to the UFW. Consumers were divided on the issue: many supported the UFW but many others saw grapes as a good economic choice during the 1974 recession. A newfound interest in nonsugar snack foods among those concerned about health gave grapes high marks. Then there were the other unions to consider. How would the Teamsters retaliate were Jewel to give in to the AFL-CIO? A trucking slowdown could cause un-

[9]Sissela Bok, *Lying: Moral Choice in Public and Private Life* (New York: Vintage Books, 1979), p. 59.

told damage for the stores. So could the drop in sales if customers stayed away from Jewel because of picket lines in the parking lots. None of these considerations could be costed out with accuracy.

Eventually, Jewel's management chose to stock both union and nonunion grapes. It could not find a single solution that it felt would substantially help alleviate the farm workers' problem. Rather, it adopted a strategy that would stand a good chance of economic viability yet be responsive to a degree to the different critics.

If the most desirable consequences cannot be determined, have I ensured that the procedural issues of decision making and implementation are ethical?

To recall Bok's advice, Jewel's managers spent as much time ensuring that the process of dealing with the boycotts was fair as they spent on deciding whether it was ethical to stock non-UFW grapes or not. Drawing on the firm's rich tradition of ethical marketing, summarized in a long document entitled "The Jewel Concepts," the top managers made sure that they listened to a wide variety of responsible stakeholder representatives before making their decision. They did not stonewall or try to denigrate their critics. A highly respected priest was a member of their board of directors. Other community representatives, among them minority and senior citizen leaders advocating different responses, were met with and heard. Top managers, Chairman Donald Perkins and President Wes Christopherson in particular, held many uncomfortable meetings with the public to communicate Jewel's concerns on this issue. They also wrote to congressional representatives urging them to adopt changes in the laws concerning farm workers. In dealing with the picketers, they set up many communication and enforcement safeguards to ensure that no store manager, in trying to protect Jewel property and customers, treated picketers with disrespect or injury. By paying attention to the process of responding to multiple stakeholders in the controversy, Jewel undoubtedly prevented many potential injuries from occurring and gave UFW supporters a safe place to have their views legally voiced.

How will the issue affect the company's reputation?

Another way of keeping the procedural issues open to examination, when the dollar consequences of a problem simply cannot be determined or seem overwhelming, is to consider the effect of the response on the corporate reputation. As Jewel and many other companies caught in a public affairs controversy can testify, a single-issue decision that has a 1 percent effect on earnings can have a 100 percent effect on reputation. Keeping this in mind makes it easier to deal with hostile stakeholders calmly and ethically rather than deceptively or even injuriously.

Problem 5. Quality Determinations

Here's a commonsense proposition: The higher the quality, the easier it is to do business ethically. If you have a quality product, you can market honestly; if you have a quality manufacturing and distribution process, you can lower the price without compromising consumer trust in the product.

Conversely, the higher your ethics, the easier it is to adopt and implement a quality strategy. Your honest assessments will get you to a value-creating product or service much faster. Your respect for others inside and outside the corporation will help you weed out inappropriate compromises and motivate other employees to adopt the same ethos toward the marketplace.

The biggest stumbling block in this proposition for quality is a bottom-line fixation, for cost considerations can suffocate the many ethical impulses that contribute to quality management. As cost of materials, say, rises, one begins to fear for the bottom line and abandons thinking about quality. One way of backing out of this hole is to ask covenantal question number one,

What value am I creating?

As Kenneth Andrews points out in his introduction to *Ethics in Practice,* "As I reflect on these articles [in the book] I conclude again that an adequate corporate strategy must include noneconomic goals."[10] Directly questioning value-creation can put understandable bottom-line considerations into a less tyrannical position and allow your decision making to create an ethical response to quality issues. Take the quality of children's shoes as an example: what is appropriate shoe quality for an ethical company? Is there an ethical distinction between the values a Stride Rite brings to its marketing strategy and that of many discount retailers? Stride Rite managers have always been self-defined "nuts" about product quality. The shoes last throughout the wearing cycle (normal predicted foot growth) or they are replaced. The firm has also had a long-standing, quasi-medical dedication to foot care, an important ethical responsibility in this market. American consumers are increasingly ignorant about shoe fit and podiatrists have seen a sharp increase in foot problems stemming from poorly fitting shoes and poor materials which do not allow the foot to breathe properly. In short, Stride Rite's choice of quality has in the past combined the following values: honest marketing, genuine value-creation for the consumer in terms of health, style, and reliability, and a good return for shareholders.

By contrast, the typical discount retailer strategy, which couples unknown brands of cheap quality with self-service, depends on exploiting customer ignorance and takes no responsibility for quality and foot care. The materials do not allow the foot to breathe, self-selection means the child will probably not be fitted well, and the customer can only guess whether or not the shoes will hold up through a wearing cycle. Moreover, the price difference is not always that great.

No manager can determine the ethical distinctions between the two strategies by restricting the discussion and managerial incentives to profit. In dollar terms, you can make a profit either way. Stride Rite's management did not confine the quality problem to cost-price terms. In seeking to avoid injuring consumers, it looked to the issue of value-creation in marketing. It coupled a new kind of retail outlet, the Stride Rite boutique, trendy shoe designs, and marketing aids to provide a

---

[10]Kenneth R. Andrews, ed., *Ethics in Practice* (Boston: Harvard Business School Press, 1988), p. 10.

total service to the shoe purchase. The boutiques were fun
and aesthetically pleasing, the designs were good, the salespeople were well trained in shoe fitting. The strategy was also
very profitable.

I asked chairman Arnold Hiatt which came first, the
dollar or the promotion of children's foot care? He refused to
be sucked into the ethics versus bottom-line, cost-benefit conundrum. He replied:

> Neither. They work simultaneously. We're a business.
> We're unashamedly out to make a profit *and* we're
> very concerned about the health of children's feet and
> posture. We run the business on both concerns.

Such an approach lays the foundation for honest marketing,
genuine value, and also innovation. These quality responses
cannot be stimulated if quality questions are approached
solely through an efficiency analysis of potential costs or benefits to the bottom line.

Problem 6. When the Bottom Line Insists
One Has to Be Unethical

Breaking out of the cost-benefit quality conundrum
can highlight a number of important ethical and commercial
issues in the process of strategy formulation. Take the issue
of bribery. Many executives deal with the frustrating preva-
lence of bribery here and abroad by asking, "What do you
want us to do, go out of business?" In other words, they use
the bottom line as an inarguable reason for ignoring their
personal sense of right and wrong or breaking the law.

This is not the argument of a mature executive: it
hardly reflects reality. Many solicitations for bribes do *not* pose
life-or-death situations for a company, they are simply a nui-
sance. Often they are a test. Johnson & Johnson executives
have asserted that by always refusing to accept bribes, they
become known in time as those you do not solicit.

At the same time, in some industries in some countries, bribery is undoubtedly a condition of doing business. It

has been seen to occur most frequently in defense industries where the stakes are high (bet-your-company-contracts), the purchaser corrupt, *and the distinctive differences between products negligible.* The real question, then, is not whether to accept bribery as a cost of doing business, but rather:

Are we in the right business and market to begin with?

Can you create distinctive value in this market? Is there a reasonable promise of a return for value, or are you dealing with a nonproductive market in which the rules are so biased as to be counterproductive? Questions like these move the analysis beyond the morally unacceptable viewpoint that bribery is nothing more than a cost of doing business and have led some companies—Levi Strauss, to name one—to refuse to do business in certain countries.

Questioning value-creation also helps managers break out of what I call the ethical red herring syndrome. Some managers, especially those operating under a survival scenario, will use bottom-line arguments to explain to themselves why they cannot possibly think about common ethical problems like honesty. They will construct absurd exceptional cases as an excuse for not considering ethical issues at all. Questions about value-creation will shatter such obstacles to moral thinking.

Here's one posed to me by someone in the railroad industry. You know that a customer can get a cheaper rate by shipping via truck. Does honesty require you to inform the customer? Doesn't empathy require you to disclose this fact to your customer? And yet common business sense would argue that a company should not be expected to shoot itself in the foot. So the railroad manager has an inarguable reason why he or she cannot let personal ethics determine the decision. He or she can make a deal that may not be the best one the customer can obtain in the open marketplace, or send the customer to the competitors and lose the business. Not a great motivator for integrating ethics and decision making.

But bottom-line blindness causes the railroad manager to pose the wrong question. The real issue is value-creation. The manager cannot come to a profitable, honest marketing approach until the question of value-creation is explored more fully. The proper operating ethical question should not be, "Is it honest not to tell a customer about a cheaper service?" Rather, it is, "What does it take to provide the customer with a genuinely better deal?" In other words, the honest solution must revolve around value-creation. What is it and can it be had in this particular market niche? By asking how to best use company resources to create value, a manager breaks through the seemingly inescapable trade-offs that are constructed between honesty and earnings.

How will the decision affect the quality of my relationship with X?

In some cases, however, it is too late to bring the long-term solutions of value-creation to short-term bottom-line pressures. A second way to break through the railroad manager's ethical impasse would be to explore whether or not he or she was creating a mutually enabling relationship with this particular customer. Certainly lying will not sustain the customer-seller relationship in the long run. What is more, the relationship with the customer may not be viable in the first place. It may be a preferable strategy to seek another market rather than stay in one that poses such financial and moral obstacles to success.

Problem 7. Setting Higher Standards Than Industry Practice

Business not only follows rules and standards, it creates them, which requires a broader, proactive approach to the marketplace than simply growing the bottom line. When basketball was just a game to be won, no time limit was placed on a play. But when basketball became a commercial business with customers to be served, new rules were instituted such as the 24-second clock and, later, dunking, in order to serve customer interests.

Every manager has an obligation to try to innovate ethical and value improvements in business. Among the many roadblocks to innovative thinking is a problem-solving focus on small adjustments to the bottom line. An interesting example can be found in the recent invention of a nonslip tread work shoe. For years, slipping in restaurants was one of the most common workplace accident claims, costing the insurance industry $250 million per year and the restaurant industry an estimated $1.5 billion in worker absences. No one approached the problem in any other terms than cost and whose bottom line would absorb it. But recently Jon Granger, an insurance claims adjustor, invented a new sole design for the $60 million market. While cost-benefit considerations were not excluded from his motives, Granger also drew on other values to come up with his creative solution. He cared. Says Granger, who essentially gave the design away to the only shoe company he could find to produce it, "I did something for humanity, that's my reward. I know that sounds hokey and altruistic, but that's the story."

For some people, thinking of humanity is not a priority when the immediate micro concerns of getting a job done and making a profit press. One way to provoke "caring" and stimulate a more proactive and responsive business ethos is to think about your immediate family. Try asking the question,

What if the injured party or intended beneficiary were my child?

Thinking about your child will often bring human needs more clearly into perspective when industry practice makes you passive.

One of my favorite examples of a proactive improvement in industry standards comes from Pfizer Corporation and the development of its "Partners in Healthcare" advertising series. The campaign provided information to the end-user about chronic diseases treated by Pfizer prescription drugs. It was written in lay person's language and appeared in popular media. The series was a dramatic innovation in pharmaceutical marketing and a far cry from the company's traditional advertising strategy. In the 1950s and 1960s, no pharmaceutical company had a stronger reputation for hucksterism than Pfizer. This small upstart had shocked the staid drug companies by handing out golf balls, pillows, even socks imprinted with the company logo to doctors. Its new campaign was so effective from a public relations standpoint that it set a new standard of consumer advertising for the whole industry. Eli Lilly developed its own series of informational ads shortly after the campaign's introduction.

Pfizer's decision to go straight to the public, even though the primary purchaser of its products is the medical doctor, was essentially based on relationship values: empathy, respect, and *delivered* value. The Partners in Healthcare campaign was an accurate and honest recognition that doctors and pharmaceutical companies alone cannot improve the nation's health. The end-user, who appeared to be very ignorant about pharmaceuticals according to consumer surveys, had to be involved in the process.

Standard industry practice assumed that the doctor should be the sole controller of the treatment process. One way to question this assumption would have been to ask the following question,

Is my relationship with the end-user one of empowering or empowerment?

The new campaign empowered consumers to participate in their own health care by providing them with information. Pfizer's marketing relationship changed from one of paternalistic superiority over the ignorant consumer, in cahoots with golf-loving doctors, to that of partner and servicer based on an informed consumer. Formulating that change involved risk and concern for more than the bottom line. Pfizer chairman Edmund Pratt noted that the campaign cost a lot more than putting pamphlets in doctors' offices; he also noted that profit and service walked hand in hand: "This series is doing good and it's good for us."

Problem 8. Avoiding Conflict-of-Interest Situations

Ironically, a bottom-line orientation can even blind you to situations in which your behavior might be *detracting* from the company's bottom line. In conflict-of-interest situations, for example, the overwhelming bias toward bottom-line thinking may cloud your awareness of other motivations that may be contradictory to the company's best interests. So strongly do most bottom-line incentive systems try to correlate an employee's aggrandizement with the company's, that sometimes it is hard for a manager to distinguish the first from the second.

Here's a familiar scenario. You are the purchasing manager in a large *Fortune* 500 company. You receive an invitation from one of your suppliers to attend an all-expense-paid, three-day informational seminar on technological change in a warm climate in February. The session happens to be located in the home town of Aunt Millie, whom you've been meaning to visit for long time. When you get to the seminar, it turns out that about two hours of hard information is being spread over three days. The rest is for sports and networking. Is it ethical for you to be there or not?

The savvy manager can turn the session into a useful opportunity to meet potential customers, discuss new uses of the product, and get some work done away from the office phone. On the other hand, your attendance may *look* bad, both to employees back home and to suppliers who assume you are on the take. It is a bad precedent and therefore poor leadership. Divided jury.

As long as one measures this activity solely in terms of tangible contributions to each participant's bottom line, it is hard even to be sensitive to the ethical issues involved. When this sort of impasse occurs, a closer look at personal motivations can help break the ethical logjam.

What other *motives are driving me beside the company's bottom line?*

No doubt the purchasing manager has no intention of succumbing to conflict-of-interest pressures when money is involved, but what about that visit to Aunt Millie? or the enticement of February fun-in-the-sun? A true test of his business ethics would be to change the scenario. What if the sessions were in Minnesota? Such simple questioning of motive can quickly ferret out the degree to which this scenario poses a significant conflict of interest.

The supplier might well conduct the same exercise on its choice of marketing vehicles. Obviously its overt motive is to make the company money, but is the purity of this intention being undermined by other, more exploitative goals? Bottom-line rationales are always employed to legitimize promotional incentives. A good test of the ethics is to ask what *other* intentions might be driving your choice of promotions.

CONCLUSION

Managers who allow a bottom-line orientation to hold sway over their decision making frequently sabotage their capacity to respond ethically to the marketplace. Usually this failure rests on the exclusiveness of bottom-line appeals. By their very ability to focus individual team effort, they invite a reductionist approach to problem solving. This can lead to a disregard, even disrespect for others as empathetic and relationship thinking are abandoned. As long as the bottom line is in the driver's seat, other ethical norms will be either decorative or suppressed. Managers who adopt such an approach to motivate themselves and others can make a company's claim to care about service and quality a joke, or even a harmful lie. Despite these risks, even well-intentioned managers will cling to a bottom-line vocabulary out of fear of diluting their powers to motivate effort and efficiency.

Although managers tend to voice the problems described in this chapter in terms of trade-offs between ethics and the bottom line, a profitable ethical solution is there to be had once the frame of reference in which such problems are addressed is opened up. People are apt to see these cases as either-or situations: either ship the flawed product or lose revenues; either bribe and make a profit, or don't bribe and lose the business. In reality, the moral quandries are reflections of systemic problems, which require systemic solutions. Bribery, for example, is a condition resulting from one's choice of markets and failure to develop a distinctive competency.

No problem-solving approach to the ethical dilemmas of business, corporate or individual, can productively integrate morality and profitability unless it takes a systemic view of the problems. It must establish a core set of goals that include more than the bottom line. Bottom-line incentives will not suffice as a substitute for the full range of considerations a manager needs to bring to ethical dilemmas at work.

A Covenantal Ethic, with its emphasis on value-creation, service, and relationships, and its view of profit as a secondary result of these qualities, helps a manager articulate in advance such a set of goals. Continually exploring relationship and value-creation questions like the ones I present in this chapter can help establish the right conditions for ethical performance *before* the trouble starts. Doing so also helps provide a corrective perspective when dilemmas threaten to become inevitabilities in the face of the pressure of the bottom line.

The stubbornness of bottom-line goal setting is being eroded today partly by a new awareness of the need to listen more closely to outsiders, from customers to public interest groups, and partly by a shift in the values that motivate people to work. Many large, publicly owned companies already recognize that the purposes that motivate business are comprised of a larger variety of values than the dollar. Says former GenRad chairman William Thurston:

> GenRad is really not a company with human aspects among other aspects; rather it is itself, in essence, a human phenomenon. . . . There is a kind of magic that sparks group performance when attitudes are right, and it is the most powerful influence determining the success of a business enterprise.

So, too, Volvo president Bo Ekman has commented that an effective degree of cooperation demands that an organization stay in touch with its members' values. "Everyone must feel that they are moving toward meaningful goals."[11] When Volvo acquired a food processing company, many employees joked about the idea of a "Volvo hotdog." But behind the joke was a real concern that the company might have shifted to a bottom-line approach, in which it would do anything to make money. This sparked an extended and meaningful inquiry into the company value system and how that should shape its strat-

[11]Bo Ekman, *Dignity at Work* (Stockholm: Streiffer & Co., Bokforlag HB, 1985), p. iii.

egy. The result was a three-pronged commitment, as stated in the corporate objectives, to: 1) strength in business through high technological content and outstanding quality, 2) industrial development and technological renewal, and 3) integrity.

Even the archetypical business advocate Calvin Coolidge, in perhaps the most misquoted speech in American history, recognized the essentialness of complex goals to motivate commercial endeavor. What he really said was:

Questions to Ask When Grappling with the Roadblocks of the Bottom Line

Who might get hurt beside ourselves?

Am I perpetuating a dishonest and fraudulent relationship?

Whose needs am I considering in my definition of the problem?

Have I tested the other person's needs directly?

Is this decision consistent with the values we wish to convey by the brand or company name?

What language am I using to set targets for other people?

If the most desirable consequences cannot be determined, have I ensured that the procedural issues of decision making and implementation are ethical?

How will this issue affect the company's reputation?

What value am I creating?

Are we in the right business and market to begin with?

How will the decision affect the quality of my relationship with X?

What if the injured party or intended beneficiary were my child?

Is my relationship with the end-user one of empowering or empowerment?

What *other* motives are driving me beside the company's bottom line?

> After all, the chief business of the American people *is* business. But there are many things that we want very much more. We want peace and honor, and that charity which is so strong an element of all civilization. The chief ideal of the American people is idealism.[12]

Many of the best companies and business leaders in America recognize that idealism is not just a sentiment for speech-making but an essential ingredient driving business creativity and responsible management. For these people, the purpose of business is not just the receipt of a healthy return, but the creation of value and maintaining respect for other people. Such purposes cannot be subordinated as instruments of the bottom line. They must stand on their own as important values motivating people on the job.

[12]Calvin Coolidge, speech to the annual meeting of the Society of American Newspaper Editors and Publishers, Washington, DC, January 17, 1925.

8

Efficiency, Expediency, and Other Short-Term Traps

Three things only are well done in haste: flying from the plague, escaping quarrels, and catching flies.*

U.S. managers are often criticized for their short-term thinking. In 1982, John Naisbitt's highly influential *Megatrends* attributed much of the unprecedented criticism which American business was receiving to the "short-term orientation of American managers."[1] In 1990, the same theme continues to be voiced. Some of the most dramatic trends of the past business decade—from the megamerger to the Damoclean layoff strategies—are those that have reaped the quickest rewards on Wall Street and in the business press. They are also most criticized for offering short-term solutions that merely paper over severe weaknesses in a company's strategic or operating approach.

Akio Morita, chairman of Sony, says he asked a New York money trader how far he looked ahead. The answer: "Ten minutes." Muses Morita, "If Americans think only in terms of ten-minute action, while we Japanese think in ten-year terms, America assuredly faces gradual decline."[2]

*H. G. Bohn, *Handbook of Proverbs.*
[1]John Naisbitt, *Megatrends* (New York: Warner Books, 1982), Chapter 4.
[2]"A Japanese View: Why America Has Fallen Behind," *Fortune*, September 25, 1989, p. 52.

But while countless pundits and war-torn CEOs are deploring the short-term pressures of the investment community, history reveals that Americans have always been particularly prone to the frenetic way of life. Remarked Alexis de Tocqueville in 1775, "It is strange to see with what feverish ardor the Americans pursue their own welfare, and to watch the vague dread that constantly torments them lest they should not have chosen the shortest path which may lead to it." (*Democracy in America* II.xiii)

The ancient Greek philosopher Protagoras confidently asserted that man was the measure of all things, but as Francis Bacon noted, economic man must recognize that "Time is the measure of business" (*Of Dispatch*). From the one-minute manager to the five-week supertakeover, the corporate treadmill turns fast and furiously. As that early American sage Benjamin Franklin put it, "Time is money." (*Advice to a Young Tradesman*)

The practical dilemmas of time management are well known. Every manager faces a paradoxical need to cultivate both a lightning response and a long-term investment vis-à-vis the marketplace. Tom Peters has succinctly described this paradoxical challenge as the "long-term capacity for change."[3] But given Americans' habitual inclination toward change and newness, the short-term side of the equation is frequently overemphasized.

A short-term bias can color almost every aspect of managerial thought, from strategic planning to the degree to which one lives up to past contracts. Nowhere is the short-term perspective more evident than in American attitudes to product development. Alan Kantrow, editor of the *McKinsey Quarterly,* points out that Americans tend to create myths about instant innovation. Like the goddess Athena, who was said to have sprung spontaneously from Zeus's forehead—in full armor no less!—some of the best-known discoveries of American management have been thought to have occurred and been implemented in a single act. But as Kantrow points out, few innovations in American business are instantaneous. Rather, they are the result of long processes of incremental

---

[3]Tom Peters, *Thriving on Chaos* (New York: Harper & Row, 1987), Chapters 1–10.

improvements. Henry Ford, for example, is usually lionized as having conceived of mass production in one stroke of brilliance and then implementing it. Not so, reports Charles Sorensen in *My Forty Years at Ford.* According to Sorensen:

> [Henry Ford] had no ideas on mass production. He wanted to build a lot of autos. He was determined, but like everyone else at that time, he didn't know how.... He just grew into it [the concept of mass production], like the rest of us.[4]

What Ford did have, however, was a vision of building many automobiles. Such visions are no more short-term than are the processes by which they are implemented.

So, too, some of America's most successful corporations have based their business philosophy on a long-term framework for decision making. Hewlett-Packard's Dave Packard, for example, recalls with pride the time HP refused to go after a defense contract because it would demand heavy hiring at the outset but heavy firing after the job was completed. In the 1920s, Procter & Gamble adopted a revolutionary direct-sell approach to the retailers in order to avoid the layoffs that occurred from short-term fluctuations in wholesalers' orders. The strategy proved to be as brilliant from a financial standpoint as it was far-sighted from an ethical one.

But although managers may know intellectually that long-term commitment pays off and short-term corner-cutting can be self-destructive, many nevertheless reason, speak, and act in short-term language. When complexity or doubt threatens to overtake a manager's confidence, efficiency, pragmatism, and impatience easily combine to create the unambiguously motivating message, "Just get the job done now."

ETHICAL CONSEQUENCES OF SHORT-TERM PERSPECTIVES

A too-expedient viewpoint not only has financial pitfalls, it can be a source of ethical problems as well. As the

---

[4]Quoted in Alan M. Kantrow, *The Constraints of Corporate Tradition* (New York: Harper & Row, 1987), p. 176.

Bible tells us in Proverbs 28:20, "He that maketh haste to be rich shall not be innocent." Instant gratification—of an individual manager's orders or an investor's expectations—is rarely a recipe for the construction of a value-creating business response and the conditions for honest business. Short-term pressures can silence moral reasoning simply by giving it no space. The tighter a manager's agenda is, the less time for contemplating complex, time-consuming, unpragmatic issues like ethics. Remarks Milton Gwirtzman about the whirlwind pace and incredible power of many multinational executives in his analysis of bribery, "This style of management has some advantages, but time for ethical reflection is not among them."[5] An efficiency message can also mislead subordinates into thinking they hear, "Get it done any way you can even if it means compromising simple ethical standards."

Thus short-term thinking is a twofold moral failure: one of vision and the other of reckoning. The manager who takes the intellectual measure of a problem with a short-term yardstick fails to adopt a vision of business purpose that adequately encompasses the dynamics of value-creation and relationship-enabling activities. Nor does he or she pause long enough to analyze past conduct. By failing to look either far enough forward or far enough back, a manager has few tangible anchor-points for conscience to attach itself to decision making in an integrated, productive way. Rather, one instinctively suppresses conscience because it only slows you down.

In one informal survey I conducted among hundreds of managers, a short-term frame for performance was consistently cited as the single greatest stress factor on personal ethics.[6] It is no coincidence that some of the most egregious examples of financial wrongdoing in the past decade occurred in industries where the time frame for decision making was extremely constricted. Insider trading, cheating on the futures exchanges, hostile and destructive takeovers, midnight massacres, and the rush to pump out generic drugs as patents expire all have an extremely fast-paced playing field.

---

[5]Milton Gwirtzman, "Is Bribery Defensible?" in *Crime at the Top: Deviance in Business and the Professions*, eds., John M. Johnson and Jack D. Douglas (Philadelphia: Lippincott, 1978), p. 34.
[6]A notable exception are those in a strong internal auditing function, which tends to show a much lower exposure and susceptibility to short-term time frames.

The impulse and obligation to stimulate efficiency corrupt a manager's moral capacity in three basic ways:

1. Once the assumption is made that expediency in its narrowest sense is a manager's first obligation, there is little incentive or legitimacy for taking a critical look at moral issues. Better to adopt a "no-time-for-ethics" pragmatism. Even when such thinking has no immediate unethical consequences, it can nevertheless pave the way to long-term abominations. The systematic crowding out of ethical considerations because they waste time is like a ticking bomb; eventually the many opportunities for unethical conduct will convene and set it off. The unsuspecting manager will not even recognize he or she is in an ethical dilemma until it is too late.

2. Short-term mindsets encourage self-delusion. Nothing succeeds like success, but often only in the short term. According to the title of Robert Frost's poem, "Happiness Makes Up in Height for What It Lacks in Length," no position, however euphorically high, guarantees protection from future mistakes of judgment. Thus the tragic heroes once taught us. You make a good deal. You're riding high. No time for a postmortem on the decision, go on to the next. Overconfident and ready to accelerate the pace, you begin to make mistakes in judgment which cumulatively catch up with you only after they are beyond your control. Only a long-term view of career and performance can provide an antidote to the heady live-for-the-present high that success can encourage.

3. Short-term orientations invite greedy orientations. As Tocqueville noted, people tend to go to curious extremes. Once they give up a far-sighted and ambitious vision, they go to the other extreme and seek only the most immediate gratification of their own desires:

As soon as men have lost the habit of placing their

> chief hopes upon remote events, they naturally seek
> to gratify without delay their smallest desires; and no
> sooner do they despair of living forever than they are
> disposed to act as if they were to exist but for a single
> day. (*Democracy in America* II.xvii)

Much of today's yuppie materialism has been rightly attributed
to an insecurity that there will be no economic rewards in the
future. Go for broke now because there will be no opportunities for wealth later. Ethical rules are suspended and there is
no future perspective to remind one of the possibility of being
caught down the line. Many managers and incentive systems
even encourage this mindset in order to make people work
harder and obey more unquestioningly. What is a survival scenario but a justification of short-term greediness at other's
expense?[7]

In many cases, companies have no built-in reminders
of penalties for such greed. Just the opposite. One of the most
destructive patterns of career advancement in American business is what I call the "Run Down-Move Up" syndrome, and it
is clearly a product of short-term orientations in management
appraisal systems. A manager takes over an aging facility, runs
it to the ground, and sows the seeds of continued labor strife.
He (understand she as well throughout) is promoted for the
improvements in return from the overmilked cash cow. In so
doing, the organization enables the manager to outrun his
mistakes, and gives him the opportunity to make even bigger
ones. Meanwhile, someone else inherits the problems he has
created, and if they are irreversible, many other people will
suffer as well through layoffs and consolidations. If a short-
term ethos is really entrenched, the company itself will do the
same thing. Run up the debt level and run down the facility
and then sell the empty shell to someone else who will lay off
the employees.

Such actions are the essence of greed, which Web-
ster's defines as "inordinate or reprehensible acquisitive-

---

[7]For the short-term mentality of greed, which seizes investors in both investment mania and
panic situations, see Charles P. Kindleberger, *Manias, Panics and Crashes* (New York: Basic Books,
1978), pp. 30ff.

ness." Common language translation: taking out more than would be commonly agreed to be a fair share, based on what you put in and left behind. Greed motivates many managers to perform, but it also corrodes the foundation of values necessary for the creation of value.

WHERE ETHICS AND EXPEDIENCY ARE BOTH ON THE LINE

While the widely agreed-upon foolishness of short-sighted management perspectives would seem to be argument enough to prevent them, managers in fact fall prey to constricted time frames on a regular basis. The following eight problems represent common moral and economic trade-offs which a short-term perspective tends to dismiss as unimportant or trivial. The questions that accompany each example suggest ways of breaking through the intellectual and emotional barriers that short-sightedness puts in the way of ethical problem-solving management behavior.

Problem 1. Complying with Policy When There's No Time

As the old saying goes, once is curiosity; twice an experiment; three times a perversion. One of the most subtly destructive aspects of short-term thinking is that it reinforces mankind's general tendency to trivialize ethical lapses. If you see each ethical slipup as an isolated incident rather than an ongoing pattern, the moral implications of your actions seem greatly reduced.

"Are we really doing the right thing?" a production supervisor wonders fleetingly as he fails to conduct a standard quality test on a part his plant is manufacturing.

"Don't worry," replies the division head, "it's nothing. We haven't had any trouble with these parts and we're behind schedule. Our buyer needs these parts. We can't afford to delay shipment."

Two years later, the indictments begin to come down. The untested parts were for the Navy, which took a dim view (translation: $1.75 million fine) about receiving untested weapons parts with falsified certificates. The production supervisor and division head are fired. The company's stock falls 87 cents on the news.

The incident, which actually occurred at a major electronic components company, is not unusual. In fact, fourteen other companies were under investigation at the same time for similar violations. The one-time slipup turned out to be a systemic pattern of lawbreaking in this industry.

With hindsight this is obviously a Type B ethics problem: everyone knew right from wrong but failed to do the right thing. Why? According to the managers involved, *the failure to test seemed unimportant at the time because the short-term production schedules loomed so large.* The only moral issue, fleetingly addressed, was whether someone was likely to get hurt by using a weapons system with the untested components. Given past defect rates, the managers were certain nobody would get hurt. They were right. When later tested, the parts were indeed up to quality standards specified by the Navy. How could one little oversight, like one little drink, hurt?

But the managers were wrong in perceiving physical injury as the only important ethical issue to consider. Honesty, accuracy, precedent, and long-term financial consequences were also up for inspection. The process of quality control was being severely undermined; the company's accounting credibility was being put at risk, and their own jobs were at stake just as much for lying as for not getting the parts out in time.

Despite these issues, which now seem obvious, their emphasis on expediency caused the managers to fixate on the tangible issues at hand: the production schedule and the reliability of particular parts. The parts were most probably of acceptable quality and the short-term consequences were beneficial to both the company and the buyer's schedule. The failure to test and the cover-up seemed trivial, a one-time compromise. In fact, it was a serious ethical lapse. As quality guru Philip Crosby notes:

> Speaking of integrity, let me make a very exact statement. I do not know of a single product safety problem where the basic cause was something other than a

lack of integrity judgment on the part of some management individual. Usually the objective was to achieve a short-range goal by cutting corners. The result was a long-range and unprofitable headache.[8]

Even the most capable and otherwise decent managers take trivializing approaches to problem solving when they only respond to expedient pressures. They focus on the tangible, immediate products of a decision rather than emphasize the long-term processes which they are perpetuating.

What if I knew there would be a full audit of every decision I made two years from now?

When the normal brakes of conscience fail to stop a corner-cutting decision, a manager needs other rational tools to reawaken awareness of how a decision may be negatively affecting long-term processes. Asking the question, "What if I got caught or audited" can be a helpful technique. The full import of adopting unethical means for short-term beneficial ends will immediately be more open to rational analysis.

The complexity of business today, with many corners to hide in, greatly diminishes the personal opportunity for being aware that you might get caught, and thus weakens your sense of the long-term consequences for unethical behavior. Even in the 1970s, when business was far simpler, there were on average 100,000 deaths per year due to occupational hazards (as compared to 18,000 murders and non-negligent manslaughters), and the majority were due to willful violations of health and safety laws. The desire to be ethical also can trick you into using short-term pressures as a way of ignoring long-term consequences. You think no one is being hurt because you wish this to be so. As long as your vision is restricted to the near future, you can continue such a charade. Forcing yourself to walk through the long-term consequences of your activities can help tease out serious injuries to less immediate constituencies as well as the effects of your decision on the less tangible, relationship-oriented aspect of a problem.

---

[8]Philip B. Crosby, *Quality Is Free* (New York: New American Library, 1979), p. 71.

Problem 2. Complying with Unethical People
to Get the Job Done

Only a simpleton or a confirmed con artist believes that the decisions made in a large organization have merely a limited and temporary effect. As Samuel Butler once said, the course of true anything never runs smooth. Most managerial decisions and actions have multiple consequences over an extended period of time. And yet the pressure for expediency is so great that even good managers can dismiss the most obvious long-term undesired consequences of their actions as inconsequential.

To return to the comparison of adolescents and the managerial mentality, which was made in an earlier chapter, one of the chief factors discovered in studies of self-destructive teenage risk-taking is that teens are uncommonly preoccupied with the present. This same preoccupation with the short term—and the excitement it brings—explains some of the riskier decisions managers make.

Take Manager Green, a facilities coordinator at a *Fortune* 500 company. Personally, Green would never buy a "hot" television or try to bribe a public official for a driver's license. But Green is responsible for constructing a new manufacturing facility, under a strict and extremely tight deadline. If she fails to meet it, there will be a delay in the company's introduction of its most important new product.

As the job nears completion, it becomes quite evident to Green that, despite her initial warnings to follow the letter of the law meticulously, the contractor has been making under-the-table payments to certain members of the city council to ensure that inspections and permits are completed on schedule. What's more, Green notices that there are about 25 percent more electricians on the job than are necessary. Street talk is that the contractor has ties to organized crime. Does Green investigate the contractor's methods or not? Should she call a halt to bribing the officials if that is in fact what is occurring? Should she question the number of electricians? Should she even discuss the issue with her boss?

Green chooses to leave matters alone. The short-term disadvantages of rocking the boat loom large in her mind:

certain delay in inspections, possible sabotage of the electrical system, and an angry boss who is under pressure from above to get the facility completed. Green explained her reasons for doing nothing: "Look, I know it's terrible, but my company expects me to get this job done. That's what they pay me for." Green has suppressed her private morality with a short-term results orientation. Ironically, her fixation on the immediate consequences of the dilemma blinds her to potentially more damaging results. Even if Green were to restrict her moral reckoning to consequences (rather than absolute obligations), her reasoning would be flawed. She is setting herself and her company up for a major exposé when the local paper decides to investigate corruption in the city council. It is instructive to recall the defense contractors who were so adamant about having to pay bribes overseas in the 1970s. The same managers saw their names plastered in the press and themselves the subject of many SEC investigations during the fervor of applying the Foreign Corrupt Practices Act of 1977.

What are the likely consequences of my decision one year down the road? Three years down the road?

Albert Carr, in a brilliant article on executive conscience, suggested that the crux of unethical versus ethical business practice was whether or not an executive took a long-term view of problems. In his opinion, "Nonethical practice is shortsighted almost by definition, if for no other reason than that it exposes the company to eventual reprisals."[9] Carr noted that one of the strongest persuasive weapons a manager of conscience has at hand is the ability to demonstrate the long-term, multiple consequences of policies and decisions. He was speaking of convincing those in whose hands one's career hangs, but the same holds true for self-persuasion. The manager who can tolerate a double standard of behavior in the belief that the first priority must be to get the job done short-term, would do well to think what that job prospect will look like after a scandal. Here is a question that will surely enlighten your own self-interest: Who is more likely to be hung?

[9]Albert Z. Carr, "Can an Executive Afford a Conscience?" *Harvard Business Review* (July–August 1970), pp. 143–153.

The boss you are pleasing or the little guy who does the dirty work?

This is *not* to suggest that the only reason to comply with private ethical norms at work is that it will pay you to do so. There is a less rational side to ethical choice which rests on the perception that you do the right thing simply because it is right. Nevertheless, when fears about your own self-interest and determination to get the immediate job done overshadow your sense of needing to do the right thing, often a second look at some of the longer-term negative or positive consequences will put your conscience back in the driver's seat.

Problem 3. Goodwill at What Cost?

Dollar costs are not the only kind of consequences to be considered over the long term. Relationship costs in the form of lost goodwill can be equally devastating to a company. So, too, the short-term cost of creating good relationships can build up a valuable asset for the future. As J&J's James Burke noted after the Tylenol crisis, "We got through the crisis because we had ninety years of goodwill in the bank."

And yet, when it comes to intangible concepts like goodwill and customer responsibility, the prospect of tangible short-term costs can make even the best manager vulnerable to shortsightedness and ethical insensitivity. Take the following case, which occurred many years ago at BankAmerica. The bank discovered that it had inadvertently made a rounding error of a few pennies on several hundred consumer loans that it had taken over from other businesses. According to California's so-called Unruh law, any error in interest charges would exempt the consumer from the entire interest payment on that loan. The kicker, however, was that no statute of limitations had been established for this kind of mistake. Bank-America's problem was uncovered during a standard internal audit and had not been noticed by any consumer. Depending on where it set the statute of limitations and how it counted the applicable loans (should boats and trailers be counted or could trailers be exempted from the Unruh requirement?), the bank would have to forfeit vastly different amounts of interest payments—the actual range was several million dollars. What should the bank do?

The board met to discuss the problem, only to discover itself at a loss for a clear-cut legal solution. This aspect of the law had never been tested in court. There was no standard practice established. Nor was there a black-and-white way to describe the dilemma, because the dollar amounts of the penalty seemed so out of proportion to the magnitude of the actual mistake. In short, a cost-benefit analysis of the bank's ethical obligations simply did not make it. Then there was the sticky issue of magnitude. If the bank chose the most generous rebate, it might make the problem look bigger and thus more embarrassing in the press. Though this seemed to argue for minimizing the way in which the bank applied the law, board members worried that it was too self-serving a viewpoint. Finally, one member turned in exasperation to Rosemary Mans, recording secretary for the meeting and technically not a participating member. What would she do?

Rosemary sat back and said simply, "If I were a consumer and I later heard that the bank might have owed me money and squeaked out on a technicality, I'd be pretty mad, and I'd be pretty sure to take my account elsewhere." The board agreed, set the limitation time generously, and ran a straightforward press announcement. The public reaction was essentially ho-hum rather than suspicious.

What is so interesting in this case is how a well-minded board, known for its concern over social responsibility, could lose sight of so simple a truth as that which Mans vocalized. Fear of embarrassment and concern over fiduciary duty magnified the short-term dollar stakes of the decision out of proportion to other issues. Consumer trust, over the long term, was the real consequence to consider. When the felt importance of long-term ethical values becomes weakened, one way to revive its force is to ask,

How will this decision affect our customers' trust in us?

Most people's—business people's included—cognitive skills in evaluating the ethical dimensions of an immediate practical problem are underdeveloped. In business, complexity and uncertainty raise so many "what ifs?" and "no ways" that it can be hard to pinpoint the ethical issue at hand or feel you have power to do anything about it. Changing technology, a globalized operations base, and gargantuan organizational structures make consequences ever more difficult to visualize. Testing for the trust factor in a problem is a good way to bring conflicting obligations and short-term needs into better perspective.

This test holds true not only for facing the costs connected with consumer trust, but employee trust as well. Often a human resource policy which makes perfect sense on paper will be so destructive to employee trust because of the context in which it is presented or the way it is communicated, that the long-term consequences can be severely damaging. Thinking about trust in the first place can help head off unintended perceived betrayals.

Problem 4. Carrying Out Someone Else's Unethical Promise

One of the most difficult aspects of managerial integrity is the problem of deference. There are many occasions when two managers disagree, and one will have to defer to the other to get the job done. Often the disagreements involve ethical issues. What is the right thing to do when such conflicts occur? Is deference always immoral if your conscience is involved? On clear-cut cases of injury or lying, it is easy to say follow your conscience; but what about those times when the issues are in the gray area of fairness? or when two moral obligations are in contradiction, as in the case below? How does a short-term perspective affect an ethical solution to such dilemmas?

Say you are the new division president of a recently acquired distribution company. You discover that during the premerger discussions your chairman promised the largest supplier that, in exchange for continuing good relationships after the acquisition, your company would drop a smaller producer of the same parts from the main list circulated to customers. You feel, however, that such a move would be unfair to the smaller supplier, who had contracted with an unwritten understanding that it would be included on the main list.

Like many other business decisions, this one involves several mutually contradictory dilemmas. Fair play demands keeping promises, but how do you reconcile the fact that the chairman has given one promise and the original contract implied another? If you seek to avoid injury, you cannot escape the fact that someone is going to get hurt in this situation, and it is not at all certain which decision will hurt your company the most. If you adopted a "least-injury" definition of priorities, you could feel secure in advocating not hurting the small supplier, obviously the most vulnerable party in the conflict. But a least-injury ethic would not give you a clue about ethically resolving the conflicting promises, which are also on the line.

When the real chairman and division president involved in this case discussed the problem, they couched it in terms of fair play and self-interest. Both approaches got them nowhere. It seemed unfair to go back on their word in either case, and self-interest depended on whether you defined the business as being supplier-oriented or customer-oriented. If supplier-oriented, then the relationship with the largest supplier seemed most important. If customer-oriented, then keeping a variety of small suppliers in order to ensure choice and substitute parts when inventories ran low was of paramount concern. Both managers told me the situation was *not* an ethical issue, even though their descriptions of it were full of moral judgments about fairness, exploitation, honesty, and trust. They were both tempted to adopt a wartime urgency mentality which said, just obey the chairman's orders, but a new emphasis on empowering subordinates and decentralized decision making had closed off this avenue of escape.

How would the decision look if it were repeated twenty times?

In the end, the decisive question for these two managers was, What if we did this twenty times? Both were then able to see how an isolated incident could be the logical beginning of a breakdown of supplier *and* customer trust. To cut off a small and loyal supplier would severely curtail the company's ability to maintain its strong variety of parts and would surely disaffect customers when inventories and price choices were

adversely affected. The question also brought into sharper relief the blackmail element. Asserted the president, "If we say
yes to the biggest bully on the block even once, we might
as well hand them the business." Thus by seeing an isolated
incident as a potential *precedent* rather than a short-term
problem, the managers were able to break through what
seemed to be an irresolvable dilemma.

Problem 5. Understanding Moral Failures

One might suggest, however, that the questions about
precedent in the previous case should not have stopped with
the discussion of external relationships. What about the process of decision making that got them into the dilemma in the
first place? Will the division president's autonomy be similarly
threatened by the chairman twenty more times? Is there a
systemic problem in the authority structure of this firm which
would make managing with integrity an impossible ideal?

Questioning the underlying conditions that have contributed to an ethical business dilemma is one of the hardest
and most neglected managerial tasks. It requires digging into
uncomfortable facts and sorting out complex chains of events.
Given time pressures, it is easy to terminally delay a critical
view of the past. How ironic that so results-oriented a profession is so loathe to look at results when morality and reality
conflict.

A starting point for this needed exploration of the past
would be the following question:

*How many times have similar outcomes happened in the
past? and why?*

This question may seem obvious, but every manager
has experienced occasions when the pressure to move on actively discourages him or her to take a second look at what
has already occurred.

Say a company states its intention to increase the representation of women and minorities in responsible management positions. Twenty years later very little progress has
been made. Insiders who fervently express the desire to "see

more women and minorities in the executive suite" confidentially voice their concern about performance inadequacies in the two groups. The next time a woman comes up for promotion, there are many good and seemingly objective reasons why she is passed over. Each promotion case seems exceptional, though most end in failure. No one in top management is twitchingly uncomfortable with discrimination issues. It knows its intentions are pure.

And yet, when questioned by disgruntled employees and activist outsiders about its minority hiring and promotion record, as was the Boston business community a few years ago, it turns out that *almost none of the companies had ever made a serious attempt to assess what actually occurred.* If any records were kept at all, they were lists of overall percentages to track EEO quota targets. These turned out to be uninformative and unconsulted records of failures, with no insight into the causes. One suspects that even the most superficial exploration of attitudes in the companies would reveal a repeated and resigned conviction that the women and minorities just didn't "fit" into the current culture. Hiring patterns and job assignments—couched in the rubric of "unique opportunities to do what no one else has been able to accomplish here"—were most likely of the nonfitting sort, and ones that only superheroes could succeed at. Questioning the practices and the assumptions behind them would provide more proactive insight into the minority and women promotions issue than fervent expressions of good intentions.

However difficult the assessment, discrepancies between good intention and poor results must be unearthed and analyzed, whether the problem is inadvertent or the result of calculated villainy. Max Weber made a distinction between the "ethics of attitude" and the "ethics of absolute ends." He felt that both were important. An ethics of attitude is crucial in establishing personal commitment to an ideal standard such as the Covenantal Ethic, but the honest executive also needs to examine results to better position personal and companywide integrity in the future.

Whether the issue is equal opportunity, safety performance, or environmental accidents, the management team of conscience has an obligation to break through the short-term, exceptional-case perspective and to make a full inquiry into whether the incident reflects a habitual flaw in its problem-solving process.

Such an assessment requires courage, honesty, and a full commitment to change where necessary. Thus high marks go to Atari's chairman James J. Morgan for his public statement, "This company is going to start delivering what it says it will deliver. Up to now, we have not done that. We have been erratic, unbelievable, and we have said things we didn't mean. That has to come to an end."[10]

Companies seeking the highest standards of conduct must be willing to acknowledge their moral warts, if they are to uncover the systemic factors of failure, and success. A frank review of past conduct can also bring a new awareness of strengths. For example, there were no women in top management positions at the time I interviewed Stride Rite chairman Arnold Hiatt. Hiatt brought the point up himself in discussing the company's reputation for integrity.

> I think it is ridiculous that we have no women managers, no mothers, working in our children's shoe division. We have tried to change, but so far we have not been able to find a match with our extremely strong culture. It is a slow process, but neither are we going to ignore these disparities.
>
> Knowing how imperfect we are in some ways makes me nervous when someone portrays us as a particularly "ethical" company. . . . Well, yes, I guess on shoe quality, on quality of fit, I can safely attest to our integrity.

Note how Hiatt not only identified the bad news but also the good news. By fully examining rather than trivializing the track record in one area, he was also able to clarify where the company was doing a good job of living up to its covenant. One might conclude that a sense of integrity is most acute when integrity is under assault. Useful as this lesson may be

---

[10]"Atari Realignment of Management Set," *New York Times*, January 24, 1984.

in motivating a second look at failures, many well-intentioned managers nevertheless are reluctant to take a long look back.

Problem 6. Life-or-Death Decisions

He who hesitates is lost, time is money, but as George Herbert said, "Good and quickly seldom meet" (*Outlandish Proverbs*). Nowhere was this more apparent than in the tragic crash of the space shuttle *Challenger*. During the Rogers Commission Senate investigations which followed, Morton Thiokol engineers were questioned about their recommendations to proceed with the launching the morning of the crash. These same engineers had originally recommended a "no go" after considering the unprecedented cold snap which hit the Florida coast overnight. But time pressed. NASA officials expressed serious concern that a delay in the launch would most likely mean further delays in the entire launch schedule for the next eighteen months. And Congress was already concerned that the shuttle project was severely behind schedule.

In the early hours of the morning, testified the Thiokol engineers, they received a new standard of judgment. Until then, every systems recommendation was tested with the following question, "Can you prove it is safe?" On the morning of the fatal launch the question was changed. Top management now asked, "Can you prove it [launching] is not safe?" By changing the operating definition of safety, the engineers and NASA came to an entirely different conclusion, with tragic consequences. The shortness of the time frame in which they were thinking, basically win or lose all in the next two hours, caused them to change their normal operating definitions.

What if I had ten times as much time in which to make the decision? Would I recommend the same thing?

Stepping back and mentally buying yourself more time may seem to fly in the teeth of pragmatism, but it is a sure-fire way of obtaining a more prudent understanding of responsibility in problem solving. If the answer to the above question is no, you are probably doing the wrong thing and need to examine your decision further.

All too often, however, a manager allows himself or herself to be victimized by a short time frame and bullied by time pressures into accepting a problem-solving approach that he or she clearly finds uncomfortable. Others will conspire to relieve the discomfort (and the prudent analytical skills which it compels) by appealing to the macho, action-oriented aspects of short-term pressures: "get it over with," and "do your job," are tantamount to throwing caution to the winds. In the *Challenger* case, even the managers who disagreed with the pressures from NASA nevertheless accepted the new definition of safety determination foisted on them under a tight schedule. Had they compared the new operating standards with those they would adopt were there more time, they might have been more aware of the risks they were taking with other people's lives.

Problem 7. Layoffs

Mentally stretching the time frame to walk through the problem from a longer-term perspective may seem a mechanical way of overcoming short-term blindness, but in the absence of real time it is a good second best for putting ethical risks into sharper relief.

In some situations, however, actually stretching the time frame is the only way in which an ethical resolution can be brought about. It is very easy, however, to overlook the fact that time can be an effective ethical weapon against seemingly intractable problems of conscience. Take the uncomfortable problem of layoffs. A Type A ethics problem, layoffs present an issue of conscience to which no one has the securely right ethical answer. No matter how necessary they may seem from a financial and organizational standpoint, the human fallout never feels quite ethical. In order to escape the moral discomfort of layoffs, many managers fall back on a short-term survival scenario: "What do you want me to do, go out of business?" The flaw in this approach is that they see layoffs as a single decision occurring in a brief time frame: either lay off (by implication, at once) or go out of business (by implication, at once).

The morally and experientially mature manager, however, sees more than one choice about layoffs, including a choice about the time frame for implementation. Testing for this choice is a good way to increase your ability to create alternatives to ensure that the layoff process is ethical. A good testing question is,

Have I actually* tried *to stretch the time frame in which to complete decision making or implementation?

Consider the case of Lex Motor Corporation's strategy of stretching the time frame which significantly improved the ethics of layoffs. John Tinker, president of Lex Service PLC's Lex Motor Division, had to implement a 75 percent reduction in his division's British Leyland dealerships from 32 to 12 in number, thereby reducing the number of people employed by half: only 1,100 would remain out of 2,200 after the franchises were divested or closed. Lex's board had delayed making the decision as long as possible for two reasons: it hoped that BL's market share would improve and it hesitated to pull the plug on a major division of the diversified company. When weighed against a national unemployment rate of 12 percent, the closures seemed particularly distressful.

Tinker was the oldest member of the senior management group and was well known for being particularly sensitive to employee relations issues. All eyes were on him and showed pity or cynicism.

Aware of the moral dilemmas involved in "making other people, not management, pay when the company makes a big mistake," chairman Sir Trevor Chinn committed Lex's resources to a stretched time frame for completing the closures. He gave Tinker three important things: time, money, and moral support. It was agreed that the layoffs and closures would be based on performance but that long-term service would be taken into consideration.

The company took well over a year to complete the closures. Contrary to predictions that the best people would immediately leave, many stayed. Tinker offered help on many fronts. In the end, about a third of the employees were transferred within Lex; 2 percent chose early retirement or redundancy; 20–30 percent found jobs in competitors' franchises in the same or nearby towns, and 16 percent were looking for jobs on the day of the last closure. Three months later the figure was reduced to 5 percent.

By taking a longer-term view and creating the cash flow to stretch the time frame of the closures, Lex's management executed a painful strategy with honor. There were also financial benefits to the time extension: Tinker could hold out for better terms on the divestments including negotiating new jobs for existing employees. Moreover, he was able to save three franchises which had been earmarked for closure when British Leyland experienced a slight turnaround with the introduction of a new model, and Lex picked up business from some of the other franchises it had closed. Meanwhile, top management had demonstrated that it would honor its strategic and employee relations commitments, which increased its credibility with those who remained.

But the moral bottom line was dignity and fairness. Said Tinker: "It takes twelve months to find a new job. If you can look for a job while still employed, with your company car and health benefits, you keep your dignity. We owed them that." Tinker put his finger on a profound truth about business ethics, and that is that morality cannot be judged only in tangible products such as the allocation of dollars or number of jobs. In this case, the layoff would never feel good from a moral standpoint, but it was greatly alleviated by the process with which it was conducted. Chinn, who has already been mentioned in this book as a covenantal leader, is fond of quoting the Jewish maxim, "Whoever saves a single life, saves the world" (Mishna, *Sanhedrin* 4:5). By stretching the time frame, Lex opened the way to a closure which tried to preserve the individual dignity of its employees and create long-term value in the employee mix. A shorter chronology for decision making would have precluded this happy transformation of personal morality into business reality.

CONCLUSION

When the legitimate pressures for expediency and efficiency dominate your thinking and your communications to others, there is constant danger of becoming nearsighted in your business approach. And yet both the concept of integrity and the basic values of a covenantal business ethic are assumptions that demand an expanded time frame. What is integrity but the maintenance of ideal standards *over time?* It is a conservative concept, often used at funerals; an assessment not so much about decisions which might be made as about actions that have been. Such a world view can seem very unbusinesslike in comparison with the fast-paced, now-oriented demands made on most people.

A Covenantal Ethic also demands an interplay *over time* between value-creation for others and receipt of a return. It emphasizes long-term processes such as relationship-building, not specific products or financial targets. Such conditions and processes cannot always be fulfilled in a single decision. That this is so argues for capacity for foresight and an analytical ability to productively engage the lessons of hindsight.

Short-term viewpoints set up both analytical and psychological barriers to such analyses. If you are preoccupied with the short term, you fail to assess long-term negative consequences, causal factors in past successes and failures, and near-term process issues such as honesty or credibility. That is a perfect mental environment for an ethos of greed and underhanded business practices. On the personal level, short-term thinking, by suppressing the awareness of cause and effect, invites self-delusion, which is a primary ingredient in the corruption of good leadership values.

A perfect example of how short- and long-term business perspectives invite differences in business morality was the 1830s railway boom in Britain. In the first stage of investment, promoters, themselves with a long-term view of the overall capital requirements of building a railroad, sold shares to those with a long-term view who not only would benefit from the railroad, but would meet future calls for payment as work progressed. These were the chambers of commerce, the Quaker capitalists, and merchants and industrialists of the time. In the second stage of railway investment, however, professional company promoters looked for quick profits from the boom—and bilked a great many ladies and clergymen in the process.

Harvey Mackay, guru of sales negotiations and author of *Swim with the Sharks Without Being Eaten Alive,* points out that an experienced manager (and consumer) knows how to wait. Says Mackay, "Deals seldom get worse when you walk away from the table."[11] The same holds true for moral maturity. The leader who can entertain a vision of the long term may not be glitzy to the financial press but this person buys the time and takes on a commitment that allows full latitude in which to meet rather than compromise moral commitments. Many of the cases in this chapter present familiar dilemmas which can only be solved satisfactorily in a company that has had the strategic good sense to anticipate in advance the essentials of value-creation and good relationships with employees and the public. Bringing these dilemmas to an ethical and profitable solution often requires extending the time frame of the problem beyond the immediate short-term goal. Such extensions take mature leadership and personal risk. John F. Kennedy was fond of quoting FDR's observation on Abraham Lincoln, which is to the point here. Said FDR, "Lincoln was a sad man because he couldn't get it all at once. And nobody can."

Where Ethics and Expediency Are on the Line, Ask Yourself These Questions

What if I knew there would be a full audit of every decision I made two years from now?

What are the likely consequences of my decision one year down the road? Three years down the road?

How will this decision affect our customers' trust in us?

How would the decision look if it were repeated twenty times?

How many times have similar outcomes happened in the past? and why?

What if I had ten times as much time in which to make the decision? Would I recommend the same thing?

Have I actually *tried* to stretch the time frame in which to complete decision making or implementation?

---

[11] Harvey Mackay, *Swim with the Sharks Without Being Eaten Alive* (New York: Ivy Books, 1988), p. 07.

9

The Seductive Power of Ego Incentives

> The reasonable man adapts himself to the world; the unreasonable one persists in trying to adapt the world to himself.*

The problem of ego is an age-old one, especially for the leader. On the one hand, strong leadership requires self-confidence and the ability to think independently. On the other, too much self-reliance deludes the strong ego into disregarding reality and becoming insensitive to the needs and rights of others whom the leader intends to help or represent.

Such delusions have always been a leader's ticket to tragedy. Oedipus was overconfident about his own problem-solving abilities because he had solved the riddle of the Sphinx and been made king. When his city of Thebes was later visited with a plague, Oedipus vowed to search out the source of pollution, despite dire warnings from the local prophet not to proceed. Tragically, he discovered that he was not infallible. Despite his intellect and good intentions to save the city, he proved to be the source of the pollution. At the height of his trading activities, Ivan Boesky exhibited a similar overwhelming confidence in his own intellect, which the press and his associates inflated even further. As one close observer explained it, "What Ivan was saying was, 'See, everybody else

*George Bernard Shaw, *Man and Superman.*

did it too—except I did it a lot better than they did.' " Boesky, too, ended up being the plague of his particular fiefdom.

Such assertions of the self go by many names—pride, hubris, arrogance, overconfidence—but, to me, the term that best describes this phenomenon is "ego." Ego is that unscientific but real impulse that causes one to confront one's own viewpoint and desires with the unquestioning adulation a baseball star receives from a child. It is an unfortunate resolution of the classic leadership dilemma: to thine own self be true versus listen and learn.

Ego is an ever-present aspect of managerial life, as many managers recognize. Managers will create wildly irrational and economically wasteful cushions to preserve a court-like attendance on an executive's ego. One astute chairman told me that he never announced a plant visit beforehand, not out of a desire to trick people, but to prevent the facility managers from needlessly ordering $10,000 paint jobs!

Corporate cultures often deliberately play on people's ego in order to motivate them to work hard and be loyal. Complex status symbols and a sometimes Byzantine social hierarchy of small fiefdoms are created in order to exploit a manager's desire for autonomy.[1] As a person of responsibility, a manager is too important to bother with the "little things." For convenience and efficiency's sake, the manager on his (or her) way up becomes more and more isolated from the daily tasks and concerns of the rest of the world. He controls millions or billions of dollars, and his decisions can affect thousands of lives, but his environment is totally removed from the reality these people encounter. Someone else takes care of his coffee cup, negotiates traffic, spares him ever having to stand in a line, get his feet wet, or persuade an obstreperous delivery person to cooperate. Meanwhile, others in the corporation massage a manager's ego in many ways. Both the press and the corporate grapevine create a culture of personality around managers: their personal hobbies become important throughout the company, anecdotes circulate about trivial confronta-

---

[1]For a sobering, if perhaps exaggerated picture of the "courtlike" atmosphere of pyramidal hierarchies, see Robert Jackall, *Moral Mazes: The World of Corporate Managers* (New York: Oxford University Press, 1988).

tions or mistakes, membership in the same golf club becomes an indication of managerial value. A recent business journal, reporting on excessive perks and inflated egos at some of the best-known takeover firms, even mentioned that the favor of the top executive's family dog can become a treasured political plum among those in the know!

Public opinion also contributes to inflating the managerial ego. Gerhard Lenski, in his classic study of social stratification, pointed out that in advanced industrial societies, political class systems have largely been replaced by occupational class systems.[2] A CEO can be more "presidential" in the public's eye than the president himself. In both Sweden and the United States, for example, public opinion polls have revealed that the head of each nation's major automobile manufacturing company has been cited as well known or better known than the head of state. Ask a group of adolescents what business leaders are like and the answer comes readily: J.R. Ewing, that swashbuckling zillionnaire whose ego is bigger than the state whose accent he wears like a red bandanna.

Even in companies where a relatively egalitarian decision-making structure exists, managers can fall prey to creating ego traps for themselves and others through the construction of self-oriented incentive and reward systems. Extremely disparate material rewards between top and bottom are harnessed to the cause of creating a strong belief that self-aggrandizement is a noble and efficient path to securing company success. Although such an incentive system seems, on the surface, to be an efficient and effective motivator, it is harder to control and manage than it might first seem. The correlations between individual contribution and company performance in a complex organization are not easily determined with accuracy. Thus assessments of contribution are particularly vulnerable to hype and politicking, turning a business into "more boast than buck," as has been charged in the financial services industry. Nevertheless, in some corporations ego is the *only* game being played on the block. Manag-

---

[2]Gerhard E. Lenski, *Power and Privilege: A Theory of Social Stratification* (Chapel Hill: University of North Carolina Press, 1966).

ers simply do not employ other measures to motivate business success.

Given the staggering degree of ego-massaging and appeals to self-interest in most organizations, every manager, not just a CEO, is a potential victim of ego-gratifying incentives. Even executives who manage to draw on a complex set of other-oriented values in their own decision making often restrict their language and motivation of others to ego incentives. Want to get something done? Demonstrate to someone that it will be directly to his or her interests to cooperate.

EFFECT OF EGO ON ETHICAL DECISION MAKING

To the degree that managers think in terms of ego, they set up tremendous cognitive and emotional roadblocks to ethical decision making of the sort described by a Covenantal Ethic. Ego corrodes empathy; it prevents a manager from keeping the "feel" for others alive, that other-orientation which is at the heart of achieving business integrity and market success. When self-motivation and ingenuity cross the line to ego, they prevent a person from seeing other points of view, and therefore from gathering relevant facts and objectively assessing information.

During the Middle East oil crisis in 1973, journalist Robert Scheer observed that it was hard for the public to believe that the oil company executives really had the marketplace's needs in mind. After all, he noted, if an oil company CEO earned upward of $600,000, how could he *feel* the effects of the crisis?[3]

Such commonsense reality is hard to retain in the heady atmosphere of managerial responsibility and privilege. A manager can easily get an inflated attitude of personal worth, which others stimulate in order to reap similar rewards. Playing up to a manager or employee's appetite for self-aggrandizement creates a hierarchical power structure where individual worth is determined solely by wealth and status.

[3]Robert Scheer, *Thinking Tuna Fish, Talking Death: Essays on the Pornography of Power* (New York: Hill and Wang, 1988), p. 197.

Some call the resulting egotism the "clown prince syndrome," i.e., a manager begins to believe that the higher up he (or she) moves, the more important, smarter, and juster he must be. He comes to think that he "deserves" extra status, and confuses position with wisdom, obedience with good decision making and teamwork.

Meanwhile, subordinates manipulate their boss's access to information to conform to his (or her) expectations, thus furthering his confidence in his own judgment and belief in everyone's dependency on his good direction. Information is processed not in terms of what is being said but simply in terms of who said it. If the source is from above, it must be right.

The assertion of self and self-interest, which ego inevitably recommends and most corporate hierarchies and incentive systems tend to reinforce, is in direct opposition to the other-oriented, service-driven, value-creation ethic which has been argued to be the contract for good and prosperous management. Left unchecked, a self-centered orientation cultivates two ego-driven attitudes:

1. I (or the company) deserve everything I desire, and
2. I'm (or the company is) so wise that I am above the law and any other rules.

These attitudes leave one highly susceptible to inaccurate, hence unethical, judgments and complacent in the face of immoral acts of greed and exploitation. A simple example would be the widespread practice of entertaining friends on the company expense account without compunction.

Author Marshall Clinard, in a government-sponsored study of white-collar crime, reported that many people inside the corporation attribute unethical business conduct to ego-aggrandizing motives: "Middle management felt that violations were more likely to arise not from poor financial situations, but from the role of an aggressive 'go-go' type of top management, especially the CEO seeking to achieve power and prestige rapidly."[4] Another Justice Department executive

---

[4]Marshall Clinard, *Corporate Ethics and Crime: The Role of Middle Management* (Beverly Hills: Sage Publications, 1983), pp. 56, 145.

survey revealed that over half of those interviewed attributed corporate criminality to "personal ambition" or "greed" at the top. One need only look at the recent egotism on Wall Street and the insider trading scandals to appreciate the accuracy of this observation.

Even the manager who would never consider participating in an illegal act can nevertheless adopt predatory or deceitful traits, lulled by the assurance that ambitiousness—however destructive—is really for the good of the company. These are the executives most reminiscent of Michael Macoby's jungle fighters: the lions who regularly engage in intimidation, bombast, and lying, or the foxes who artfully flatter and grovel to manipulate in order to get ahead.[5]

Today's quick personnel turnover dramatically confirms and even accelerates the corrupting impact of ego by destroying opportunities for self-criticism and accountability. Fast-track promotions and very high salaries for junior stars, or frequent job changes of senior people, allow managers to "outrun their mistakes." They are never around long enough for their poor judgments and inadequacies to be fully detected and addressed. Not only are others fooled, they fool themselves, trusting overmuch in their own judgment.

The legal system tends to reinforce the delusion of infallibility. An individual engaged in corporate wrongdoing is neither as easily detected nor as likely to be punished as are other types of criminals. Fines and other punishments for corporate crimes are far less harsh than for street crimes. A drug addict who stole a bicycle in Central Park received a four-year prison sentence. A drug company whose managers covered up the fact that one of its products had resulted in four deaths and many illnesses paid a $25,000 fine and no individual was indicted for criminal charges. Until recently, the insider-trader who stole millions while his company laundered drug money received a slap on the wrist.

In an ego-driven environment a manager's capacity for retaining sensitivity and a respect for others is seriously undermined. Reinforced by a totally inequitable culture and compensation system, along with ego-massaging perks, a

---

[5]Michael Macoby, *The Gamesman* (New York: Simon & Schuster, 1976).

manager can mistake corporate hierarchy and financial position for good judgment and ethical conduct. When reality is this muddled, it can seem unremarkable to condone conflict-of-interest activities, cheating, cover-ups, mudslinging, bribery, gouging, price-fixing, exploitation of the little guy, and unsafe production processes, all of which stem from an inability to respect the other person's rights and needs.

FORMULATING AN ETHICAL RESPONSE TO EGO

When expressed as starkly as this, it is relatively easy for most people to resist the forces that overstimulate ego, but in the real world the process is obviously much more subtle and the dilemmas of ethical leadership less easily tested for an inappropriate ego bias. Ego distortion of ethical sensitivity and rationally sound judgment has far-reaching effects on the way managers define and pursue their basic goals, the way in which they gather, assimilate, and report information, and the way in which they handle relationships inside and outside a company. The following cases illustrate many facets of this process. The questions help keep ego in perspective and provoke a covenantal outlook.

BREAKING THROUGH THE EGO BARRIER

Problem 1. Determining Appropriate Sales Incentives

Even if a manager is careful to keep his or her own ego in perspective, he or she can be instrumental in corrupting another business person through use of ego-massaging incentives. In certain functional areas, the subversion of other managers' judgment by appealing to ego is a normal part of doing business. Sales incentives for corporate purchasers is a perfect example. In the travel industry, to pick a typical case, it is standard practice to make a pitch for business by offering gifts and incentives. With the rules of gift-giving ambiguous, it is easy to feel no qualm about enticing high-volume purchasers of travel services to do business with a particular hotel or agency by playing to their ego. That's the way it's done. Fur coats, free airline tickets, free "familiarization trips," and so on are offered to the purchasing agent in return for his or her corporate business. Of course, such reciprocity is only implied—otherwise the incentive would fall in the area of bribery, which is illegal.

But are such legal incentives ethical? First rule of customer service, make the customer feel important, right? Not from a covenantal viewpoint. Because value is not being provided to the *real* buyer whose interests the purchaser represents, these companies are deliberately clouding a purchaser's judgment, and normal rules of paying for what you get are suspended.

Such incentives deliberately set up a conflict-of-interest situation that depends on a lie for its rationalization and ego for its execution. It is self-deceptive for a purchaser to think that his or her terrific free experience is an accurate indicator of what other paying guests will receive. Such incentives subtly cultivate a sense of entitlement, which can bring about an equally subtle corruption of a manager's attitude toward the use of company funds and time. He or she will begin to feel no qualm about channeling them to personal use.

Despite the obvious problems in the above example, setting the appropriate level of personal incentive in sales is still a difficult decision. What is appropriate is in part culturally rooted. What is more, many of the practices that play on a purchaser's ego are not illegal and are acceptable marketing tactics industrywide. Technically a sales manager can argue that such gifts are not bribes because there are no rules against them and no one signs a noncompetitive agreement in advance. We might then hang ourselves up on the ethics of a specific corporate incentive policy by arguing over the exact wording of gift-giving rules. But such a discussion usually ends up in the gray area of moral doubt, which leads to the recommendation to change nothing and go along with industry practice.

What is my intention?

One way to get back to an other-servicing, honest sales approach is to question your intent. Questioning intent punctures the moral complacency of the manager who stays within the letter of the law but not its spirit. Say you are considering running an advertisement in which a model holds a fur coat in each hand and suggests the reader book his or her next corporate conference at your hotel in order to receive this volume bonus. You think your hotel offers sound value, and such incentives are a normal part of the industry ethic, so what's the ethical hang-up? Ask the simple question, What is the intent of the ad? Clearly the intention is to entice the purchaser to make a choice based on an egotistical sense of entitlement and his or her own personal interest (rather than the company's).

In the 1950s, when the Oklahoma legislature was considering a resolution to discontinue the prohibition of alcohol, two groups held an all-night vigil on the steps of the statehouse: the preachers and the bootleggers. Same actions, very different intentions. Were their ethics the same? Hardly.

Problem 2. Processing Uncertain Information

Former Raytheon chairman Thomas Phillips, under whose leadership the company prospered without scandal in the scandal-ridden defense industry, remarked that he felt the most destructive aspect of a top management role was ego. He cited the strategic assessment of a potential merger or acquisition as a typical example.

Phillips personally found that even for a well-intentioned manager, the merger game can quickly become an exercise in ego gratification rather than an objective consideration of sound financial strategy. A CEO discusses a potential acquisition that looks good on paper. The board of directors, on behalf of the shareholders, is pleased at the idea of a bigger company and the concomitant boost to their own prestige. The CEO, formerly unknown, suddenly receives front-page attention in the financial press because of the gains in power and size which the acquisition would represent. Everyone on the acquiring end is gangbusters over the idea and certain that the certain increase in prestige holds an equally certain promise of value-creation.

But as Phillips points out, at the initial stage of merger

discussions no one really understands the financials. In many cases what looks like a good fit turns out to be less attractive once the books are carefully scrutinized. When this is so, says Phillips, it is the hardest thing in the world for a CEO's ego to go back to the board and the public with a recommendation not to proceed. One need only look at the RJR-Nabisco or Campeau-Federated negotiations to see the truth of his observation. These takeovers, with their dizzying numbers and strong personalities, became national exercises in ego assertion. Meanwhile the fiduciary issues were glossed over as the major players assumed a glitzy air of self-confidence.

Ego transforms the reality of not being omniscient into a personally deflating admission of failure, a sign of weakness. For those who succumb to the delusion, the prospect of strategic failure and the widespread perpetration of excuses and cover-ups when the effects of poor decision making begin to surface is as probable as the sound of thunder after lightning. Instead of plain talk, the manager develops an etiquette of euphemisms. Convicted Singer Company chairman Paul Bilzerian's language was not unusual when he publicly asserted that his statements to the SEC were "less than candid." Such face-saving goes on all the time and proves to be a powerful tool for blunting personal conscience.

Embarrassment reinforces these attacks on a manager's ability to process and communicate information accurately. If your company persona is one of invulnerability and omniscience, it is degrading to admit failure, and embarrassing, or downright suicidal, for others to inform you of your mistakes. Lower level managers, especially loyal ones, will contribute to the playacting by covering up bad news or doubts about a safety issue rather than imply that a mistake has been made.[6]

Have I invited and tolerated dissent?

Covenantal thinkers like Tom Phillips deliberately work at offsetting the seductive power of ego by developing

---

[6]Professor Robert Payton, former head of Exxon Education Foundation, reminds me that the etymological origin of the word *hypocrisy* is "playacting." See John MacMurray, *Persons in Relation* (New York: Faber and Faber, 1961), p. 172.

the emotional capacity to listen and respect others. One way is to cultivate a deep sense of humility and recognize the potential for fallibility. To be effective, such a capacity must go beyond attitude to actions. Or, as the legendary head of Boeing, William Allen, once said, "Be just, straightforward; invite criticism and learn to take it."[7] The above question provides the well-intentioned manager with a concrete litmus test for one's critical abilities.

Have I rubbed elbows with subordinates?

Another way of keeping your own views in perspective is to set up an egalitarian office environment. One of my favorite examples comes from Mitchell Kapor, famed founder of Lotus Development and current CEO of ONTechnologies, Inc. Kapor recently started a new firm and proudly announced that it was about to hire its first woman engineer. I asked him if he anticipated any problems in the all-male group. "Nope," he said, "as long as she plays ping pong, we'll all get along at the table."

Kapor's ping-pong management style seems flippant until one reads of the ritual beer busts at Tandem Computer or Hewlett-Packard's kaffeeklatsch tradition in its work areas. If there are no ego barriers, information flows, ideas percolate, and criticism becomes natural rather than personally threatening. Providing value in the marketplace, personal self-respect, and the ability to market honestly are some of the more desirable performance and ethical results.

In short, to foster the leadership attitudes that invite constructive self-reliance, the covenantal manager has to avoid total self-reliance and its attendant ego dangers. Inviting dissent and sharing experiences, elbow to elbow, with so-called subordinates prevent a leader from developing an over-inflated view of his or her opinions and worth.

Lincoln Electric's sensational performance over the past forty years was achieved through its egalitarian approach to industrial management. Lincoln's thoughts on this topic are a moving example of empathetic management reasoning:

---

[7]Kirk O. Hanson and Manuel Velasquez, "The Boeing Company: Managing Ethics and Values," in *Corporate Ethics: A Prime Business Asset* (New York: The Business Roundtable, 1988).

If those crying loudest about the inefficiencies of labor were put in the position of the wage earner, they would react as he does. The worker is not a man apart. He has the same needs, aspirations and reactions as the industrialist.[8]

Problem 3. Failure to Face Up to Potentially Damaging Information

Ego can not only falsely color one's assessment of objectives, it can also exaggerate the impulse to dismiss other people's advice if it contradicts your way of doing things. The impulse to gloss over one's own ignorance is strong when one operates in a public context. Take, for example, the Beech-Nut senior executives who received a memo from the director of research indicating some doubts about the purity of their supplier's apple juice concentrate. They took no action, dismissing the report and others which followed as inconclusive. When Beech-Nut staffers visited the supplier's plant and were denied access to the processing facility, no follow-up visits were initiated. According to later reports in court, the top managers' attitude was both aloof and "I know better." They told the head of research that even though it could not be proven that the concentrate was pure, they would not think of changing suppliers until research had conclusively proved it was impure (an impossible task at that time). *BusinessWeek* later called their response one of "rationalization, self-delusion and denial."[9] All these emotions are sustained by the self-orientation of ego.

What have I omitted from my analysis?

As Ben Franklin once said, "Half the truth is often a great lie." Whenever you find yourself trotting out the old rationalization that no one can prove it, that's a good time to stop and take a second look. Are there contradictory facts you

---

[8]"How Lincoln Motivated Men," *Civil Engineering—ASCE* (January 1973).
[9]Chris Welles, "What Led Beech-Nut Down the Road to Disgrace," *BusinessWeek*, February 22, 1988, pp. 124–128; see also, James Traub, "Into the Mouths of Babes," *The New York Times Magazine*, July 24, 1988, pp. 18–53.

may have omitted from your assessment for convenience sake, or to bolster your own position? Oftentimes your ego is clinging to the comforting delusion that because you have not *deliberately* fabricated something, you're being honest and upright. But failing to ask questions about what you don't know is just as irresponsible and misguided as a deliberate fabrication.

I used to hear managers defend their own occasional insider-trading activities with the argument that nobody gets hurt. But their own secrecy in the matter should have given them a clear signal that there were important ethical issues and facts that they had omitted from their argument in an over-keen consideration of their own interests.

What if I get caught?

Another, slightly inelegant but extremely effective, way of prompting a second look at potentially contradictory omissions is to imagine yourself the subject of an outside investigation. Sunshine is well known to be the greatest disinfectant. An outside investigation would most certainly bring to light those uncomfortable facts you might be glossing over. Had Beech-Nut's senior executives been able to imagine the kind of public inquiry and censure that later occurred, they might have been less blind to their own analytical biases.

A mature sense of ethical responsibility does not guarantee moral perfection. Business activities are often complex and frequently their consequences can only be expressed in probabilities rather than certainties. It is very difficult to determine "the truth" in such activities as reckoning the value of a nonessential product and determining the safety of a previously untested operation, or the potential injury embedded in a complex manufacturing process. But despite the elusiveness of conclusive information, it is imperative to *acknowledge* mistakes and uncertainty rather than sweep them aside as being trivial. The ancient Greeks had a proverb, "Learn through suffering." It was the self-enlightenment which came from suffering that transformed tragic heroes from sad misfortunates to heroic figures. Scrutinizing errors and imperfections in a previous analysis provides insight into what is both responsible and questionable about your own integrity and your business effectiveness as well.

Problem 4. Dealing with Hostile Criticism

One day I was visiting a defense industry company. The gossip of the day concerned the fact that the chairman's wife was participating in an antinuclear demonstration in town. The reaction ranged from humor to resentment. How could she embarrass him this way?

It is very difficult for anyone's ego, including an executive's, to be buffeted by public ridicule when one's private life turns out to be less than perfect. It is even harder to tolerate being publicly described as a social menace. Whether the issue is weapons, pollution, marketing to the third world, or producing a product with debatable health benefits, there will be decisions of corporate leadership that not everyone will find acceptable. And not all outside critics of corporate policy play fair; some distort the facts and play on antibusiness sentiments for political reasons.

Formulating an ethical response to this chaotic environment is one of the hardest tasks a manager faces. Ego can be one of the chief obstacles to the responsible fulfillment of this task.

A public interest group accuses you of personally orchestrating the pollution of a nearby river. A staunch nature lover, you resent the implications of the charge. It would be tempting to brush the problem under the table, giving it as little attention as possible, secure in the knowledge that you personally are on nature's side and that the scientific evidence concerning the source of pollution will be indecisive in the foreseeable future.

Have I listened to other opinions? Can I tolerate hearing them directly, or only filtered through company communication channels?

When ego prevents you from facing up to critical opinions directly, chances are you're ignorant of important aspects of the problem. That there will often be no definitive, objective determination of right and wrong is a reality which every manager has to accept. One of the best ways to get closer to the truth, however, is to invite as many informed opinions as possible. The full impact of these views cannot be determined if they are sanitized by the corporate communications networks to meet a manager's ego needs.

Every company and every manager needs a moral equivalent of a Monday morning quarterback against which to bounce off decisions. Willingness to expose one's ideas to personal and external scrutiny is one of the vital principles of a sound and moral social system.

Furthermore, if you take service to others as the first point of reference, as a Covenantal Ethic recommends, it is far easier to tolerate the full scrutiny of complex issues involving multiple stakeholders. For example, when former Knight-Ridder chairman Alvah Chapman invested company funds in a lobbying effort against the introduction of casino gambling in Florida, he did not refuse to meet with a delegation of *Miami Herald* reporters who felt that the practice was wrong for a supposedly impartial newspaper. Chapman told them, "My job is to stand by what I think is right for this company and the community. I think it can be demonstrated that casino gambling will be bad for local business and is morally questionable from a social standpoint. Your job is to report on these issues fully, including disclosure of the funds Knight-Ridder has allocated for this issue."

Chapman's ethic of personal risk for the sake of truth has been shared by Knight-Ridder's new vice chairman and former *Miami Herald* publisher Richard Capen. In summing up Capen's contribution to the *Herald*, investigations editor Jim Savage wrote: "He has never interfered with any story, even when they involved his personal friends and the interests of Knight-Ridder. He has always been totally committed to honest journalism."[10] Such risks not only require personal courage, they require backing up that courage with a record of good judgment and chasing after the facts. They cannot be undertaken by someone who is taken in by the personality cult which many companies construct around top managers and which isolates them from dissenting opinions.

[10]Quoted in *The Miami Herald*, August 6, 1989.

Problem 5. Keeping Skunkworks Ethical

Peters and Waterman made "skunkworks" a household term for many managers. In their book, *In Search of Excellence*, they advocated creating pockets of cash as a quick resource for innovative efforts that would otherwise be stymied by a company's budgeting process. Such off-book or disguised expenditures were, of course, intended to be put only to the best of uses: the advancement of the best interests of the company.

In reality, however, the best interests of the company are rarely clear-cut. On the one hand, it seems right to create a mechanism that is more efficient, especially if it is directed toward innovative, value-creating purposes. On the other hand, the results of these efficiency measures are not guaranteed to create value. When things do not work out according to plan, the lack of external accountability, an inherent part of a skunkworks operation, can encourage a manager to gloss over mistaken decisions which may have occurred along the way. Ego will push him or her over the fine line between creative secrecy and unethical refusal to be accountable to others.

In her analysis of secrecy, Sissela Bok suggests that at the heart of most conflicts concerning secrecy there is an issue of power:

> Conflicts over secrecy . . . are conflicts over power: the power that comes through controlling the flow of information. To be able to hold back some information about oneself or to channel it and thus influence how one is seen by others gives power.[11]

The power of a skunkworks or other covert operation is obvious. No doubt the frustrations and inefficiencies of large corporate bureaucracies systematically undercut a manager's ability to get the job done. A secret effort can give a team the time and money to take risks and see innovative ideas through to completion. But ego can trick a manager into mistaking

[11]Sissela Bok, *Secrets: On the Ethics of Concealment and Revelation* (New York: Vintage Books, 1984), p. 19.

occasions of unjustifiable secretiveness for noble pragmatism. The following comment of a divisional president is a telling example of how personal ego and corporate size provide managers with a convenient excuse for intentional distortions and cover-ups of important information under the guise of noble skunkworks:

> Once we were acquired, we were told to put in a corporate controller. Well, that's going to slow us down. He'll want to fish around, we'll have to waste time getting out records. I know there's nothing wrong with our books, but I don't want to waste the time with some bloke who doesn't know what he's doing. So I'll just stall that one for about a year while I take care of the customers.
>
> The whole thing is, when you get bigger there are lots of advantages, but trust is not one of them. When I say something, I can't be sure it's necessarily true—corporate may have other ideas. So there's a lot of things I don't volunteer to my employees or corporate.
>
> I've become a lot more closed about certain ways I believe we should be doing the business. When I know corporate is going to slow me down, I just find a corner to get it done quietly and well. I still feel I'm an ethical person, but I can't afford to speak up, can I?

This manager's "I-know-better" attitude feeds a cover-up of information which could be illegal but is certainly a disincentive to the free exchange of ideas in his company. It also prevents accurate planning and assessment. As such, the ethics are obviously doubtful from the point of view of business integrity, *and yet the manager feels his behavior is above moral reproach.* In fact, he is rationalizing his own refusal to cooperate because he is unwilling to give up power, as he would certainly have to do if he established an independent auditor or went to his superiors for funding of risky projects.

Ego is the cancer gnawing at his better judgment, and no doubt it has been reinforced at every step along his meteoric rise in the company. Combine a self-regarding manager with an ego-rewarding incentive system, and one risks large-scale distortions of the truth in order to get the job done quickly. Skunkworks and other sabotages of normal reporting channels create a tightrope which few managers can walk ethically without strong supporting intellectual paraphernalia. Two very good questions for testing one's justification of secrecy are,

Did I address the facts? Precisely what value am I creating?

The ethical manager must always keep a close watch on when innovation, risk-taking, and cover-ups cross the line and result in potentially injurious or simply bad business decisions. Conducting meticulous fact checks on every assumption one makes in a skunkworks-type operation is a good way of preventing yourself or discouraging others from crossing that line. No one else will be able to check the facts, so it is your responsibility to do so. If efficiency and value-creation are being claimed, then both ought to be demonstrable. If safety is a factor, then it needs objective verification.

Everyone's judgment is fallible. How many companies have devised meticulous measurement mechanisms for product defects or pollution only to discover that someone deliberately failed to report the results of those procedures? Perhaps an individual somewhere along the line simply decided that the numbers were not significant and a report would only slow the organization down. Usually such judgments result from a manager's overconfidence in his or her own technical skill and opinion.

Another way to get a moral sounding on skunkworks and other cover-ups is to ask,

At whose expense am I creating value?

Needless to say, if the skunkworks has to obtain resources by hurting another part of the organization, then you're not being ethical, just greedy. If an investigation into your maneuvering around the reporting channels will ultimately lead to financial penalties and a decrease in shareholder return, then you are clearly putting your own aggrandizement over the company's and are breaking your contract with the company and the public.

Problem 6. Communicating Unpleasant Information Upward

Not all ethical problems are a result of trying to protect or inflate one's own ego. Many instances of unethical decision making arise from trying to protect the *boss's ego*. The corrupting power of hierarchical ego considerations was brought home to me in a dramatic way during one of my management seminars on ethics. One participant, call him John, had suggested that safety was his number one ethical issue at work. He was concerned that new cost constraints and disaffected workers would increase the probability of carelessness and neglect in the operations for which he was responsible.

His presentation sparked tremendous controversy among the group, roughly divided between staff people and operations managers. Out of the discussion there emerged a detailed assessment of the important trade-offs that were being made and that possibly compromised safety. It was a frank discussion of how a tougher competitive environment was affecting individual managers' sense of power to carry out their responsibility in the safety area and their honesty in reporting problems. Some of their observations about the industry were confirmed a month later when a competitor experienced a major accident in which ten people were killed. The incident was a direct result of poor safety compliance.

At the end of the session another manager approached John with an air of confidential chumminess and politely warned him that he'd better erase his presentation from the front board. "You know," he said, "the boss has declared safety our number one issue—he wants us to be known as the safest company in the industry—and he'd have a fit if he saw that list!"

Every company risks encouraging such deceptions. Many of the failures of conscience and communication are based on the fear of damaging the boss's ego. As Delbert Staley, former chairman of NYNEX told me, "Some people think they have to cover up bad news. That's the *last* thing I want. I can't make any decision unless I can trust the information I'm getting."

But how does the ethical manager bring bad news to a boss or peer in an ego-oriented, hierarchical organization? Often the problem is less fearful than one assumes and a straightforward and extremely open declaration of *facts* rather than opinion will prevent the message from triggering an ego attack.

Have I articulated factual information in as objective and impartial a way as possible?

A clearly presented and impartial statement of facts reopens channels of communication and prompts someone higher up to take a second look at the problem. In many companies, top managers express a strong commitment to ethical conduct but are convinced that their subordinates do not have the same commitment. Meanwhile, people lower down in the organization bemoan the fact that they'd like to be ethical but the boss wants things otherwise. Middle managers feel literally stuck in the middle: unsure of the signals from the top and unsure of how ethically their own policies will be carried out further down. In most cases, the problem is not with people's morality but with the communication process. Clarifying expectations and probable results through straightforward disclosure of the facts is an effective way of reestablishing stricter standards in everyone's mind.

The same technique is a particularly powerful tool in those instances where ethics are in danger of falling victim to someone else's inflated ego. Someone higher up in your organization seems to be condoning or demanding unethical practices. Accusing him or her of being a liar or cheat will only make matters worse for you and will not solve the problem. A straightforward statement of the problem can be a tool for dealing with the situation more effectively.

Your boss suggests you charge your time or a purchase to another account for efficiency's sake. He (or she) tells you, "Don't worry, I'll take responsibility." You know better. It's your signature and you are responsible. A simple voicing of the facts, sometimes two or three times over a two-day period, can be an effective way of increasing everyone's ethical awareness. "Let me get this straight; you want me to charge this work on contract A to contract B?" Such a question has a way of stimulating second thoughts and objective judgment which one hopes for in the first place without putting anyone else's ego on the line. It gives the other person a chance to back down without losing face.

Problem 7. Rewarding the Technically Effective but Egotistical Team-Destroyer

The owner of an up-and-coming information systems company told me about one of his senior managers, named Ralph. Ralph was an extremely creative fellow in his early thirties who had been with the company for two years. On several occasions Ralph had found an engineering solution for a client when no one else in the company could solve the problem.

Ralph knew he was good, expected top dollar for his competency, and often had expansive ideas about how to grow the company quickly. He was very materialistic and frank in admitting that money was the only thing that drove him to work. While his boss had qualms about that attitude, his only real complaint was that Ralph was extremely impatient and rude with other employees. Ralph made it very obvious that he thought he was smarter than everyone else. Not only did he point out other's mistakes, he was smug. His lack of team spirit bothered the owner. When confronted with these observations, Ralph shrugged them off, telling the boss that he never had trouble with people who did their job well, and that he simply didn't like incompetency. "After all," said Ralph, "if someone isn't pulling their weight, that takes away from *my* bottom line ultimately, and I don't think that's fair."

Other employees were less sanguine, although they hesitated to make their views known to higher ups for fear of provoking a counterattack from Ralph. They felt that Ralph frequently took sole credit for jointly developed ideas and wrote out his personal assessment reports with too sharp a pencil, leaving out the long-term problems he was ignoring.

If they were on a project with Ralph, they tended to hold back ideas or cooperate only to the degree necessary to avoid making waves. What Ralph saw as incompetence was at least partially attributable to his ego-oriented management style. He did not respect other people simply as individuals, but only in terms of the qualities they had that could help *him*. This egotism was partially disguised by his gung-ho pursuit of "the good of the company," a quality that the owner noticed, admired, and rewarded.

Are my decisions or behavior having a negative impact on the relationships involved?

One of Ralph's chief drawbacks as a manager and as an ethical person is an inability to see problems in terms of anything except efficiency. By measuring performance (his own and other people's) only in terms of tasks completed and revenues taken in, he is not aware of his own destructiveness. His ego reinforces this outlook because on his terms, he always comes out on top.

One way to help a Ralph break through his (or her) own ego bias would be to provoke a more relationship-oriented approach to the assessment of business problems. The question above puts this neglected aspect of business and covenantal responsibility back on the table.

By Ralph's own admission the company stands for nothing more than power and a paycheck. To him, the company is not an organization of people nor even an entity for creating something of value. It is a means to his own self-aggrandizement, and to the degree that it so contributes, he remains loyal to it. With an ego-calculus driving his work life, he seldom cultivates relationship-building skills. It is very unlikely that Ralph would help another employee during a personal crisis or create the kind of team loyalty that sustains everyone's hard work and cooperation in a competitive environment. Meanwhile he is demoralizing and disabling others.

By assessing himself only in terms of tasks completed and paycheck, however, he fails to be aware of these other responsibilities of management. Ralph is an extreme, and the mere voicing of the question I have posed would probably give him little pause. But every manager is susceptible to some degree to thinking, like Ralph, in exaggerated terms of tasks completed and personal rewards. Testing for one's contribution to or disablement of a relationship excites a fuller sense of responsibility to others.

Am I rewarding ego-dominant, relationship-destroying attitudes in others?

It is particularly important to test not only your own relationship-building skills, but how well you motivate these qualities *in others* through reward systems. To create an ethical business climate, every manager is responsible for not becoming a Ralph, and seeing that Ralph-like behavior is not rewarded. The incentive system in this company, and many others, was biased toward rewarding the Ralphs as long as they produced concrete results. Business is about productivity, and as Charles Kelly points out in his book *The Destructive Achiever*, the egotistical manager is often very effective in gettings things done. You may not *like* a Ralph's way of dealing with other people, but if he isn't breaking the law and is getting things done, how can you justify penalizing him? Besides, he is very convincing about his desire to advance the company's interests. Strong leadership requires strong character, so that the abrasive or abusive sides of such a manager's personality may seem distasteful but an inevitable price to pay for his or her effectiveness.

Many of the qualities that build or impede ethical business performance cannot be cast into traditional performance measurements such as revenue increase or cost reduction. The ethical manager has a responsibility for seeing that the less quantifiable, relationship-enabling characteristics of a manager, such as "ability to cooperate" or "success at empowering other people," are taken into consideration in hiring, training, and assessing subordinates. This is one of the most difficult and important responsibilities of a well-intentioned manager, for as long as an incentive system encourages relationship-destroying behavior, it will never motivate ethical conduct and good business decisions among employees.

Once one thinks of performance in relationship-enabling terms, it is easier to justify not rewarding Ralph's egotistical management approach. His way of solving problems is not just a matter of style, it is a fundamental statement about the values he brings to a problem. Some of these, such as pragmatism, are consistent with a business concerned with service and value-creation, but many others are not. Ralph is not really concerned with long-term business health; he has merely been smart enough to find a way of making a quick return for the company in a growth industry. One would have to question how well his value system would sustain his innovativeness and effectiveness if the company were to hit bad times or tougher competition and could not promise him as high an immediate reward. What will stimulate his effectiveness ten years down the road, when the personal rewards of his extreme materialism begin to hit their limit?

Given his inability to question himself and his scorn of others, it is quite likely that when his first few rounds of creative ideas die out, Ralph will begin to blame the customer or colleagues for lost sales or service complaints. Should he be told of a potential problem in one of his products, it is likely that he will not regard these reports as significant unless they are 100 percent provable. Ralph is incapable of creating enabling relationships with others because he cannot see the worth of other individuals. Without this ability, he will never be a good leader.

Although Ralph's boss had great qualms about Ralph's undermining the traditional reward system at his company, he eventually told him he would have to rethink his management approach or he would never be made a partner in the firm.

CONCLUSION

Ego blinders go up every day in a thousand subtle ways for most people, and especially for the business leader whose strength of character is his or her first resource for problem solving. Any occasion on which one's way of doing business or one's ego gratification dominates thinking is ultimately a moral failure to fulfill the fiduciary trust which a manager assumes. These occasions can quickly become face-saving exercises in dishonesty and bombast as well.

A Covenantal Ethic is inherently oriented away from ego and toward the service of others, but even the covenantal manager can easily become sidetracked by ego. When the Covenantal Ethic works, its legitimate rewards can carry their own danger of misleading a manager into feeling justified in trusting overmuch in his or her own viewpoint.

Many of the most common incentive systems, ways of communicating objectives, and hierarchies of position only increase the ego factor at work. To stimulate a second look at the potentially unethical fallout of failing to move beyond one's ego, one can draw on any of the questions suggested in this chapter. Though they will not address every dynamic of the problems described, they will provide quick and workable ways for mentally breaking through the ego barrier by

- introducing a stronger note of objectivity
- focusing on value-creation rather than greed
- inviting dissenting opinions to correct for a self-interest bias
- developing relationship reasoning and skills.

Because ego is much less an analytical phenomenon than short-term thinking or bottom-line bondage, it may seem simplistic to suggest that a list of questions will be effective in countering so basic a character trait. But for most people, ego is a *dilemma* of leadership, not an unambiguous corrupter, and the questions suggested here help introduce a more balanced view of one's place in the universe of managerial responsibilities. Often the mere voicing of an issue provides one with the stronger power of character needed to put on the moral brakes.

None of these moral sonar devices, however, is fail-proof. Ethical managers who have not fallen prey to ego have a realistic sense that they are not omnipotent, despite indications to the contrary from the corporate culture. But they also have the self-confidence to know that they can survive mistakes—some of them moral—learn, and move on. One last question, then, to disarm the potential pomposity and blindness of ego:

Have I laughed at myself recently?

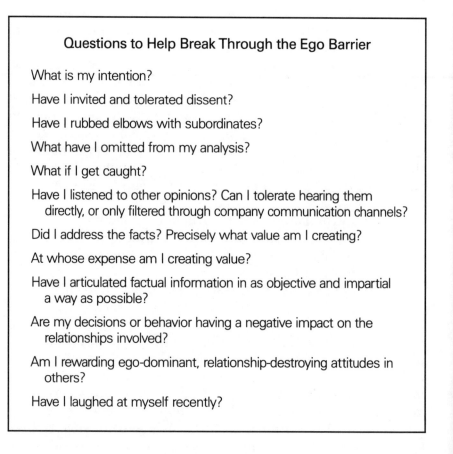

Questions to Help Break Through the Ego Barrier

What is my intention?

Have I invited and tolerated dissent?

Have I rubbed elbows with subordinates?

What have I omitted from my analysis?

What if I get caught?

Have I listened to other opinions? Can I tolerate hearing them directly, or only filtered through company communication channels?

Did I address the facts? Precisely what value am I creating?

At whose expense am I creating value?

Have I articulated factual information in as objective and impartial a way as possible?

Are my decisions or behavior having a negative impact on the relationships involved?

Am I rewarding ego-dominant, relationship-destroying attitudes in others?

Have I laughed at myself recently?

10

Wearing Two Hats: When Private Conscience and Corporate Viewpoint Conflict

> I always seem to be wearing two hats: my private hat and my corporate hat. On questions of conscience, they often tell me to do two very different things.*

In *The Lonely Crowd*, David Riesman argued that American society was changing from being one in which men operated from an inner-directed orientation on private feelings and sentiments, to an other-directed society in which the feelings of others and their perceived expectations motivated individuals. In *The Fall of Public Man*, Richard Sennett turned Riesman's argument around by suggesting that the cultivation of a public persona was rapidly becoming a thing of the past, at great cost to an individual's capacity for intimacy and other social activities. Despite their different theories, both scholars were addressing a fundamental problem of modern social experience, namely the discrepancy between one's private self and the person you become as part of a larger organization.

To cope with the fragmented social experiences

*Remark of a senior executive at the Harvard Business School, Advanced Management Program.

which an individual encounters, he or she normally cultivates multiple personas, each with its own reference point and values. The relative strength of any one persona, or role, is in constant flux. It is not remarkable to be at the same time a family person, a skilled technician, a company ambassador, a loyal citizen, a participant of a religious sect, and a supporter of a public interest group.

Because these roles do not necessarily carry identical values, their very multiplicity raises ethical difficulties for an individual. The fragmentation of the self, an inevitable aspect of modern life, can frequently present a person with conflicting moral impulses, as the executive quoted above so rightly noted. To cite an extreme but recurring example in history, one may as an individual believe that it is wrong to kill, but as a member of a religious cult feel it is right to murder a dissenting member.

A manager continually faces internal conflicts between what he or she would do as a loyal representative of the company and what a private individual, friend, consumer, or citizen would think is right. To paraphrase the old joke about an ambassador (one who lies abroad for his country), an executive is one who lies abroad for his company. Keeping the conflicts between one's noncorporate perspective and one's managerial obligations in a state of balance, or even integration, is one of the most difficult responsibilities of the ethical executive.

A friend and subordinate comes to you confidentially to ask for advice. She has just been offered a job with another company and wants to know what you think she should do. You know that your own unit has just been given a three-month lease on life. Improve performance or headquarters pulls the plug. Your friend's input on this project is crucial; you cannot afford to lose her now. But if you tell her the facts, i.e., there is a good chance that her job will be obsolete in three months, you will probably lose her. Even if she stays, the information may leak out and demoralize the rest of the team. Do you tell your friend the facts of the matter, which obviously pertain to her dilemma, or not?

One could play out this scenario in many ways. The employee could be testing you to get a readout on her own status. Her ability to keep secrets may be impeccable, thus lowering the risk of demoralizing the rest of the team. If you tell her the truth, she may so respect your honesty that she will decide to take the risk and stay in order to work with such an upright boss. If you conceal the information, you may be weakening the company down the road by contributing to a culture of deception in employee relations, which will surely catch up with you sooner or later. However destructive or beneficial one imagines the effects of concealing or revealing the facts, the heart of this issue remains the same: as a friend who is concerned for a friend's welfare, and a manager who is concerned for the corporate welfare, and an individual separate from both, how does one be honest? Do your two or three hats tell you the same thing, or not? If different, which is right?

Some managers would argue that the conflict described above is bogus, that the dictates of private conscience are always more ethical than the instrumental considerations of the corporate welfare. Others would argue that you owe the corporation your secrecy, no qualms about it. An employee shouldn't expect you to do anything against the company's obvious interests. But for most people, such choices are ambiguous and painful. Dealing with real people as a representative of an abstract entity or power structure raises an inevitable sense of dilemma, which often hinges on the conflict between one's private and corporate persona.[1]

Every would-be manager of integrity needs to address the issue of corporate persona and the factors that make it so powerful, for as a loyal manager one continually defers to this persona in order to promote the company's needs. One of the chief ways in which the company viewpoint is established and made powerful is through the creation of a strong corporate identity. Call it image, reputation, or simply culture, corporate identity can exert a tremendous influence on a manager's perspective and sense of purpose. "The Widget way of doing things" is a phrase that has real meaning to a Widget employee. Not tarnishing the Widget name is a goal which every Widget manager understands as important.

---

[1] A covenantal solution to this case is suggested at the conclusion of this chapter.

The obligation to protect and promote the *image* of a corporation is particularly relevant to the moral dilemma of wearing two hats in business. In one survey of over two hundred mid-level executives at three companies, I found that "creating a good company image" was the most frequently cited perceived corporate expectation after "making money." *Interviewees viewed the morality of this goal with great ambiguity.* On the one hand, managers were well aware of how consideration of the corporate image could wrongly encourage a "sweep-it-under-the-carpet, get-it-done-but-don't-let-me-hear-about-it" climate. On the other hand, these same cynics were keenly sensitive about any outside criticism of their own company's standards of conduct. Their desire to be loyal to the firm and to put its best face forward in public was both reasonable and well intentioned. Not airing dirty linen in public is a sentiment widely shared by the members of any organization, and is not necessarily intended to excuse unethical behavior. That considerations of image can provoke unethical behavior, however, was also widely recognized.

As the ambiguity described above indicates, protection of the company image and deference to the company viewpoint is not bad per se. A well-known corporate name carries a cachet. While it is hard to quantify, there is unmistakable goodwill and competitive advantage in a good brand name or company image, which can be a plus in many ways, from product recognition to recruiting. Conversely, the company caught in a public scandal knows how irrationally punitive people can be toward anyone or anything connected to a tarnished company name.

Internally, strong image and identity can be a powerful organizational motivator. Philip Selznick pointed out that the identification of self with organization, which a strong corporate identity provokes, has a powerful motivating effect on individual employees:

> Whenever individuals become attached to an organization or a way of doing things as persons rather than as technicians, the result is a prizing of the device for its own sake. From the standpoint of the committed person, the organization is changed from

an expendable tool into a valued source of personal satisfaction.[2]

EFFECT OF CORPORATE IMAGE ON ETHICAL DECISION MAKING

The motivational power of corporate image closely resembles charismatic leadership on an institutional scale, with the same moral strengths and limitations that Max Weber identified as confronting the charismatic leader (*Economy and Society*). The cultivation of a corporate name and personality can create an effective legitimization of an individual's (or company's) power in the face of unsettling economic or social changes. People, believing in the idealistic images of the charismatic leader's personality, will defer to the leader's direction. In times of social disorder, charismatic leadership can be an efficient catalyst for social cooperation. In managerial terms, the more charismatic the corporate image, the stronger is employee loyalty and commitment to the company's interests.[3]

On the other hand, the unquestioning loyalty which a charismatic leader (or corporate image) is able to command almost inevitably introduces a corrupting element into his or her leadership. Personality, not law or moral consideration of the issues, dominates one's sense of what is the right and wrong thing to do. Corporate charisma can prompt managers to put on their "corporate hats" and never take them off; they will fail to draw on private views or judge issues from a broader standpoint. In psychological terms, a manager subordinates his or her private identity to that of an institution. In dealing with the dictates of company image, a manager can confuse company loyalty, which is a reasonable duty, with *unquestioning* loyalty, which is not.

In his famous essay on the psychology of nationalism and its moral corruptiveness, George Orwell noted that the root of nationalism was to be found in "the habit of identifying

---

[2]Philip Selznick, *Leadership in Administration* (New York: Harper & Row, 1957), p. 17.
[3]See, for example, Terence E. Deal and Allan A. Kennedy, *Corporate Cultures: The Rites and Rituals of Corporate Life* (Reading, MA: Addison-Wesley, 1982), pp. 16ff.

oneself with a single nation or other unit, placing it beyond good and evil and recognizing no other duty than that of advancing its interests." Significantly, he called this way of thinking a process of making judgments "solely in terms of competitive prestige" ("Notes on Nationalism," in *Decline of the English Murder and Other Essays*). Wearing the corporate hat closely resembles nationalistic thinking: one's primary duty is taken to be the promotion of corporate interests, usually in self-aggrandizing terms of competitive prestige. The way in which one then solves problems takes on the characteristics of a wartime mentality. Strategy (its original Greek root means "leading the army") operates out of a survival, win-lose wartime scenario. Anyone outside the top management team, which is most closely allied with the corporate image, becomes an "enemy," including in some cases hourly employees, whose dissent is considered tantamount to treason. Other competitors are fair game for "guerrilla warfare" and the suspension of rules which that term implies.

This kind of thinking depends in large part on the corporation's ability to isolate its members from the objective and subjective realities of the outside world. One *seems* fair and trustworthy and concerned about people because, in a closed universe, these things are so. But because such principles are applied selectively to advance only those loyal to the corporate "nation," one still engages in unfair, dishonest, and exploitative behavior. A classic parallel is the bigot who is meticulously fair and honest with members of his own religious community but cheats and hates everyone else.

Corporate egoism can breed the same kind of bigotry. By confining the universe of managerial concerns to the corporate welfare, one closes off important motivations for honesty and fairness in the marketplace and community, even toward one's own employees further down the corporate hierarchy. The needs or injuries of others are unreal in comparison with the company's ambitions or need to create an image of goodness. Should a corporation adopt policies that weaken a manager's ties to external groups, it can further encourage the kind of closed social perspective that bigotry represents.[4]

4For descriptions of this socialization process, see Christopher Stone, "Controlling Corporate Misconduct," *Public Interest*, no. 48 (Summer 1977); Carl Madden, "Forces Which Influence Ethical

Such attitudes represent morally distasteful business approaches, and they also cultivate market blindness. David Halberstam's explanation of Detroit's self-destructive car strategies in the 1970s—"Detroit listened only to Detroit"—illustrates such thinking.

Putting a good face forward, not airing dirty laundry in public, keeping the company's good name—these efforts at image-making are admirable as long as managers make a clear distinction between not advertising problems and ignoring them. But when image pressures dominate one's thinking to the point that one wears only the corporate hat, the distinction is lost. Not only will managers then look the other way on ethical problems, they will also use fear to intimidate subordinates into suppressing information that "might look bad for the company." Such behavior is an open invitation for cover-ups and toleration of injurious or unfair practices.

Whether the issue is quality, caring for the customer, good corporate citizenship, or financial stability, managers tend to place their claims of corporate public affairs within an aura of respectability and status that even Caesar's wife would find hard to rival. Many of the claims are not deliberately false, but merely exaggerations of a manager's sincere intentions to identify with a fine corporate reputation. Managers mistakenly substitute images of company prestige for more objective indications of sound decision making.

Combine this cushion of good intentions and respectability with the gamesmanship of public opinion, stir in a wildly fluctuating baseline of public expectations for corporate conduct, and bake it in the pressure cooker of changing legal definitions of harm and benefit, and it is hard *not* to step over the line between truthful and deceitful corporate representations. But when corporate image becomes the overriding goal, avoidable deceptions follow.

Take the large computer firm that failed to announce the indefinite delay of a long-awaited new product until the day before the scheduled rollout. Surely the decision was

---

Behavior," in *The Ethics of Corporate Conduct*, ed., Clarence Walton (Englewood Cliffs, NJ: Prentice-Hall, 1977), pp. 31–78; and Marshall Clinard, *Illegal Corporate Behavior* (Washington, DC: National Institute of Law Enforcement and Criminal Justice, 1979), p. 8.

prompted by a desire to stave off the time when it would lose face. But the deception of the financial markets and customers was clear and wrong, and could have been avoided if embarrassment had not been so strong a factor.

So, too, when *Time* magazine editors chose not to include an immediate report on the bumpy details of the Time-Warner merger out of consideration of the feelings of some of the corporate executives involved, they were strongly criticized by several professional journalism schools and by the general public for failure to provide objective news coverage. That *Newsweek* scooped the story, to the even greater embarrassment of *Time,* only added a poignant penalty to their misguided attempts to protect the company image.

DEVELOPING AN ETHICAL RESPONSE

Every manager is confronted with a contradictory responsibility: to help feed corporate charisma by helping create a company image of strength and likability, to defer to its interests on many occasions, and yet maintain the autonomy to judge issues independently and from outsider viewpoints. David Ewing has written a number of informative books on the problem of whistle-blowing and freedom of speech in the corporation. He sums up the moral dilemmas of managerial loyalty as follows: "Loyalty in harness with conscience is a truly admirable human resource, either for individuals in organizations or for organizations in the larger society. But once decouple the two and we all are in for it."[5]

The following cases illustrate a number of common managerial problems in which the twin desires to advance the corporate image and be true to one's private conscience may come into conflict. In many such cases managers erect, consciously or otherwise, a barrier of hypocrisy between their work and sense of right and wrong. The question or questions at the close of each problem can help a manager recover an important perspective on the ethics of the issue without discarding his or her "managerial hat" altogether.

[5]David W. Ewing, *"Do It My Way or You're Fired!": Employee Rights and the Changing Role of Management Prerogatives* (New York: John Wiley, 1983), p. 174.

Problem 1. Accurate Advertising Content

Truth in advertising has never been a very sober proposition. As the old sales joke goes, if you can just fake sincerity, you've got it made.

It's not very hard to determine the moral inadequacies of some fly-by-night operation that plays on the ignorance of widows and children to sell as many shoddy products as it can before the FCC or Better Business Bureau puts it out of business. But when the company in question is a well-established member of the Rotary Club or *Fortune* 500, the idea of its executives deliberately engaging in unethical marketing seems implausible—at least to those inside the company. To the degree that all advertising is a combination of image and fact, corporate identity and specific product, a company's margin of respectability can soften an individual's acuity in determining whether corporate image promotion is inviting misleading claims. The hyped-up language of advertising is a clear indication that the practice of "strategic misrepresentation" in corporate communication has developed into an art form, much of it determined by the image a company wishes to project. A Rolls-Royce does not break down, it "fails to proceed." Such best-foot-forwardisms are not venal when the fantasized language is understood to be just that and the real-time consequences are not harmful. But the impulse to massage corporate ego can push such window dressing over the line into a habitual orchestration of other people's ignorance.

In many cases, the exact position of the line is extremely difficult for a manager to determine. In the late 1960s and early 1970s, consumer movements pushed very hard for a seller-beware ethic. Today most consumers express a more balanced expectation of buyer-and-seller responsibility. But definitions of fairness and value or claims of benefit and harm will vary between the two constituencies. The resulting conflicts of opinion make objective determinations of truthful advertising nearly impossible, and raise undeniably difficult dilemmas for a manager.

Take the newest trend of claiming druglike health benefits for breakfast cereals, an issue which has been hotly debated in the media. The difference between nutritional and medicinal value is so vague in the public mind that a company can be regulatorily right but morally in doubt when it comes to marketing a low-cholesterol or high-fiber food product. Should one follow FDA drug guidelines or food value standards in making health claims? It is a lot easier and cheaper to secure FDA approval on the latter, but which strategy is right?

This issue is often argued in terms of regulatory appropriateness. Are companies following the right set of rules? Are the federal rules themselves in need of revision, since the standards of application are inescapably ambiguous at the moment? But judging from the tone of the cereal ads, it appears that the desire to do the right thing should also be examined in terms of corporate image. It is very complimentary to a corporate image to assume the status of quasi-medical advisers, as the rules of product labeling currently appear to allow. Not only does playing doctor stimulate consumer trust and interest, it also has an inherent status in our society. To the degree that corporate ego is flattered by the idea of being a quasi-physician, managers are more vulnerable to making less accurate and responsible judgments on the cereal labeling questions.

If I were on the receiving end of this communication, would it make me better informed and able to make a personally beneficial choice?

Putting oneself on the receiving end of a corporate communication is a good way of ferreting out how far corporate image may be coloring an analysis of marketing claims. Status-enhancing statements are not inherently wrong, but they do tempt people to overlook factual discrepancies between image and actual results. I am particularly drawn to an eloquent and fact-oriented understanding of marketing ethics in an automobile review which once appeared in the *Boston Globe*. The editor made an ingenuous statement of the need for facts: "We judge cars on the basis of how well they do what the manufacturer claims they were designed to do." Forget hype and ego, tell the facts. Are the stated health claims accurate or not? Do they enable a consumer to make an informed and healthful purchase? Corporate ego demands that any doubts about these questions be resolved in favor of the company image. Ethics demands that the answers to these questions be based on fact—including the fact that the facts are in doubt!

But what about those wildly imaginative ads where factual claims are not being made? How do you test them for truth and value-creation? Take the question of advertisements in the brewing industry. What age group should be targeted? A determination of potential injury is obviously in order, but the facts about the effect of such ads are very controversial. This is a typical Type A ethics problem in that there is not a universally agreed upon definition of right and wrong. To begin with, not every state agrees on what drinking age is the "right one." Second, the correlation between advertising and a decision to drink or not has never been determined conclusively.

So what is the ethical course of action for Anheuser-Busch's Bud Light campaign, featuring Spuds, the charismatic English bull terrier? Spuds was featured in a media blitz as "the original party animal" and most of the parties looked to be in the college or late high school age group. So successful was the fantasy that Spuds was named one of the ten best-dressed Americans by *People* magazine and she (that's right) sparked a whole new licensing franchise of Spuds items.

In both image and bottom-line terms it worked very well. Spuds represented a likable, playful image, far removed from typical stereotypes of uncaring, unsmiling corporate behemoths. Not only did students buy Spuds T-shirts, mugs, and key rings in great quantities, they helped put the beer ahead of Coors and right behind Miller.

On the other hand, Anheuser-Busch's public image was tarnished. Schools, parents, consumer and public health groups, even Sen. Strom Thurmond raised objections to the campaign on the grounds that it was contributing to adolescent drinking. An ethical approach to the problem will not be found in a political arena at this point in time, given the historical reluctance of Congress to impose age-related restrictions of any sort on advertising. A strictly legalistic approach would be a cop-out, a way of capitulating to the simplicities of a narrow corporate interest rather than dealing responsibly with the company's obligations to others. The motivations behind this particular campaign need to be explored more fully, including the corporate image motivations. To the degree that the ads manage to associate the company with fun-loving but harmless party animals, admittedly a powerfully attractive image, the more trivial the admittedly ambiguous health issues seem by comparison.

Are you enticing people to injure themselves?

When belief in an advertising image threatens to blind a manager to potential ethical difficulties in advertising, this simple question often cuts the mustard quite nicely. The "party" ads with luscious women going wild over an ugly dog are an enticement to abandon sensible thinking about drinking. If one argues that no one of mature age is hurt by such ads, it is important to recognize that they may be enticing immature people to do themselves injury. Your image of yourself as a harmless, well-intentioned, and technically legal marketer may be contradicted by the facts.

Problem 2. Assimilating Unwelcome Information

It was suggested in the previous chapter that ego can turn enlightened self-interest into a self-first-always viewpoint which tends to suppress undesirable facts about consumer or supplier behavior. For the loyal manager who is overly concerned with creating a seamless company image, outsider dissatisfaction can be dismissed rather than soberly considered. Executives are right in thinking that a public admission of vulnerability runs the risk of bringing on a wholesale indictment. Trying to put a corporate error into perspective is like trying to convince someone that you are only a little bit pregnant. Given the stakes, many executives prefer to stonewall on errors.

The unfortunate and often unintentional result, however, is that they condone further wrongdoing. "What does the consumer know?" is an all-too-common excuse for ignoring significant problems. Take the case of Cordis Pacemakers. In the early 1980s, Cordis managers so strongly believed in the beneficial qualities of their previously successful products that they systematically ignored outsider claims that one pacemaker was defective. When the board of directors raised questions, management tended to dismiss the complaints as uninformed. Since the legitimacy of other viewpoints simply did not register, managers were able to convince themselves of the superiority of their own good judgment; they became blind to the magnitude of the problem, which had real, life-threatening implications. After an outside director delivered an extremely strong lecture at a closed session of the board, an investigation was launched. Cordis discovered widespread cover-ups in almost every aspect of its reporting channels. The product was recalled. The stock plunged and did not recover for over four years.

How does it look on the other side of the fence?

Every manager needs some kind of best-friend outside opinion to keep his or her sensitivity to other viewpoints alive. In Cordis's case, a conscientious director delivered this perspective on a platter, and to the credit of Cordis's managers, they listened. A simple way of testing the corporate party line is to ask, How does it look from the other side of the fence? If you *really* can articulate the answer accurately (in most cases this will require testing your assumptions face-to-face with outsiders), then it is a lot harder to ignore these concerns.

The English essayist William Hazlitt once wrote, "Ignorance and impudence always go together; for in proportion as we are unacquainted with other things, must we feel a want of respect for them" (*Manners Make the Man*). Testing the viewpoint of others is not just an exercise in objectivity, it can also be a sterling consciousness-raiser about the need to respect the other party whom you claim to serve. Operating out of this respect, you are much less likely to choose *symbols* of perfect decision making over factual evidence of service or injury.

Problem 3. Negotiating a Big Deal

Nowhere is the tendency to put on the corporate hat and engage in corporate partisanship stronger than during negotiations. The gamesmanship, bluffing, and uncertainty of such situations make image and corporate interest particularly compelling guidelines for decision making. But as Harvard Negotiation Project director Roger Fisher points out, this kind of enemy mentality can put a severe limit on the value of the negotiating process.[6] A more open, win-win strategy makes more sense for the long-term resolution of conflicting objectives. Having the perspective to adopt such a strategy, however, means moving beyond the dictates of one's "corporate self," which tends to opt for the quickest, most obviously aggrandizing solution.

Consider the following case, which describes two managers in the same company, and their different approaches to negotiating. The first manager, Steve, cannot suspend his personal "hats" and thus finds the situation ambiguous and ethically disturbing. The second manager escapes internal conflict by sticking adamantly to a corporate viewpoint. It will be argued, however, that Steve not only makes a morally more responsible decision, but by listening to his private conscience he brings a number of value-creating managerial qualities to the table. These characteristics, however, raise difficult tensions in the exercise of his corporate role as chief negotiator on a big deal.

> Steve, the new president of a large division of a publishing company, was about to complete an acquisition of a privately owned, well-respected but financially faltering firm. His elation at winning a tough round of bidding had been severely dampened by the details of the negotiations. In the third and final round of negotiations, Steve discovered that the bidding had been narrowed to himself and the current president of the press, who wished to buy out the owners. The fellow was a highly respected editor who had built an impressive authors' list from scratch. Steve clearly had deeper pockets on which to draw for his bid, and he won.
>
> When asked what he thought of the outcome,

---

[6]Roger Fisher and Scott Brown, *Getting Together: Building a Relationship That Gets to Yes* (Boston: Houghton Mifflin, 1988).

Steve reported mixed emotions. "I'm thrilled at the acquisition," he said, "but I really had to question what I did. I really felt for the former president. It was hard to be the one to take the product of his work away. He'd put his life into the company and the authors he'd attracted were devoted to him. It finally came down to a choice of either doing my all for my company or resigning."

When a member of the board of directors heard of this story, he snorted: "I don't see that there was any issue at all here. We paid the best price, and that was what was best for that firm." The director's comment was, to quote the philosophers, partly right and somewhat wrong. The price *was* better and legitimately fulfilled the rules of the game of ownership. In speaking of "the good of the firm," he obviously meant the financial good of the owners, but he also was referring to his unquestioning belief that his company was "better" from a management standpoint. But by failing to acknowledge the emotional and ethical issues Steve faced *as a person*, the director failed to pay attention to and cultivate areas of managerial competency that would be crucial to the long-term success of the acquisition. The director wanted to reduce the arena of problem-solving vocabularies to a minimum. But in the process he was signaling to himself and others that the company's financial interest and size—not private conscience or even other kinds of competencies—were what counted. As Steve put it: "I was totally alone in this decision. They simply wanted me to win the bid. Had I told them my qualms they would have questioned my abilities as president."

What are the legitimate strengths and desires of the other party?

Even when you disagree about the final outcome of a negotiation, it is important to separate the outcome of the issue from the people involved. Asking an empathetic question such as the one above will help keep a manager from considering outsiders as enemies. Steve's sensitivity to the president's feelings represented an approach to business that was more than just soft fuzzies for the other guy and not a sign of negotiating weakness. His personal qualms were not simply a matter of not being tough enough, as one manager later suggested. Behind Steve's feeling for the other president was a perceptive analysis of that person's competitive strengths, an appreciation of what it took to create a good list of authors, and, most important, an active sense that right and wrong *mattered* in the transaction.

The keenness of his moral sensitivity was a direct result of keeping both hats on rather than rejecting the promptings of individual conscience. Steve abandoned neither his role of negotiating on the company's behalf, nor his private moral underpinnings. Out of this awareness, Steve conducted the acquisition with an honor that has been noticeably lacking in many takeovers today, to the destruction of public and shareholder trust throughout the financial community. The first person to tell the former president about his loss of the bid was Steve himself. The owners, who saw the event solely in dollars-and-cents terms, had not even bothered to call him.

The "people values" which Steve's empathy evoked also served him well after the acquisition was completed. He personally visited every author to discuss the changes in his own strategy and marketing plans. Only one author removed himself from the list, despite the fact that many had been close to the former president. Without such people values, it is unlikely that Steve could have kept as many authors, and the value of the acquisition would have been diminished.

Problem 4. Reporting Wrongdoing

It is hard enough for the ethical executive to try to avoid wrongdoing; but once wrongdoing is established in a large organization, it is a daunting task for a single person to set it right or even pass on the information that there is trouble in paradise. Passivity in the face of unethical or illegal practices is one of the most problematic areas of moral challenge for a manager. If the growth and diversity of the large organization has introduced the visible hand of management, it has also introduced the hypocritical hand into corporate communications. Out of fear of making the company look bad, a manager will choose not to be the one to pass on information about a questionable practice.

For instance, say some managers are engaging in accounting abuses. Another manager, call him Jim, tries to communicate the information in-house. He is stonewalled by his superiors, who refuse to believe anything bad about the company. They decline to investigate and even go so far as to call his own integrity into question. In frustration, Jim blows the whistle and reports his findings to the IRS.

His decision seems obviously ethical from an outsider's standpoint, whether that of a shareholder, the IRS, or a bilked customer. Theoretically, it should seem ethical inside the company as well. The corporation should be proud and grateful that Jim is such an honest and courageous employee. And yet, according to expert David Ewing, the majority of executives condemn a whistle-blower who goes outside the company *even in cases where executives agree that the criticism was justified.*

Their reason? Corporate image. Most executives justify such an opinion in the belief that whistle-blowing hurts a company's reputation out of proportion to the misdeed. Reputation, image—not law abiding or ethics—drives such thinking. As long as protection of the company image is a primary concern, it is very difficult for a manager to stimulate a direct, close-up look at problems, ethical or practical.

What if I were leaving the company tomorrow?

By removing the personal stakes involved, you greatly increase the possibility of making a more objective assessment of what is the right course of action. Imagining yourself out of the game is a fast way to get at the truth in those many Type B instances of wrongdoing, where a decision would obviously be wrong from a private outsider's standpoint but helpful from a company one. Articulating what is wrong is the first step toward doing something about it. This question also helps remove that "doing-it-for-the-company" attitude which screens a manager from seeing important alternatives. In Type A ethics problems (the acute dilemma) where there is no unambiguously right judgment, a step back from company loyalty opens the door to other commonsense points of view.

Ironically, nowhere is the desire to protect the corporate image a greater factor in managerial moral passivity than in many corporate ethics programs. Well-intentioned managers write codes and corporate policies to ensure high standards of conduct. There is nothing wrong with the technical content of these codes from a moral or legal standpoint. And yet the same company later discovers that even the simplest cases of false reporting are being condoned by well-meaning employees who fear for their careers should they communicate their suspicions of colleagues' or superiors' cheating.

A look at the language with which most of these programs are articulated gives great insight into how corporate image can prevent employee communication of corporate wrongdoing. Most company codes are worded to massage the company image to make it appear that never a suspicion of doubt or dilemma has crossed the corporate path. The record would be perfect were it not for a few bad apples. Often, managers contribute to this fantasy of moral certainty in the way they present such codes to their subordinates. Seeking to create a clean corporate image, they unconsciously convey the message that they will not tolerate any individual doubts that might cast a shadow over company policy or a superior's orders. As one manager put it: "We're an ethical company, and this code is what we stand for. If anyone has any doubt about signing it, we *make* them sign!" But, of course, in the real world, individual managers are continually aware of ethical dilemmas. Finding the ethical course is not as easy as the corporate image would make it seem.

Every manager needs to be aware that no image issue is worth the price of a don't-make-waves attitude among employees. Eventually, the cover-ups will be uncovered, at least some of them, and the company image will suffer more than it would if there were an internal investigation. If you ask yourself how you would act if you were leaving tomorrow, chances are your private conscience will find a stronger voice.[7]

---

[7]Obviously other measures, including stronger monitoring mechanisms, are also needed to create code effectiveness. A 1985 survey by *Purchasing* magazine found that where companies with gift-taking policies used internal checks or audits to measure employee compliance, almost 50 percent uncovered policy violations. When Bentley College's Center for Business Ethics surveyed 1,000

Problem 5. Addressing Public Criticism

There is a terrible irony in many managers' approach to corporate public relations, an irony that hinges on the power of corporate image. The protection of a good corporate image can make a manager extremely sensitive to the creation of strong symbols of corporate power internally, and yet extremely insensitive to the symbolic value of corporate activity in other people's terms. Obvious shortcomings in the company's response to outsider criticism or to the problem itself will be overlooked out of a firm belief that the company is technically in the right.

To the degree that public criticism is approached in tangible and technical terms, rather than symbolic ones, a management team fails to develop the kind of strong outside relationships that can sustain public criticism. Often it is the company's own symbols that blind a management team to the symbolic value other people place on its activities. As such, relationship reasoning is precluded and an important avenue to the resolution of public criticism closed off.

One of the most dramatic examples of a corporation's failure to perceive the relational and symbolic aspects of its ethical stand was Nestlé's handling of the infant formula boycotts in the 1970s. After much research and personal discussion with the executives involved, I am convinced, as was former senator Edmund Muskie, that Nestlé had been "had."[8] Its infant formula marketing was not as irresponsible or as exploitative as many public critics would have the public believe. The company had engaged in clearly unethical and overaggressive marketing campaigns in the early 1960s, but it had corrected the overwhelming majority of the problems very quickly and long before the height of the anti-Nestlé campaigns. Nestlé stuck to the ethical rules of infant formula marketing, but it failed to address the relationship side of its problems. Its failure could be partly attributed to the strong

---

corporations about their ethics programs, of the 295 that responded, 90 percent had developed codes but only 22 percent had developed a way of measuring their effectiveness. See Michael Hoffman, "Are Corporations Institutionalizing Ethics?" *Journal of Business Ethics* 5 (1986), pp. 85–91.

[8] I am extremely grateful to Jacques Paternot, former general manager of Nestlé Products, for his time and help in making material available to me.

influence of corporate ego on managerial thinking. When Sen. Edward Kennedy before a Senate subcommittee asked publicly how the company could market throughout Africa a product that depended on sanitary or even sterile conditions and a literate consumer with discretionary income in order to be used safely, a Nestlé representative began his reply by reminding the senator that he did not by law have to answer the question. After all, he represented a Swiss company. The rest of his response was totally inadequate in addressing the issues of the case. The public was outraged at the callousness of his reply. The company's failure to give a straight answer in a public forum could only be interpreted as an act of arrogance or guilt, or both.

Failure to think in anything but legalistic terms caused Nestlé to shoot itself in the foot many times during the extended boycotts. Clearly the company had lost the confidence of the public. There were many reasons why the company allowed this situation to continue, but, in my opinion, the cover-up of unethical marketing practices was *not* among them. Nestlé's management had carefully investigated the facts and was confident in its position, even though the issue would always be controversial. What they failed to do, however, was offer an adequate public explanation of the facts. Curiously, they insisted before a senate subcommittee that they owed the public no explanation, lumping concerned consumers with some of the radically anticapitalist groups which had targeted Nestlé for attack.

The public, however, did not care about legal technicalities. Consumers already had a transactional relationship with the company that was based on trust, and the basis of that trust had been called into question. While the African infant formula market was only of small concern to the company in dollar terms, it carried strong symbolic power to outsiders, who were testing the company's entire consumer relationship based on its response to the controversy.

Nestlé management failed to see that the issue on the table was not just the facts of its marketing practices, or the technical legalities of public inquiry, but the company's *relationship* with the general public, far removed from Africa. By failing to think in relationship terms, Nestlé managers exacerbated the mistrust of its consumers in the way it responded to their criticism. It failed to recognize the issues which were important not to Nestlé but to outsiders.

One way it might have provoked a greater sensitivity to these issues would have been to ask the question,

What is the symbolic value of our activity in other people's terms, whether they understand our motives or not?

By failing to assess the symbolic truth of its behavior in the eyes of the public, management sabotaged its own past efforts to create and ethically exploit consumer trust. For whatever reasons, paternalism or paranoia, it did not acknowledge that legitimately there could be different interpretations of a single act or decision which demanded further public scrutiny.

It may well be that Nestlé's failure to assess the symbolic power of its unresponsiveness on the infant formula issue was motivated, ironically, by the strength of its corporate symbols inside the company. Nestlé had always cultivated an image of competency, scientific quasi-medical service to public nutrition. Its corporate strategy was based on the quality and reliability of its products and fantastic sensitivity to the consumer market. Henri Nestlé's first success had been, of all things, the development of a nutritious infant formula to provide poor families with a safe alternative to wet-nursing, which was expensive and not always available. The targeted customer was the impoverished mother who had to work and could not nurse. In the recent infant formula controversy, critics claimed that the company was injuring precisely the same person. Nestlé managers disagreed. Based on the company's history and the kind of products it had produced, Nestlé managers saw themselves as benevolent producers of healthful products, concerned about mothers and infants.

As they investigated infant formula marketing in Africa, they saw no reason to revise that view. In fact, the more medical-like the conditions of marketing, the more responsible the use of infant formula. It was in the uncontrolled, illiterate environment outside the hospital where potentially harmful results could occur. Thus they adjusted the labeling and advertising of formula for these conditions, advocating nursing above formula and printed all instructions in pictorial form.

Given its past relationship with the marketplace, one would have thought that Nestlé would have been very responsive to a public inquiry into its infant formula marketing policies in Africa. To keep the trust of the consumer, Nestlé had an obligation to clarify the facts of the controversy. Nestlé's blindness to the symbolic importance of the controversy to consumers resulted in a devastating blow to the company's reputation, which suffered for many years. The controversy was not resolved until the firm created an independent forum, headed by former senator Edmund Muskie, for acknowledging the public's concern as its own and investigating the specific charges made against the company.

Asking what the symbolic value of a company's stand is, especially if misunderstood, can open the way to perceiving significant aspects of a controversy *from the antagonist's point of view* in a way that concentrating on the problem in terms of facts or legal rules cannot. Management decisions carry symbolic messages that can profoundly affect trust levels in a relationship. Sensitivity to the symbolic value of a decision is crucial for both ethical and practical reasons. One can be morally secure about the facts of the matter from a private standpoint, but relationally irresponsible if the symbolic issues are not addressed. And yet, as in Nestlé's case, security about the facts may make answering public criticism seem in its own way a betrayal of the corporate image, especially when both the facts and the image are benevolent.

Problem 6. Cooperating on Important Public Welfare Issues

Whether the issue is global warming, endemic poverty, or clean water, there are many public problems connected to a corporation's activities over which a single company has no control. Progress can only be made by cooperative ventures between many corporations and nonbusiness institutions. Often this kind of cooperation will require that two or more competitors put aside their traditional enmity. While such cooperation may seem logical to a public interest group, or to a private citizen, it can meet with mystifying resistance in a company.

Part of the reason for such foot-dragging is corporate nationalism and competitive prestige, as described in the opening part of this chapter. Within the closed universe of a single company, it seems counterproductive to stop trying to "best" other competitors, and unfair of the public to expect the firm to assume responsibility for costs that it may not have incurred in isolation.

Thus what appears to be a reasonable proposition and pressing issue to a private citizen seems unfair and unnecessary to the same person when his or her company's participation and possible dilution of power is involved. Clinging to a charismatic corporate image of a strong, benevolent, but independent company, a manager fails to see the corporation as part of a larger community and does not develop the will to cooperate with outsiders.

Take, for example, the question of air bags in automobiles. Industry critic Clarence Ditlow and many others had long argued that air bags would significantly reduce the incidence of certain kinds of head injuries. Throughout the 1970s and 1980s automobile companies resisted pressure to include the bags, for two basic reasons: surveys consistently reported that the public was not willing to pay for the bags at cost, and the additional safety margins were uncertain.

As long as the companies framed the problem only in terms of cost distribution and the isolated economic effect on their own bottom line, no progress was made on the development of air bags. Nothing could create the will to break down the them-us, my-pocket-or-yours mentality which informed the articulation of the problem. There was no will to establish a more creative *relationship* with the public and government in order to find a way of sharing the costs. And yet air bags could be viewed as a management's ultimate ethical test, for no moral responsibility in business is more pressing than the avoidance of unnecessary injury, and no moral responsibility more difficult to determine than how much further in the value-creation process a company should go. Successful and responsible business is not only a satisficer but also an innovator. Its decision on safety issues will profoundly affect national well-being and act as an indication of a company's commitment to safety and quality.

Although the overall importance of the air bags issue was clear, the actual details of the decision involved a typical Type A ethics problem: no one could agree on who should pay for safety, or even on what constituted responsible safety equipment. A cost-benefit calculation failed to enlighten the issue sufficiently. To cost out a life at $800 (the potential decrease to the bottom line or price increase for an unwilling consumer) instinctively did not seem to be the right approach, although the $800 price tag was frequently cited as reason not to proceed with air bags. Similarly, the potential long-term competitive effects of such a measure in the United States vis-à-vis foreign manufacturers did not seem directly comparable to the safety factor under discussion. As long as U.S. companies framed the problem in terms of competitive ability and competitive prestige, there was no cooperation between companies and public representatives to find a solution.

What if my child were the customer or citizen directly affected by the problem?

When macro issues of public welfare bump up against the inexorable concern for company autonomy, there is usually great managerial reluctancy to take positive action. Asking the above question will help a manager slip on that private hat which puts the urgency of the problem in a stronger light.

When Ford Motor Company began its "Quality Is Job 1" campaign in the early 1980s, it tried to provoke a greater sensitivity to private opinion in all its managers. Engineers were asked if they would personally buy the design they were suggesting, and so on. This same perspective informed its stand on air bags. Ford changed its approach to the problem from one of arguing over cost distribution and scientific doubt about the potential benefits to one of putting itself in a potential victim's shoes. In 1984, Ford was the only company to offer automobiles at cost to the U.S. government so that it could make a more accurate determination of the potential safety benefits of air bags. In my opinion, this was a changed and more ethical approach to the air bag problem. Once the company and the government moved away from the cost-benefit approach, which had stymied progress, and toward determining the customer's best interests first (cost came later), the air bag issue began to be resolved. It is not concluded, but as of 1990 most upscale cars include air bags as standard equipment and the overall industry trend is clearly in this direction.

CONCLUSION

Every manager wears several hats in life and even in the fulfillment of his or her corporate duties. The same manager can be boss, facilitator, subordinate, friend, counselor, consumer, technician, and renegade. While many business problems are the cause of potential conflicts between private values and corporate roles, the felt force of any one of these roles varies as circumstances change. The simplistic, resigned, or cynical manager may try to resolve the conflicting voices of conscience by simply adopting the corporate hat at work and leaving private conscience for home life. The well-intentioned manager might try constantly changing hats: one moment a friend, the next a corporate ambassador, the next an advocate for the consumer, the next an advocate for company costs, and so forth.

A third strategy is to seek a more *integrated* approach to personal ethics at work, to bring one's other hats into the consideration of business problems from the start, rather than seeing them in terms of either/or. For example, instead of viewing the aggrandizement of corporate power and image as the first value and purpose of a manager, a manager directs legitimate consideration of the corporate image toward the service of others, as was argued, for example, in a Covenantal Ethic. This is precisely what a Tandem Computer or IBM achieved so effectively in the cultivation of corporate images of service and employee responsiveness. *Achieving this redefinition of corporate purpose and identity automatically requires an integration of normally private values such as caring for other people and relationship-thinking into one's business role.*

In order to achieve integration, a manager must place strong limitations on the legitimization of the corporate viewpoint. Rather than expecting individuals to suppress their conscience at work in deference to the institution, the expectation is that personal conscience and the moral norms it represents *inherently limit* the power of the corporate image. Covenantal managers, by directing their obligations toward the service of others, encourage an extension of corporate identity to include people outside the corporate community, thereby entertaining the notion of less-restricted nationalism.

It was with this approach that Procter & Gamble, long known for its high standards of conduct and its market sensitivity, addressed the difficult issue of environmental hazards resulting from its production and marketing of disposable diapers. P&G could have turned its back on the problem out of a desire to keep its corporate image as distant from the suggestion of wrongdoing as possible. That would have been both insensitive to its stakeholders and irresponsibly indifferent to its own potential contribution to significant injury of the environment. Instead, P&G thoroughly researched the issue; it acknowledged that disposables presented a problem, and began to develop creative solutions ranging from a recycling plant in Seattle to obtaining more facts about the relative performance of different biodegradable materials in landfills. The problem is not yet completely solved, but P&G is putting its size and image toward creating value for its customers and community rather than allowing these symbols of identity to pose obstacles to environmental responsiveness.

Further, consider the example of employee wrongdoing. Ethical leaders do not try to gloss over problems out of a fear of tarnishing the corporate image. Rather, they feel it is important to expose company problems to the light to tease out the grains of truth that might be gained from the exercise. As ITT's Rand Araskog said, "I can't expect that the entire company will never get in trouble. What's important is that employees and the public see what we do when someone acts unethically." So, too, when two Johnson & Johnson executives were discovered through internal auditing procedures to have misused certain expense allowances, they were not just fired. A letter went out from the chairman to all senior managers stating clearly what happened, what was wrong about it, and how everyone needed to be more sensitive to this type of problem.

Humor is another great way to resist being overwhelmed by service to the corporate ego to the neglect of one's private conscience. Take the recent dissemination of "Boeing Trivia," a 214-page collection of embarrassing anecdotes by former PR man Carl Cleveland. It's an egg-on-the-face, grin-and-bear-it exercise in reality tests. Anyone who reads it would have a hard time swallowing the "perfect corporation" image which so many managers are expected to cultivate to the neglect of their better judgment.

In short, to achieve ethical conduct in the marketplace, it is important to keep both hats on, private and corporate. By maintaining the paradox that one is neither private citizen nor a moral cog in the corporate wheel, the values and obligations of company and individual are better melded. Thinking in relationship terms, staying other-directed, universalizing one's opinions, listening to outsider viewpoints, putting yourself in the other person's shoes—all these approaches are not foolproof or the way to an automatic solution of ethical dilemmas at work, but they will help create the will to put supposed corporate infallibility into broader perspective.

To return to the case example at the opening of this chapter, where a friend and employee seeks confidential advice on a job offer, how would a covenantal manager with both hats on resolve the dilemma? Would he or she inform the employee of the potential closure of the operation or not? Would he (or she) be a good friend or a loyal manager?

In this case, the covenantal manager has more than one relationship to think about: not only his (or her) friendship with the employee, but also his relationship with other employees, who may be demoralized should the news get out. He also has to think about his relationship with the company itself. There are implied obligations, or contracts, attached to each relationship, which can all be boiled down to the corporate covenant: to provide value and receive a fair return for so doing. This manager must provide value to the friend, to other employees, and to the company itself. He has a right to expect a return from all of them.

Taking this viewpoint, he would probably cast the problem differently to begin with. The first issue is not secrecy but welfare. How can the interview be turned into one that will provide value for all parties? Without revealing the company strategy, the manager should see this valued employee's request as a potential source of information about what motivates her, how well the company serves her needs, and how well she contributes to the team. Few employees are motivated solely by job security and there is no reason to restrict the discussion to this issue. (To the point of this dilemma is a survey by the Wyatt Company in which workers rated "a boss you respect" as the job value they most regard as extremely important.) Directing the discussion toward the full panoply of reasons why she looked elsewhere may offer the company valuable information and the employee better insight into how to create a more productive and satisfying work environment.

At the same time the secrecy issue cannot be sidestepped. Any relationship depends in part on fairness, and secrecy is potentially an unfair use of power over another. It is easy to see how it would be unfair to use secret information to mislead the employee into thinking that she had total job security. But it is no more unfair to keep a company secret—if you do not mislead the employee—than it is unfair for the employee to ask a friend/boss that he keep her request for information and her job hunt confidential. The boss should point this out, and pave the way for agreeing that both of them have secrets which they are obligated and trusted to keep. He should tell her that he simply cannot tell her about job security, but he should then expand the discussion as suggested above.

At no time, however, is he forced by this solution to abandon his dual role as friend and corporate supervisor. In forming friendships at work, long before this particular request came up, he should have been very careful never to try to keep switching hats, being a special friend to an employee one day to the exclusion of his corporate role and impartial "boss" the next, or the above solution would be impossible to carry out.

Like most covenantal perspectives, this one takes a long-term view of the problem at hand, rather than restricting understanding and analysis of the issue to the single decision. The ethical wearing of two hats rides on the same long-term thinking and behavior: with a covenantal strategy of value-creation and continual attendance to relationships, those dilemmas between private conscience and corporate loyalty are less likely to be intractable conflicts.

Epilogue

Meeting the Moral
Challenges of Business

It is often easier to fight for principles than to live up to them.*

After the many debacles of greed and dishonor which punctuated business performance in the Roaring Eighties, it is easy to see at the opening of the 1990s that the ethical climate of business must improve, and hard to know just what will best bring about improvement. The Covenantal Ethic posed in Part II and the roadblocks and questions in Part III offer specific intellectual road maps for steering a course through the temptations of power and short-term profit toward a more constructive approach to the marketplace. While rejecting the "do-good-to-do-well" incentive, it has been suggested that good business questions can lead to good ethics and vice versa. By replacing profit-driven motivations with value-creating ones, and subordinating the pursuit of efficiency to a sense of service and relationships, managers will increase the probabilities of being able to sustain their personal ethical norms and build business strength.

Some ethical problems are more tractable to this approach than others. A quality strategy is a helpful focus for issues of honesty, exploitation of ignorance, and potential injury. The Covenantal Ethic is less directly applicable to macro

*Adlai E. Stevenson, speech in New York City, 1952.

questions of distributive justice concerning, say, corporate tax rates or business contribution to education in America. Widespread progress on the first set of issues, however, would clearly create a national climate of business credibility which would help the public and the corporate worlds find better resolutions of the second.

What has been left out of the analysis? Are there problems and factors in business misconduct that have not been addressed here that are crucial to the success of any effort to improve business ethics?

In asking these questions I am reminded of a wonderful short story by James Thurber, entitled "The Owl Who Was God." This remarkable bird appeared to know all sorts of unknowable things. First he spied two ground moles passing by in the dark. When they reported to the other animals that the owl was the greatest and wisest of all animals, the secretary bird was sent to examine him. When the owl answered each question correctly with a "To wit" or "To woo," his reputation soared and he was made leader of the animals.

One day, while all the animals were gathered in the middle of the road to listen to the owl's pronouncements, a truck came speeding toward them. The owl, blinded by the daylight, appeared unconcerned, and so none of the animals moved out of the way. They were all immediately run over. Thurber's moral: "You *can* fool too many of the people too much of the time."

Throughout this book I have claimed that good managers can be fooled by their own good intentions, a managerial problem-solving approach, and sometimes financial success into complacently accepting a business ethic that falls far short of their private ideals. To my profound discomfort and education I was caught short by my own good intentions as I was completing this book.

I was teaching an executive seminar in business ethics and some of the group were presenting their analysis of a dilemma which regularly occurred in their functional area. I was nonplussed when everyone agreed on a do-nothing strategy in the face of obvious wrongdoing. "No dissents?" I asked incredulously, knowing that such seminars usually bring out the most idealistic recommendations. Apparently there was one. When questioned further, he explained, "Well I'd do something if I knew the boss wasn't going to penalize me, otherwise I'd go along with everyone else."

Like the owl and his followers, these insights into moral intelligence at work are shattered by a larger environmental truth: if the corporate environment penalizes or simply threatens to penalize ethical decisions, many managers will be unwilling to apply these moral—or any other—frameworks. If the only choice for a manager is private moral norms or career suicide, then very few managers will have the courage to stick to their principles, and even fewer will be fully aware of how often they compromise them. I am not confident, however, in solely condemning the individual manager for this state of affairs. It should be remembered that Polonius's platitude in *Hamlet,* "To thine own self be true and . . . thou canst not then be false to any man" was spoken to a madman. And as Alexander Pope once reminded us, the worst madman is a saint run mad. It would be a saintly madness to dismiss as irrelevant the very real systemic roadblocks which a poor strategy, short-term investment pressures, and a corporate hierarchy run amok can impose on individual ethical power.[1]

Two responses to the problem seem appropriate here. The first is that we need to go beyond the analysis of this book for a full reform of business behavior. The voting power and patterns of the investment community, the organizational structure of business, and the reward patterns of many corporations are all in need of change. Each of these areas is a subject for separate and full discussion.

The second point, however, is that none of these reforms can be affected unless there is also, and perhaps first, a personal transformation of the business mindset to coincide more closely with a Covenantal Ethic. No amount of technical reform in the marketplace or corporate organization chart will create the individual capacity to care and be sensitive to the opportunities for meeting the needs of others. Only a basic

---

[1]For eloquent discussions of the force which corporate hierarchies exert on individual sense of responsibility, see Marshall Clinard, *Illegal Corporate Behavior* (Washington, DC: National Institute of Law Enforcement and Criminal Justice, 1979), p. 7; Kathy E. Kram, Peter C. Yeager, and Gary E. Reed, "Decisions and Dilemmas: The Ethical Dimension in the Corporate Context," in *Research in Corporate Social Performance and Policy,* vol. 11 (1989), pp. 21–54.

change in one's business priorities can bring this about. What environmental changes can do is to create the conditions for encouraging individual managers to translate caring into profitable action.

No systemic approach to business ethics can succeed without personal insight and leadership from the very people who are both creators and victims of the corporate system. I recall Calvin Coolidge's warnings against increased regulatory oversight of business. Coolidge acknowledged that there were indeed abominable abuses throughout the moneymaking system. But, he reflected, these abuses are the result of human greed and immorality. If government hires other humans to oversee these activities, humans with the same degree of greed and immorality as anyone else, what is to prevent them from succumbing to the same practices? Ethical lapses throughout the public sector in its dealings with business have confirmed Coolidge's prediction.

This is not to argue against stronger oversight mechanisms. I believe that the threat of getting caught is a primitive but effective deterrent on many occasions. Rather, it is to say that every person in business—from investor to plant worker—needs to have in place a sound understanding of responsible business behavior and the intellectual tools for breaking down the most common assumptional barriers to achieving it. The second section of this discussion analyzed the stars by which many responsible business leaders are seen to steer, and the third tried to provide the hammer and wedge for shattering some of the most commonly ignored obstacles to this kind of covenantal thinking.

No doubt as we progress into the last decade of this millennium, the need for covenantal expertise will become more acute. Changing markets and changing workplace demographics will challenge managers to form alliances that they never imagined would be appropriate. In the scramble to reorganize the pace and structure of the financing-manufacturing-delivery process, trust will become an increasingly important commodity. Consumers will pay a premium for a corporate name that can be trusted to deliver on what it promises, even though the specific products will change rapidly. A labor force in short supply will only remain loyal to the organization that can be relied upon to demonstrate and deliver on a mutuality of interests and respect for all individuals in the firm. World environmental problems will pose extraordinary investment demands with no guarantee of success, and these conditions, too, will make necessary new alliances between unfamiliar partners with contradictory economic cultures to boot.

In the face of such institutional disruption, the role of individual integrity will become increasingly crucial to the practical success of commercial efforts. New and often hostile business environments will test the decency quota of even the most strictly reared managers.

What is more, for many it will be the first test. Most of today's new managers have experienced no substantial trial of their value system before donning a white collar. Some of them have already given up idealism, certain before they ever enter the work force that they must "sell out" to ensure the economic security they so sorely seek. Others have found themselves capitulating to this proposition whether they like it or not. Take this comment from a successful grad of an Eastern business school, now in his forties and a multimillionaire:

> Now that I've been out working for twenty years I see all these other things that are important that we never talked about in business school or in my company. You know, the "people values." And I do not want my kids to be this arrogant when they grow up. I want them to care about other people, be honest, make a contribution to this world.
>
> But I do not see how these things will ever be important to my firm or any of the others I have worked in. I would get out tomorrow and start my own company, but I'm too tied in to our life-style. It wouldn't be fair to my wife and kids.

Should business leaders succumb to this kind of cynicism and self-interest, we condemn democratic capitalism to a fundamental moral bankruptcy, which encourages the exploitation and cheating that every economic system offers. Without a

strong demonstration of personal integrity from managerial
leadership, and an explicit acknowledgment of its role in business success, this nation will surely sink under its own desperate search for self-aggrandizement and economic well-being.

Many new managers today are strongly committed to
the idea of self-expression and independence. The challenge
now is for them to direct these same strengths to strengthening personal integrity. It is crucial for top leadership in today's
corporation to take a more active role in setting high, meaningful, other-oriented moral standards for the rest of its employee group and to show how good business questions and
personal conscience go hand in hand.

This cannot be done with platitudes. Nor can it be
done with utopian generalizations about business ethics. It
must be achieved by a frank reexamination of those common,
everyday problems that put the business person's basic values on the line, often without he or she noticing. As Nobel
Prize–winning scientist Peter Medawar observes, successful
scientists do not always spend their time on the ultimate questions of existence. Rather, they are constantly experimenting
with the tractable questions. They tinker with the best wheel
available to advance our knowledge of the world. In the case
of business integrity, the best wheel is one that helps succeed
in breaking down and redirecting the forces of self-centered
business behavior: ego, narrowly defined profit targets, an I-
win-you-lose mentality, and short-term time frames.

The best wheels for doing this rest on knowledge.
Ethical conduct at work can only stem from a full personal
understanding of the values and assumptions that make
"good" business a reality in both the moral and economic
sense of the word. The fifth-century Athenian statesman
Pericles asserted that the democratic citizenry had a distinctive competence from both a moral and military standpoint for
the very reason that it was an *informed* citizenry. Unlike the
Spartan soldier, tyrannized into performing feats of bravery,
the Athenian fought with special zeal because he knew what
dangers he faced—and faced them anyway.

So, too, the corporation that seeks to achieve ethical
compliance by coercion or appeals to self-interest alone can
never hope to establish a resource of management integrity

that goes beyond compliance to create win-win solutions. Such a resource depends, like ancient Athens, on individuals being informed; informed of the important ethical assumptions that drive good business behavior, informed of the intellectual and emotional pitfalls that hinder its accomplishment even among the best intentioned. This process must be a collective undertaking to pursue self-knowledge and find the will to bring the basics of morality to the basics of business success.

While most of the jokes about the ethics of business people assume that the average executive has about as much moral insight as a banana, it has been my experience in countless seminar discussions that the well-intentioned manager who engages in an act of self-scrutiny and moral questioning finds new insight into creative business thinking, personal courage, and the will to change. If the thoughts in this book cause even one moral insight that results in positive change, it will have served a purpose.

But that will be nothing compared to the change that the ethical corporate leader can incite in American business behavior by successfully demonstrating the legitimacy of covenantal viewpoints and shedding the most cherished management traditions that deflect a company from this goal. Many have already done so. What this book has tried to do is make those activities more visible and supply some labels by which many more may recognize the process of business integrity at work.

Index